Playwright Versus Director

Recent Titles in
Contributions in Drama and Theatre Studies

The Age of *Hair*: Evolution and Impact of Broadway's First Rock Musical
Barbara Lee Horn

The Gymnasium of the Imagination: A Collection of Children's Plays in English,
1780-1860
Jonathan Levy

Every Week, A Broadway Revue: The Tamiment Playhouse, 1921–1960
Martha Schmoyer LoMonaco

The Simple Stage: Origins of the Minimalist *Mise-en-Scène* in the American Theater
Arthur Feinsod

Richard's Himself Again: A Stage History of *Richard III*
Scott Colley

Eugene O'Neill in China: An International Centenary Celebration
Haiping Liu and Lowell Swortzell, editors

Toward an Aesthetics of the Puppet: Puppetry as a Theatrical Art
Steve Tillis

George Sand's *Gabriel*
Gay Manifold

Confronting Tennessee Williams's *A Streetcar Named Desire*: Essays in Critical Pluralism
Philip C. Kolin, editor

Challenging the Hierarchy: Collective Theatre in the United States
Mark S. Weinberg

The Dawning of American Drama: American Dramatic Criticism, 1746–1915
Jürgen C. Wolter, editor

The Actor Speaks: Actors Discuss Their Experiences and Careers
Joan Jeffri, editor

Richard Wagner and Festival Theatre
Simon Williams

Playwright Versus Director

Authorial Intentions and Performance Interpretations

Edited by **Jeane Luere**

Sidney Berger,
Advisory Editor

Contributions in Drama and Theatre Studies,
Number 54

GREENWOOD PRESS
Westport, Connecticut • London

Library of Congress Cataloging-in-Publication Data

Playwright versus director : authorial intentions and performance
   interpretations / edited by Jeane Luere ; Sidney Berger, advisory
   editor.
      p. cm.—(Contributions in drama and theatre studies, ISSN
  0163–3821 ; no. 54)
   Includes bibliographical references and index.
   ISBN 0–313–28679–5 (alk. paper)
   1. Playwriting. 2. Theater—Production and direction. I. Luere,
Jeane. II. Berger, Sidney. III. Title: Playwright versus director.
IV. Series.
PN1661.P62   1994
792'.01—dc20   93–44134

British Library Cataloguing in Publication Data is available.

Library of Congress Catalog Card Number: 93–44134
ISBN: 0–313–28679–5
ISSN: 0163–3821

First published in 1994

Greenwood Press, 88 Post Road West, Westport, CT 06881
An imprint of Greenwood Publishing Group, Inc.

Printed in the United States of America

∞™

The paper used in this book complies with the
Permanent Paper Standard issued by the National
Information Standards Organization (Z39.48–1984).

10 9 8 7 6 5 4 3 2 1

Every reasonable effort has been made to trace the owners of copyright materials in this book,
but in some instances this has proven impossible. The editors and publisher will be glad to receive
information leading to more complete acknowledgments in subsequent printings of the book and in
the meantime extend their apologies for any omissions.

It is a task for the historian of culture to explain why there has been in the last four decades a heavy and largely victorious assault on the sensible belief that a text means what its author meant.

E. D. Hirsch, Jr., *Validity in Interpretation*, 1

[The] meaning of a work [or of a text] cannot be created by the work alone; the author never produces anything but presumptions of meaning, forms, and it is the world which fills them.

Roland Barthes, Preface, *Critical Essays*, xi

Contents

Illustrations

Preface

Polemic in the realm of drama is striking at underlying issues of authorial intention and performance interpretation. The theatre world is reassessing its position on production hierarchy. The longevity of the issue of what constitutes a play's text, who determines its meaning, and who controls its transfer to the stage equals its magnitude. Aristotle could not have approached more studiously his era's enigma about what constitutes a human being—its chemical make-up or its functional properties. A cursory look in this preface at the make-up and function of a script may ready the reader of the text for theoretical distinctions between play and performance.

In the first half of our century, actor-director Antonin Artaud, remembered for his blasts at the "tyranny" of playwrights, stated paradoxically, "The author must discover and assume what belongs to the *mise en scène* [the placing on stage] as well as what belongs to the author, and become a director himself in a way that will put a stop to the absurd duality existing between director and author" (112). The polemic over what is text and who interprets it began even earlier in a discipline separate from drama—literary criticism—where its theorists produced reams of discourse for libraries and universities on the essence of text and the expanding potential for interpreting it.

By the 1960s a conservative literary philosopher, E. D. Hirsch, placed any text's meaning and intent solely with its author: "the notion of a sense beyond the author's is illegitimate"; it would be possible only if one were to grant the conception of a "sensus plenior," a divine sense beyond the human author's (126). The notion that a text's meaning could "go beyond anything the human author could have consciously intended is, of course, a totally unnecessary entity" (126). For Hirsch, valid interpretation is always a "re-cognition of what an author meant" (126). Thus he held to the position that "unless there is a powerful overriding value in disregarding an author's intentions [i.e., original meaning], we who interpret as a vocation should not disregard it"(quoted in Smith, 133).

But a severe and opposing position had also circulated in literary criticism with the advent of translations of Roland Barthes in the 1960s. Barthes held that authors cannot fasten their texts nor give them a "definite meaning" (Barthes, "Literature and Signification," xi). In the 1970s, theorist Michel Foucault, too, loosened authorial control: "Authors create a possibility for something other than their discourse [and] make possible not only a certain number of analogies, but also and equally important, a certain number of differences from their intended meaning . . . often the possibilities for the formation of other texts" (Foucault, "What Is an Author?" 154). The validity of these pronouncements in academia's literary parley hinged on definitions of concepts like "makers, creators, interpreters" and "text" or "work"; their implications permitted readers, lecturers, or professors, to consider themselves co-creators—auteurs—as we took a volume of literature in hand. Since the 1980s these critical distinctions have been seeping into theatre discourse to qualify the appropriate style of playwright/director interchange. Today, in production parley, vexing corollaries like "text, script, play, performance, author, auteur," cause anxious inferences such as this: "The traditional idea of the [playwright] as the creator of meaning must be re-examined" (Rabkin, 152).

Related issues in play production hinge on "the certitudes of law and questions of interpretation as well as allegations of censorship and theft of text" (Savran, "The Wooster Group," 101). Though solid and valid collaboration between director and playwright routinely occurs, disputes do arise, revolving around two areas: "the legal and the extra-legal, with the former dependent upon copyright laws and the latter upon more equivocal, subjective notions of artistic freedom" (101).

To make golden-mean choices between radical stances like protectionism and deconstructionism, or even between "text" and "hors texte" (outside or extratext) as Jacques Derrida put it (Young, 6), requires care and groundwork as the theatre world subsumes the early, ticklish discourse of literary criticism. But "isms" that began in other disciplines years ago as positive challenges to (or supports for) the integrity of text may now have overreached themselves. In *The Death of Literature*, Alvin Kernan cautions that literary criticism's radical approaches to text—and by extension to play and performance—may place us in "a last apocalyptic period in which the angels of death were not visitants from some other world but exaggerated versions of positions which, positive in their earlier forms, became destructive in their extremes" (213). Opportunity may be rife for a launch to a new galaxy where play and performance sit propitiously side by side.

The contents of Part One of this volume draw from definitive articles in literary journals as well as from more recent corollaries in theatre journals, to give the reader basic concepts and terminology of postmodernism and poststructuralism.

Part Two has interviews with or commentary from playwrights and directors whose views prove the complexity of the issue of production hierarchy. Part Three features five compact studies of playwrights and directors who faced production crises bringing scripts to audiences.

The contractual aspects of collaboration appear in Part Four to define the Dramatists' Guild's protection of playwrights' texts before and during production. To skirt authors' control over their art or to squelch directors' creative urge—either is deplorable. But with the Dramatists' Guild's contract signed by authors *and* producers, why do problems appear? This question—whether contract and copyright alone can foster solid collaboration between dramatists and directors, or whether an accessory approach must be studied—is critical. Can law itself differentiate between *interpreting* and *distorting* a play? Can law delineate the fine aesthetic line between the two functions without downplaying essential talents of directors? A positive approach and a possible solution appear at the end of Part Four in an article on American law and performance theory.

Acknowledgments

I should like to voice my appreciation and respect for my co-editor, Sidney Berger, Director, School of Theatre, University of Houston, and for Sandy Judice of his staff, who lent skill and humor to this undertaking as I ran for the borders with it—by phone, fax, and air.

I wish to thank the Alley Theatre for permission to transcribe the Playwright/Director Panel Discussion and for the care and enthusiasm of its literary director, Christopher Baker.

Also, I am grateful to the English Department at the University of Northern Colorado for making this book possible. Our chair, John Loftis, was more than generous with time and advice. Colleagues John Harrison and Ben Varner graciously supplied stylistic assistance as I prepared the manuscript. Without the aid of the secretarial staff under Pat Chandler, the completion of this work would not have been so smooth and enjoyable as it has been. Lidia Casarez, Sandy Pope, Nicky Loncorich, Mike Schmeeckle, and Russell Iverson tendered their top-notch skills to keep my pages neat and ordered. For reference assistance, Maurice Zane, librarian at Kahului Public Library on Maui, Hawaii, was invaluable. To Maureen Melino, editorial staff at Greenwood, and to her guidance and taste, I am indebted. A special thanks to Lois Morris, Lynda Groves, and Barbara Taylor of the Dean of Arts and Sciences' staff for technical assistance.

PART ONE

Theories of Authorship and Interpretation

Literary Assumptions about Text

In disciplines afield of theatre, theorists like Roland Barthes, Michel Foucault, Alvin Kernan, and Barbara Herrnstein Smith have singularly challenged our traditional certainty of what constitutes text in poetry, prose, and drama. The earlier, humanistic view of literature held that authors were prime movers who communicated through texts to their audiences. Text was sacrosanct, inviolable; the reader's duty was to delve into the language through which the author had expressed himself. The goal was to discover the author's intent; for in literature, as in the Bible, everything began with the word. Theatre text, in part, and fairly or not, was held to derive in like manner.

ABANDONING THE TEXT TO THE WORLD

Using a semiotic ground, Roland Barthes qualifies the old assumptions about literary text, professing that "the meaning of a work cannot be created by the work alone; the author never produces anything but presumptions of meaning, forms, and it is the world which fills them" (Barthes, "Literature and Signification," xi). Texts, then, resemble "the links of a chain of meaning, but this chain is unattached," so that someone else—in time, the reader—must "fasten it, give it a definitive meaning" (xi).

Barthes implies that readers, interpreters, or critics are "not responsible for reconstructing the work's [original] message" (260), for at the heart of any reading of a critical work is "a dialogue of two histories and two subjectivities: the author's and the reader's" (260)—and the dialogue is shifted toward the present, Barthes believes. With that emphasis, the meaning that comes to the reader is as individual as the language the writer chooses to speak, which does not "come down to him from Heaven; it is one of the various languages his age affords him . . . in his exercise of an intellectual function which belongs to him in his own right, an exercise in which he puts all his 'profundity' "; therefore reading or probing is "not an 'homage' to the truth of the past or to the truth of 'others' [e.g., authors]—it is a *con*struction of the intelligibility of our own time" (260). Note that for Barthes, meaning comes from *con*struction of the interpreter's mind, not from *re*construction of the author's intent.

In schemata like Barthes', then, the writer abandons his text to the world, which "always restores his work to him as a motionless object, provided once and for all with a stable meaning" (xiii). The abandonment of the work by the writer is forced by necessity, for "the present of writing is already past, its past always pluperfect" (xiii). The chronology seems sound to Barthes, for an author does not write for himself but for others. For this reason, "the ownership of language is impossible" (xiii).

From his semiological base of words as signs, Barthes implies that a literary work is not bound to what is signified by the writer but opened to what the reader signifies from it. We infer, then, that the function of a piece of writing, of a group of counterpointed signs, "is not to transmit a positive message" but "to show that the world is an object to be deciphered" (263). The reader, not the author, is the decipherer, the signifier. While language, words, and speech are all signs, "do they always signify the same thing? Do they combine in a single meaning" (262)? If not, then the meaning of a work (which Barthes qualifies as "generally an insipid notion identified with the author's 'philosophy' ") hinges "not on a sum of intentions and 'discoveries,' but on what we should perceive as an intellectual system of signifiers" (263). Barthes refers for support to Bertolt Brecht, who "elaborates the tautological status of *all* literature, which is a message of the signification of things and not of their meaning" (263). In his use of the concept of signification, Barthes insists that what he is naming is "the process which produces the meaning and not this meaning itself" (263). His tight differentiation is germane to our notions of the origin or existence of meaning in script.

DELEGATING AUTHORITY TO THE READER

From his first writings in the 1970s, Michel Foucault's work has been called opaque and provocative by critics; yet he is said to be "the most powerful figure in French intellectual circles today" (Harari, 431). Foucault follows a "devil's-advocate" style of exposition.

Foucault suggests that it is in the nature of literature that "the author should appear to be absent . . . delegate his authority" to others (Foucault, *Archaeology of Knowledge,* 93). Yet writers want to own their texts, do not wish to be "dispossessed" of "what they say" (211). Most feel that "at all costs, they must preserve that tiny fragment of discourse . . . whose fragile, uncertain existence must perpetuate their lives"

(211). Herein lies their "trace," their immortality; they do not want to believe that "the time of discourse is not the time of consciousness extrapolated to the dimensions of history, or the time of history present in the form of consciousness." Hence they protest, "Must I suppose that in my discourse I can have no survival?" (210). Such awareness antedates dramatist Edward Albee's contention in 1987 that "There is a kind of proof of existence that print gives" (Albee, "Introduction," vii).

Foucault plays with the idea that the author-function can be filled "by virtually any individual when he formulates a statement" (Foucault, "What Is an Author?", 93), and hence is not "the expression of genius and freedom" (210). Thus Foucault treats words that make up composition and discourse "in terms *not* of the gentle, silent, intimate consciousness that is expressed in them, but of an obscure set of transformations, of anonymous rules" (210). He consoles the maker of discourse who must watch someone "cut up, analyze, combine, rearrange all these texts . . . without ever the transfigured face of the author appearing" (210). He regrets that the author expended "so much piety in preserving them and inscribing them in men's memories," yet with "nothing remaining of the poor hand that traced them, of the anxiety that sought appeasement in them" (210). He appears to deny the authors of textual discourse "their exclusive and instantaneous right to it" (209). However, if (or when) the writer "acquires some 'importance' " in a culture, then Foucault proposes that the author might justifiably have more control of the ramifications of what he has written (154).

CHALLENGING THE TEXT'S INTEGRITY

A more contemporary theorist, Alvin Kernan, discloses how Barthes' revolution in defining language and text took form and flourished, and why he fears the revolution's result. Whereas literature was earlier valued and empowered, it is now regarded as one of "the most corrupt institutions of capitalism" (Kernan, 213). He warns that we need a "new way, plausible and positive . . . to claim for the traditional literary works a place of some importance and usefulness in individual life and for society as a whole" (213).

Kernan's *Death of Literature* covers the early attacks of deconstructionism on the integrity of text: "Deconstructors show the emptiness of literary language and texts" (212). They reach back to the eighteenth century and disallow Samuel Johnson's edicts on authorial ownership of language, though his stance "still stands as the magna carta of [many a] modern writer" (159).

Deconstructionists devalue the authority of language and claim rights to open readings of text since language itself is "empty," lacking in any "absolute connection between words and things, or words and ideas" (154). Hence they refuse to "posit some linguistic essence in language" (154). Words are not "fixed in some permanent way in and of themselves, but are always changing . . . to suit the needs and interests of those who use them" (155).

Kernan writes that feminists, too, challenge the authority of text; they constitute "one of the big revolutionary first moves in the linguistic power game," namely, "to demonstrate the arbitrary and insubstantial nature of the received standard language" (157). With one blow, they also demonstrate "literature's use in the past wrongfully to suppress the female" (212).

Other power struggles over the essence of text Kernan terms "battles in a class war" (72). Rooted in radicalism, literary iconoclasm was "a crucial part of the struggle for democratic freedom" (72). Kernan bares Barthes' objections to the old mode of criticism that put the usually upper-class writer on top and cast "the reader or audience in the role of the oppressed proletariat" (Kernan, 72). Before the battle, "the writer (was) the only person in literature" (72). But after Barthes' revolution, newer reader-response modes of discourse set readers ever freer "to interpret in any way they saw fit texts which in themselves either had no meaning, or were deficient in meaning, or contained infinite possibilities of meaning" (Kernan, 73). In this approach to text, "the author . . . whose creative imagination was once considered the validating source of all art, was finally sent to the guillotine" (73). Kernan warns that these "radical criticisms of recent years [are] only hypertrophied extensions of old literary values," and he finds it difficult to see how "literature that has been stripped of any positive value can be considered worth reading and interpreting" (213).

SUPPLYING A TEXT'S MEANINGS

With authors—as Kernan jokes—guillotined by Barthes' revolution in critical theory, the reader "arose" as literary interpreter with a new code of ethics popularized by Barbara Herrnstein Smith. In her volume *On the Margins of Discourse*, Smith claims the "inference or 'supplying' of meanings" to a text is part of the individual reader's "engagement with and experience of literature" no matter how "invalid or unvalidatable" the interpretations seem (154). Whereas the more traditional theorist E. D. Hirsch held that the "uses of language" are "all ethically governed by the intentions of the author" (quoted in Smith, 134), Smith exhorts us to be leery of Hirsch's protectionist argument. She questions his broad and overlapping use of concepts like "original meaning," "authorial meaning," and "intentions of the author," which she argues are not "equivalent at some points but not all points" (Smith, 136). Their misuse as equivalencies, she thinks, misleads Hirsch and us into overstressing the power of authors.

To clarify the distinction between authorial meaning and intention, Smith divides the many uses of utterance into two categories: natural discourse and fictional discourse. Smith sees her division as necessary to help us recognize that "although the intentions of all authors are historically determinate, the meanings of all utterances are not" (137). Natural discourse embraces conversational remarks and philosophical treatises, and their initiation is an historical act and event. Therefore some of their meanings, at least, can be "inferred by the listener on the basis of linguistic convention, and the propriety of those inferences can be challenged or supported by appeals to those conventions" (137).

In contrast, Smith's second category, fictive discourse, which covers literary texts like poems, novels, and playscripts, should be distinguished from other utterance. She does acknowledge that "[b]ecause the composition [n.b., *composition*] of the words is a historical act or event, *some* of the meanings of *that* act or event . . . are at least theoretically ascertainable on some basis" (138; emphasis in original). These ascertainable meanings might encompass "everything from the author's most intimate motives in composing [the work] to all the social and intellectual circumstances that could be conceived of as having occasioned its composition or shaped its form" (138). However, "[b]ecause a fictive utterance is not itself a historical act or event . . . was not 'performed' and did not 'occur' in the historical universe, some of its meanings are *historically indeterminate*" (138; emphasis in original). Smith's qualification gives the reader a measure of interpretive leeway into composed (fictive) texts, which theorists call "open texts." The potential that Smith's "open text" furnishes for open interpretation now looms in theatre polemic as a measure of sanction for directors' unconcern with authors' text (Suchy, 80; Vincent, 6). For Smith encourages the reader (in theatre, the first "reader" is the director) to search the written text—with confidence and without guilt—for emergent meanings, and to infer and supply them freely. To do so "is not to override—ignore, mistake, or betray—something that is *there*, but to acknowledge the fact that something is *not* there" (138; emphasis in original). What we have here is Smith's liturgy of evolution either consoling or repelling us (as our culture or counterculture has slyly directed our thinking).

In sum, Smith's analysis leaves the meanings in a literary text open; they await our creativity and cognition as readers/listeners/audience; and our unconcern with authorial intent (or our mistaking of it) is not "morally unregenerate behavior" (150). In fact, when we "evoke other meanings from a verbal structure" than those the author "presumably or even certifiably intended," what we do is ethical; for we have merely "re-given [the text] to ourselves and thus re-authored" the fictive utterance (150). Our feat is not inequitable, for "the composer of a verbal structure does not, and presumably does not expect to, retain eternal proprietary rights to the manner of its employment" (150). Authors rise or fall. For what looms is Smith's warning to mulish purists or text-protectors forever searching for what the author meant: "[T]he works that survive [in any culture]—the plays that continue to be produced, the poems and novels that continue to be read—are those that evoke and exemplify *emergent* meanings" (151). If texts are to endure, "they must continue to have meanings independent of the particular context that occasioned their composition, which will inevitably include meanings that the author did not intend and could not have intended to convey" (151). For literature to live, it must be open to "individual cognitive activity" (154). Smith's life-giving drill may be better therapy for texts than for authors.

2

Literature's New Criticism Applied to Theatre

The theatre world has begun to reckon with shifted literary aspects of text and with reader's rights of interpretation. The new definitions of open and closed text, of meaning and intention, are testy and inexact; but familiarity with them may help dislodge old blocks between authorial rights and directorial freedom in production. Today's theatre journals flash enticing titles and lead-ins on issues of textual authority played out on our stages.

ART BY FRAMING

In "Author, Authority, and the Pedagogical Scene," Michael Vincent writes that the text of a play can lie beyond the print on its pages. Vincent spotlights *Elvire Jouvet 40*, a work that plays on Barbara Herrnstein Smith's categorization of fictive versus natural discourse (Smith, 137). This play, "an example of art by framing," conceived and directed by Brigitte Jacques, is a "literal re-enactment of a series of drama lessons given by actor and director Louis Jouvet in Paris in 1940" (Vincent, 6).

In Jacques' play, an *objet trouve*[1] becomes art through the artist's "transformative gesture" (7). The transformation occurs through what Smith has called category switching; for Jouvet's natural discourse, the discourse of his pedagogy, becomes Brigitte Jacques' fictive discourse. By appropriating the drama teacher's (Louis Jouvet's) discourse, the transformer—director Brigitte Jacques—"becomes the 'author' of this play even though she herself did not write a word of it" (7).

Moreover, Vincent feels, the performance of the text is even improved when the
" 'body language' and intonation of the actress contradict the literal sense of the
text" (9). This departure from the usual supports the logic of the concept "supplement" as detailed by Jacques Derrida in his *On Grammatology*. A "supplement" is
"added to what is already in some sense complete, and compensates for a lack; it
also supplants, displaces, and replaces." (Vincent, 8).[2] Thus Vincent declares that
the print on the pages is not the whole text of a play.

THE STAGE DIRECTION

Patricia A. Suchy's article, "When Words Collide: The Stage Direction as Utterance," asks whether the concept of "text" includes stage directions and must,
then, be adhered to by directors. Tossing neither author nor director atop the theatre stack, Suchy suggests that today, with authors' more extensive use of stage directions in their texts, we encounter "simultaneously opening potentials for the
director's interpretive authority" (80). Clear problems also arise with playscripts,
making it virtually impossible to separate a prior production's "stage directions"
(as they evolve in rehearsal) from the author-conceived ones. Suchy uses Smith's
terms—fictive and natural discourse, authorial force, and legitimate interpretation—to exemplify how stage directions can take the form of "a cryptic 'trigger'
inviting experimentation" (80).

Suchy cites Aristotle's emphasis on plot, character, and thought over diction to
support Samuel Beckett's position that stage directions rather than the text's "diction" often *are* the play (73). (Beckett's *Acts Without Words I and II* are nothing but
stage directions.) Suchy reasons that "in modern times, with the concept of the
'sub-text' or the idea that much of the play's meaning can be discovered beyond
the surface of its language, the uttered lines of a play seem skeletal, only *suggestive* of dramatic life" (73). She quotes lines from Pirandello to support her reason-
ing: "Nothing in this play exists as given and preconceived. Everything is in the
making, is in motion" (Pirandello, 373). Hence a stage direction often takes the
form of "a loose scenario inviting experimentation in the creation of *mise en
scène*" (Suchy, 80). Suchy sees theatre moving "increasingly toward greater self-
consciousness," which demands that in staging, what is needed is "the freedom to
interpret [stage directions] as part of the [play's] fiction" (80).

AUTHORIAL POTENCY

Judith Roof's "Testicles, Toasters and the 'Real Thing' " addresses "the credo
of authorial potency," and proposes that a playwright's anxiety over loose interpretations of text is a potency-problem (108). Roof hypothesizes a playwright who
pauses to reason, then immediately worries: "If a text defies analysis, it [might
stand] for itself as its own best irreducible version" (109). Hence the playwright
"grabs his testicles, attaching himself simultaneously to the intentional fallacy—
what he says goes—and to a belief in his power to generate 'real' impenetrable

characters" (108). Roof sees our reader-role as that of penetrating and sizing up characterization on our own rather than assuming it is authentic by reason of its author's intention alone (111, 112). Her forceful call for action in this article is aimed not at author versus director problems alone but at our need to "release ourselves from the onus of sex-role stereotypes" (113) which she accuses playwrights of foisting on us.

TEXT AND PERFORMANCE

An article by Gerald Rabkin, "Is There a Text on This Stage?"—subtitled "Theatre/Authorship/Interpretation"—discusses Umberto Eco's classification of closed versus open texts in his work, *The Role of the Reader*. Closed texts "aim at pulling the reader along a predetermined path, carefully displaying their effects so as to arouse pity or fear, excitement or depression at the due place and at the right moment" (144). Rabkin suggests Arthur Miller and Samuel Beckett as, perchance, in this category, and examines media coverage of their hostile reactions to directorial license. Eco's alternative category, the open text, is, Rabkin says, one in which reader and audience interpretation "is demanded by the text in order to complete understanding; it compels us to make the work together with the author" (144). In Eco's view, text is not "an artifact that has been granted canonical privilege" (Rabkin, 149). In the 1960s and early 1970s the text "as a sacred, inseminating source which commanded devout fidelity was overthrown in the name of a revolution of physical presence" (Rabkin, 143). But Rabkin stresses that if we deny the author's "patriarchal authority over his text," we must also recognize "the importance of protecting his personal rights to his work" (155).

To insure this recognition, Rabkin finds no help for authors in our current tendency to divide "text" into two entities: the written text and the performative text; for then, if the first is the author's and the second the director's, our vital theatrical problem immediately becomes that of the hierarchic relationship between the two (155). And surely the actors and designers contribute as well to the evolving work. In this connection, Rabkin brings in Richard Schechner's paradigm of the performative process. Schechner elevates script above text by separating the two, making text one of many components of "drama" along with score, scenario, plan, or map (Schechner, 8). The category itself (drama) is but the smallest circle of the four in Schechner's whole performative process—drama, script, theatre, and performance (8). Of these four slots, performance—not drama—is the largest. Rabkin is not enthusiastic about Schechner's assemblage, which makes text "a function of language" circumscribed by "Drama, the narrowest circle of Performance, which is privileged in [text's] place" (Rabkin, 150).

Other theorists, too, have remarked on the prestige of the term "performance" in contemporary culture, complaining that "[t]his clearly subversive modernist valorization of performance over the meaning that would dominate it cannot help also recapitulating modernity's imperialistic grasp for authority over the event" (Benston, 437). Rabkin does not support the downplay of text by Schechner nor other theorists, but suggests instead that we broaden the concept of textuality "so that the mediating level of performance is neither privileged NOR deprivileged" (Rabkin, 150). Rabkin concludes that "The playwright's intentionality is, then, not irrelevant [but is] perceived within a complex matrix of interpretation" (158).

As one reads theatre items conversant with literary criticism's parley, claims like the following can turn readers into Foucault-styled devil's advocates: "The script is something to be used and discarded as its textuality is corporealized in performance" (Suchy, 74). To such a statement, any reaction, however cantankerous, seems better than placidly watching the legitimate theatre resign itself to the plight of the movie world, wherein "[t]he true author of the film text is the director, who authoritatively 'writes' the film with the help of the narrative and thematic material provided by the writer" (Rabkin, 155). Though theatre directors need to be master designers, critics, and stylists as they work with playscripts, a good director's interpretation will not override the text but will reflect "a sincere attempt at finding an author's ideas in a play and at rendering them honestly and appropriately through the theatrical arts" (Hodge, 10).

Once society, worshiping its artists, poets, and playwrights, named them "shaman," spared them the necessity of compromise to sell their work. And patronage was born—but died. To many, the Samuel Becketts, Buckminster Fullers, and their like became heroes for staunchly clinging to their text and its intent. Having one's words changed or cut, whether on page or stage, may seem to a playwright the ultimate affront, arousing more hostility than tampering with other facets of performance. Albee's view that print gives playwrights "a kind of proof of existence" (Albee, "Introduction," vii) seems sound; authors go deep inside themselves to find precise phrasing—a more intimate or intense search, perhaps, than a designer's for a sleeve-line or an architect's for a stair. Since playwrights come up with their words and metaphors after struggle, directors may be perceived as insensitive when they fear that some of these hard-won lines or phrases may not work as theatre. What authors may fear is that if they free up what they formed out of blood and inspiration, they'll lose their text's essence. And we may ask why we wish to shatter their shaman status when art needs leaders today.

NOTES

1. *Objet trouve*—an object picked up from somewhere else; something lost and found; hence here it is a "found" object in one field of art (lessons) transformed into another (performance).

2. Vincent explains the double meaning of Derrida's "supplement" thus: "Teaching, we know, is by nature a supplementary, parasitic practice. The teacher's teaching adds to the matter of the course, makes it consumable, even palatable to students" (8).

PART TWO

Remarks of Playwrights and Directors

We think we know what playwrights are and what they do, but what *directors* are and what they do is less understood. Historically, the playwright/director relationship under classic codes was clear: writers from Sophocles to Shakespeare controlled production. But by Europe's neo-classic age, the plays performed in theatre were not necessarily true to their authors' texts. "Restoration and eighteenth-century audiences in England found many of Shakespeare's scripts [plays] unacceptable and preferred adaptations of them" (Brockett, 353). Directors altered plots and generalized the scenery.

By the mid-nineteenth century London's Charles Kean had popularized the director as a leading figure in theatre (Brockett, 505). Even Richard Wagner's performance theory held that an opera's success as a piece of art rested not on the written composition alone but on its performance; therefore the music's composer should direct every aspect of production. Composer-master pianists may occur but not often. The argument here is primarily the rarity of combined and generally equal talents in two disparate areas like composition and performance or playwriting and direction.

European theatre figures like Saxe-Meiningen, Max Reinhardt, and Vsevelod Meyerhold saw directors as *creators* who might and should adjust and redo a script at will. Like Adolphe Appia and Gordon Craig, their rationale was the compression of multiple facets of drama into one artistic end. Our culture's subsequent nudge toward a director's creative posture may spring from such beginnings.

However, contrary notions of playwright-director roles in the early 1900s still argued for an author's control of text and meaning: in France, Jacques Copeau insisted that directors were but translators who must render the playwright's intention precisely. Such support for playwrights' potency has prevailed in our legal system. The backing lies in Dramatists' Guild contracts and in copyrights protecting authors' material from overt theft—if not from aesthetic misstatement—by theatrical groups who wish to produce a work; protection extends throughout a playwright's lifetime and for fifty years thereafter.

Still, by 1984, the theory of directorial primacy had reenergized enough in our culture that Robert Brustein, artistic director of a leading repertory company, could proclaim that "a director's *normal* rights of interpretation are essential in order to free the full energy and meaning of the play" (Freedman, E6). And by 1988 a university text defined a director as one who "brings out the life-force of a breathing and pulsating story on the stage" and captures for the audience "the wild tropical bird of the play" (Hodge, 10).

The issue is complex and its ramifications vast. Yet today's theorists and journal writers too seldom address what Brustein's "normal" means, nor tackle specific, nagging questions on floating concepts of "text" and "control" like these:

Is theatre a medium that naturally requires productive collaboration?

What measure of subjectivity may a director bring to the interpretation of a playwright's text without diminishing the author's intent and/or the play?

How can directors envision and execute a new set of images as they direct a text yet still leave the meaning untouched and intact?

Does the ethic of respecting a text and its author's intent rest mainly on adhering to the scripted dialogue and action; or does the concept of ethics reach into aesthetics of setting, costuming, casting type, tone, ambience—areas beyond those usually covered by legal contracts?

How can the playright's intentionality be perceived within a complex matrix of performance but still not be thought irrelevant? (Rabkin, 148)

How can we broaden the concept of textuality so that the mediating level of performance is neither privileged *nor* deprivileged? (Rabkin, 150)

Must the result of direction be a "glossy" (photograph) of the script—or can it be a less mimetic reflection?

Can an ethical director turn a *King Lear* into a *King Lear and I*, or produce a *Lady in the Dark at the Top of the Stairs*? or *The Music Man for All Seasons*, or *Guys and Doll House*? (Review of *Prospero's Books*)

How much do stage directions "open up" the text to the director's authority? (Can directors choose or choose not to heed texted stage directions?)

Is the script primarily cerebral, a textual entity into which the director can help the actors pump emotion to create the meaning of the play?

What about tone? Can the director ethically encourage an actor to "improve" the performance of the text by letting "body language" and intonation contradict the literal sense of the text?

What responsibility does a playwright (and/or director) have to "watch dog" the production?

Can the director alter circumstances of the story to broaden its thematic reach?

Who suggests and controls rewrites? At what stage in the play's development does the rewriting end?

Does the director translate to the stage only what is already in the play?

Could the stage directions rather than the text's "diction" ever *be* the play? What would the director's function be in this instance?

Are directors working with scripts principally creators, interpreters, or guides?

Can the director alter the ending to get a more theatrical or a more commercial finish?

If it is acceptable to shorten *Hamlet* and put the play in modern dress, where is the line in altering the work of a living playwright? Is the ethic of altering a play dependent solely on the legal phrasing of the contract?

To hard questions we cannot pour out easy or obvious answers; a stream of language is not sufficient. Both playwright and director will readily grant that a produced play is the "physicalization" of a playscript; and "it must be cohesive and integrated in all its aspects, from the manipulation of the actor to the manipulation of the stage space and all the material used on it" (Hodge, 10). Yet a watershed of divisive factors still blurs the authorial and directorial positions.

Indeed, more than a decade prior to the interviews that follow, the eminent English film and stage director Peter Brook said that his view of "what a director does and why" had shifted over the years. In the 1940s he had believed that "the work of a director [is] to have a vision of a play and to 'express it' . . . to make the play live for a contemporary audience" (Berry, 117). A director is "always a man of his time . . . [who makes] a new set of images" for the play (117). But the danger Brook soon found was that directors could "allow their love and excitement and enthusiasm" to lead them into proudly presenting "very subjective versions of the play" in a vain belief that their version was "the play as made into sense by such-and-such an individual" (Berry, 116). Brook warned that such pride and enthusiasm "have to be tempered by a cool sense that anybody's personal view of the play is bound to be less than the play itself" (Berry, 117). His thought evolved until he felt that a play goes "far beyond the unity that [a director's] image could give"; his interest then advanced beyond "liking the play, and therefore showing my image of the play," to a different process "which starts always with the instinctive feeling that this is [but] the play for *now*" (118). Thus the director's version is a contemporary one and not assumed to be the definitive one.

These are not simple concepts; but it is ingenuous to dam a flow of discourse on production hierarchy with such pat definitions as "a playwright provides a text and the director produces it." If we go to the source of the spring, we should get clear and fresh answers to hard questions. Following are letters, transcriptions of interviews, and forums in which these topics were tackled by contemporary playwrights and directors in professional, repertory, and university theatre. Their comments may solidify our view of what a playwright does; moreover, they may furnish us with what we unquestionably need: a working definition of what a director does (and is).

In America's theatre, as in England's, whether for authors' tried or untried plays, the view of what a director does—and of what power or authority lies in staging— is still evolving.

3

Alley Forum: Playwrights, Directors, and the Postmodern Stage

The forum was held at Houston's Alley Theatre on January 27, 1992.

Christopher Baker: The gentleman to the right of me is Gregory Boyd, artistic director of the Alley Theatre since 1989. Among the plays that he has directed are his own and also many classic plays—*A Flea in Her Ear*, *Jekyll and Hyde*, *Svengali*, *Three Sisters*, *Measure for Measure*, and *As You Like It*. Before coming to the Alley he served as artistic director of Williamstown's Other Stage, Stagewest in Massachusetts, and Playmakers Repertory in North Carolina. He has taught on the faculties of Carnegie Melon University, the University of North Carolina, and Williams College.

Gregory Boyd: Thank you. I'd like to introduce the other members of the panel. To my far right is Edward Albee, whose plays include *The Zoo Story*, *The Death of Bessie Smith*, *Who's Afraid of Virginia Woolf?*, *Tiny Alice*, *A Delicate Balance*, *Box Mao Box*, *Counting the Ways*, *Seascape*, *All Over*, *The Lady from Dubuque*, *The Man Who Had Three Arms*, and *Marriage Play*. Among the many awards he has received are two Pulitzer Prizes, the Tony Award, the New York Drama Critics Circle Award, the Obie, and the Gold Medal in Drama from the American Academy and Institute for Arts and Letters.

Edward Albee: [interjecting] It wasn't gold. The first year they decided not to give the gold medal out *not* made of gold. I get it! [Audience laughter]

Gregory Boyd, artistic director, Alley Theatre, 1992. Courtesy of the
Alley Theatre.

Boyd: He is president of the Edward Albee Foundation, a member of the Council of
the Dramatists' Guild for the past twenty-five years. For the past four years he has
been Distinguished Professor of Drama at the University of Houston, where he
teaches playwriting and is particularly active in the development of new plays and
young playwrights. Mr. Albee is also a director, having staged productions of his own
plays as well as plays by Sam Shepard, Lanford Wilson, and others. His production of
his own play, *Three Tall Women*, opened recently at Vienna's English Theatre. His recent work at the Alley includes his production of *Who's Afraid of Virginia Woolf?* performed here as well as touring the United States and the then Soviet Union; his
production last season of two plays by Samuel Beckett, a playwright he particularly
admires; and his current staging of the American premiere of his *Marriage Play*.

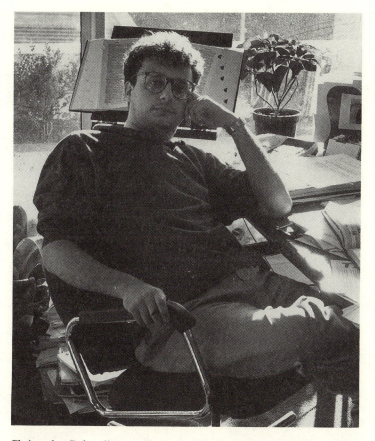

Christopher Baker, literary director and dramaturge, Alley Theatre, 1992.
Courtesy of the Alley Theatre.

To Mr. Albee's left is Ron Link, who has won the L.A. Drama Circle Critics Award for production of Bill Cain's *Stand Up Tragedy* at the Mark Taper Forum and at Hartford Stage, and subsequently on Broadway. Internationally he has directed plays by Neil Simon, Herb Gardner, and others in Europe and Australia. Recently he directed the premiere of *Jake's Women* by Neil Simon. In the beginnings of his career Off-Off-Broadway, he directed over twenty-five productions, working with the then-incipient talents of Robert De Niro and Sylvester Stallone. He is currently an associate artist at the Mark Taper Forum in Los Angeles.

To my left, Christopher Baker, dramaturge and literary manager of the Alley Theatre, responsible for our playbills, lecture series, and forums such as tonight's symposium. He is the author and director of *Calliope Jam*, and directed the Alley's touring productions of *Twelfth Night* and *Julius Caesar*. He's been a guest lecturer at Harvard University and is an alumnus of Northwestern University and the American Repertory Theatre Advanced Training Program at Harvard.

Edward Albee, playwright-director. Courtesy of Fred R. Conrad/NYT
PICTURES.

To Mr. Baker's left, Robert Wilson, author, designer, and director of nearly one hundred theatre, opera, dance, film, and video works. Since 1970 Mr. Wilson has been at the forefront of innovation in international theatre; he is perhaps best known for such creations as *Einstein on the Beach,* his 1976 opera, a collaboration with composer Philip Glass, for *Death, Destruction, and Detroit* and *Death, Destruction, and Detroit II* in Berlin. Recently he has directed *King Lear*, an opera based on Thomas Mann's *Doctor Faustus*, and *Orlando*. Mr. Wilson has toured his works throughout Europe, the Americas, and the Near and Far East, and is the recipient of the Drama Desk and Obie awards, two Guggenheim fellowships, and two Rockefeller grants in playwriting. His Alley production last season of *When We Dead Awaken* was chosen by *Time* as one of the ten best productions of last year. He is currently in rehearsal for *Parsifal* for the Houston Grand Opera opening February 6, 1992. In October 1992 he will direct *Danton's Death* at the Alley.

Will you join me in welcoming the panel tonight. We've taken so much "noise" about the title of this program that what we want to start out with is asking Mr. Baker what postmodernism is. Any ideas?

Baker: The important thing that the label of "postmodern" indicates is a questioning—or calling into question—of certain ideas, both culturally and artistically, within the last fifty years. I think briefly, in terms of art, the term "postmodern" calls into question the idea of causality and logical progression, but more important, the idea of hierarchy—the hierarchy between art and popular culture. Postmodernism also calls into question the hierarchy in a work itself: of the text and the playwright and the production and the idea of content and meaning as being somehow the deeper, more significant level of a work. This notion—a romantic notion that we still retain—of an author's intention that we try to "get at" or interpret is called into question as being primary.

What are *the* most important parts of a theatrical production of a work? Is it indeed the verbal text or are there other things that are more important? I think—and as you notice I phrased my answer "calling into question" rather than "these are definitely the changes"—that's why postmodernism is in the title. It calls into question something that I think certainly (at least in the American theatre), we wouldn't have questioned a hundred or even fifty years ago: the primacy of the text.

Boyd: [Teasing] Mr. Albee, postmodernism? [Audience laughter]

Albee: [Chuckling] Well, I have no problem with anything that he says, except as a semanticist I must argue with the title. I have various arguments with some of the concepts, but it's the title that bothers me. What he really means is, "Let's examine some new stuff that is going on, some new ideas about theatre." The whole concept of the title "postmodern" bothers me because "modern" is really that which is contemporary, that which is going on. It bothers me in architecture; postmodern architecture seems to be architecture about architecture rather than architecture about building buildings. It's a kind of masturbation in architecture and in many arts, if you will. There are many things in a healthy art scene, many things that are going on. There are even plays that are written that are supposed to be acted and directed with respect to the text. This is still going on. It's merely the term that bothers me.

We can have a discussion—I think we should—about all this stuff as long as we don't have to use that awful term.

Boyd: Well, let's phrase it another way and ask the big question. In terms of a theatrical production, what is the primary focus of the production? Is it service to a text that exists, is it interpretation of that text, or is the text merely one of the elements that come together to make a theatrical event, and no more or less important than costume or scenery or acting or music or sound?

Albee: It depends, does it not, on the piece that you're doing? If you're doing a new play that is through-composed, if you will, which is written with a full text, which does not ask for improvisation, which does not ask for variance from the text, then I think your responsibility is to do what the author wanted. That's merely one kind of theatrical experience. If you're taking a very, very famous play by either a completely dead or half-dead author, then why not experiment with it as long as you respect the text if the author wants the text respected? However, if you are creating a theatrical experience—and some of the most interesting theatrical experiences I've come across in the past twenty years have been the stuff that Robert Wilson's been doing—if you're creating a different kind of theatre, the rules are different. With a play that wants its text respected, respect its text; with a play that is a set of improvisations or that approaches theatre from a totally different point of view, then do it that way. I've never thought anything was the wave of the future except possibly diversity.

Robert Wilson: I think what we see is what we see and what we hear is what we hear; and frequently for me in the theatre it's difficult to do both of those things simultaneously. In directing *Parsifal* right now I'm trying to set up a situation where one can hear music, hear text, and see. So the two primary ways that we relate to one another are through our eyes and through our ears—through other senses as well, but primarily I think it's through our eyes and ears. So what I've tried to do in the theatre that I've made is to set up a space where a text can be heard and where what we see can reinforce what we hear—but doesn't always have to be subservient, or decoration, or an afterthought to what we hear. Theatre is a work, I think. I like the fact that you referred to the theatre as a work. I always like to think of it, actually, as opera—in the Latin sense of the word meaning opus or work. I also don't understand what is meant by the term "postmodern." I think always for me the responsibility is the rediscovery of the knowledge that is within me or within all of us. Socrates said that the baby was born knowing everything. I think that it is the uncovering of this knowledge that is the avant-guard—the rediscovery of the classics.

Albee: What, well, you're doing all of *Parsifal,* as Wagner wrote it?

Wilson: Yes . . .

Albee: Thank heavens.

Wilson: We have no cuts.

Albee: Well, I don't know, it's a very long first act. Good. This is not an improvisation on *Parsifal* or cuts from *Parsifal*—it's *Parsifal*?

Wilson: It's *Parsifal*! And it's actually a work that I've thought about for many years. It was controversial when I did it in Hamburg last Easter. But actually I had thought a lot and read a lot about some of the things that Wagner had said. He said once in a letter to a lady friend, "People misunderstand this work; it's not a work about a Christian ceremony, but it's a work about human strife and struggle and spiritualism." Many things Wagner talked about! He said that for the most part the singers shouldn't move around a lot. They could just stand and sing and sustain the tension of these long lines, and that was enough. He talked about movement and stillness, the idea of continuum of the line of sound, that it is always there, that it doesn't begin and end. My production is different from any other production that has been done in the history of *Parsifal.* Some people thought that it was against Wagner, but I felt it was in its way very much with respect for the text, the audio text and the music. It's very different from my own work, but here I was given a text, music, and I tried to create a visual book around this that would reinforce it, support it, give us space so we can hear and see.

Boyd: Ron, when you work with a new play—and most of your work has been with new plays and playwrights who are current and in the rehearsal room with you— what do you feel your responsibility is?

Ron Link: I always feel that my first responsibility is to serve the writer. I feel it's like the European tradition. If you have not serviced the writer, then you haven't done your job. Plays either attract me on a very visceral level like music—language is music—and if I don't service that and the writer is not happy because I don't pretend to want to be a writer, then I haven't done my job. I happen to enjoy working in tandem with the writer very much. I love that process, and I find that all the plays I've done are brought to life. I have to take almost an entrepreneurial attitude. In other words, let's say you get a play like *Stand Up Tragedy* or *The Kiddie Pool*, and let's say you get it on its voyage of a long life, and that doesn't mean just going to Broadway. It usually takes about two years out of your life. So you have to love it, and the writer had best be happy with that. I think the first job that you have as a director is to cast very well. Many actors come to me and say, "Oh, I want to be involved with your next project," and they are nowhere near ready to come along on a new work. Because they suddenly want to do Samuel French–type plays, they say, "Oh my god, you mean you're still going to change that?" They're talking to you and the writer at the same time. They're not prepared for the voyage; the voyage is very difficult on a play. And having produced—I don't produce anymore—but having produced in New York, you often have to take on a play, not only from its very beginnings as "text" and its look, interpreting it to designers, and therefore hopefully you have designers who have a painting vocabulary as well as a great imagination. You often have to worry about things, I find, like logos, advertising. I've certainly found myself with plays in New York where the advertising agency was selling a play down the drain by trying to push something visually on the public. But above all, and we can go into many things about the marriage between a director and a writer, I think it's to serve up the play that is in the writer. It often isn't there in the first draft of the script. And above all, I would like to get out that it has to be accessible to the public. I think that's a great deal of what's wrong with the theatre today—it's not accessible. Robert's work, for instance, does something magical that makes theatre an event, which is a great deal of what has dropped out of the theatre.

Boyd: So the chief responsibility, though, is to the writer—to the text?

Link: To the writer. In my instance, I have never started a play that didn't change drastically by the opening night. Sometimes, let's say in the voyage of *Stand Up Tragedy*, it opened at the Mark Taper Forum workshop, then it went to the Mainstage, then to Hartford, then to San Francisco, and then on into New York. With each one of those ventures the writer kept working on the play and changing it for the better.

Boyd: This is something that is common now. The piece that I've done recently, *Jekyll and Hyde*, has changed maybe 75 percent from when we first did it here. But, Edward, as a playwright, I don't want to put words in your mouth, but I think I've heard you say at times that it's not for you a question of rewriting through a series of productions; you know what the play is pretty much after the writing process. Is that so?

Albee: When I write a play on paper, I have spent a lot of time with it in my mind; and when I write a play down on paper, I know what it looks like and sounds like as a performed stage piece. So I see it as I write it, as a piece that is performed by actors on a stage in front of an audience. This may save a little bit of time. [Laughs] I heard a distinction made that I didn't quite understand: the distinction was between responsibility to the playwright or responsibility to the text. It seems to me—well, first of all, nobody should go in rehearsal with a play that they don't respect. We're talking about a play with a composed text. You should not go into rehearsal assuming that the piece is going to be written during the rehearsal procedure because in the commercial theatre, anyway, there is no time in the four weeks to accomplish that. I claim that my plays don't change very much in rehearsal; I lie a little bit when I say that. I cut my plays because I overwrite. I get infatuated with the sound of my own voice and I put in all sorts of scenes and speeches that I am very fond of and I will probably use in another play if I take them out of the play that they are in. But I don't reconsider the play, because I think about it very carefully before I write it down. The responsibility to the text of a serious, useful play is the same thing as the responsibility to the audience, it seems to me. If you mutilate, revise too much a play, the changes that take place in the commercial theatre of a play on the way to opening night are usually oversimplifications, removals of grit; they homogenize, they make it very, very smooth and less an act of aggression against the status quo; and these are very bad things that usually happen in the commercial theatre. Theatre is there for a playwright to give us his vision of what the world is, not the vision that the audience wants to have of the world.

Wilson: No, I don't think we're in disagreement there.

Link: No, we're not in disagreement. I think what you do is incredibly brave, because you take on other writers when you get in there and wrestle—as long as there aren't too many dramaturges with the yellow pad brigade. It's wonderful with other writers to see them blossom in that situation that you don't need to go through.

Albee: You know, having just defended authors, I've now got to defend directors because I direct not only my own work but the work of a lot of other people. I have in mind now, for example, a production of the nameless Shakespeare play, you know, the Scottish play, I will call it *Macbeth* and see if the ceiling falls down. I have thoughts about that play which are going to be, I think, quite startling. However, I don't intend to second guess Shakespeare. I think he did a pretty good job in most of his plays. But I have to do something that Robert was talking about before, to let us see something freshly—which is enormously important with the work that everybody knows. Let us see it from a different perspective; let us do it with a different refraction—that's fine! You take chances sometimes and sometimes you're right. When I directed the two Beckett plays, *Krapp's Last Tape* and *Ohio Impromptu,* last year downstairs at the Alley, something very interesting happened during *Krapp's Last Tape*, where the character Krapp goes off-stage to get his drink several times. The last time that he goes off-stage was bothering me a great deal because it broke the dramatic action; and I suddenly said, "You know, well, I'm going to do something here that I probably shouldn't do. I'm not going to let him go off-stage that last time before he comes back and rips the tape of the past off and starts recording in the present! I'm going to let him get halfway off-stage, stop, think, look back at the tape, and then come back and do it. I'm not going to let him go off-stage that last time." Now this was probably in violation of Samuel Beckett, I thought, but I was very pleased to learn as an aside—they didn't say it in public, damn them, but as an aside— one guy during the Beckett symposium said, "That's very interesting what you did there, because when I saw Beckett direct it, that's what he did." That was nice; that kind of second guessing worked. And in that same evening of Beckett, I took this seven-minute play (less— this six-minute play) *Ohio Impromptu*, and decided to do it three times, which is certainly not rewriting Beckett; it is merely giving us more of Beckett than Beckett gave us; and I thought that worked.

Boyd: There are lots of ideas in what you've said, Edward. There's no question when one sees the production of *Marriage Play* that it is *your* production, *you* are the *auteur,* to use another hateful word like "postmodernism." There is no question that it is your production, you wrote it, you staged it. Similarly, I think, in terms of Mr. Wilson's work, most audience members are struck by the fact that each of Bob's productions is very distinctive, very much his authorship, whether it be an opera by Wagner or a play by Ibsen. Ron has spoken of the closeness in the relationship with the living playwright. I'm interested in the distinction between fidelity to the text and fidelity to the writer, when the writer no longer is with us. No one can know the state of Shakespeare's mind, really—what a fairy looks like for Shakespeare, what he meant by writing a fairy in *Midsummer Night's Dream.* So we're forced to fall back on our own devices and to create some context where a fairy can exist. Battling the totally unknowable state of Mr. Shakespeare's mind, we don't know what his intentions are; we have his text, and to quote Bob's quote of Socrates, there are truths in us perhaps from the time we're born that are reflected in that text and at different periods we find different things to embrace. Since you brought up Beckett, let's pursue him just a bit. Here's a playwright who is very much writing the visual stage picture as well as the language, the verbal aspect of the play. We've heard your story about whether there is a responsibility to adhere strictly to his suggestions when he's very specific about what the stage looks like at any one moment, or very specific about the movements the characters make. At what point does this simply become slavish and perhaps not lively? Peter Brook once said that if we let his play speak for itself, it may not make a sound; and our job is to try to conjure the sound from the play.

Albee: I saw a production of *The Tempest*, Peter Brook's production, his French language production. I saw it in Vienna last spring. It was fascinating, as everything Peter Brook does. All of his wonderful things were happening in it, including some of his excesses, but it doesn't matter. I know *The Tempest* very well. The experience for me was exhilarating to see somebody who respected the text, not second guessing Shakespeare, but allowing me to see it in a totally fresh and totally different way. Any production of Shakespeare is second guessing since we don't know, we have no standard of performance to go from. Anything that illuminates without distorting, anything that reveals without distorting it, is absolutely wonderful, no problem there. You get somebody like Beckett, who is enormously specific; I can think of no playwright who is more specific in duration of silences, who understands more than maybe any playwright besides Chekhov the value of both sound and silence in theatre. He is enormously specific about what he wants. The only time that I know that Beckett or Beckett's estate really fought greatly was that experience up in Cambridge, was it not, where this play *Endgame*, which is meant to take place sort of, certainly above ground, in a ruined world, was taken by the director and put down in a subway, as I believe. Beckett was concerned about this; I imagine he was concerned as much as anything by assuming "If you do that, what else will you do, or what else won't you do to the play!"

Boyd: Bob, what about your experiences in dealing with the Shakespeare or the Chekhov texts? How do you approach those—or is that an awfully general question?

Wilson: I did, actually, do Shakespeare and Chekhov back-to-back a couple of years ago, *King Lear* and a very short play that Chekhov wrote called *The Swan Song*. Actually in thinking about it, it never occurred to me until just now that what I did with *King Lear* is very similar to what I've done with *Parsifal*. I wanted to tell a very simple story. I think theatre has to be about one thing first and then it can be about many things. Susan Sontag said in her essay against interpretation that the mystery is in the surface, and I think the surface should remain simple and accessible for anyone. So this story of King Lear for me had to be on the surface something very simple, and then it gets more complicated. I wanted a space where one could hear the text. I used an old translation that was spoken in verse. I wanted actors that could speak in lines, not phrases, to sustain the line of the text, to be able to speak the text not in an interpretive way, but in a way that the audience could read through the text the way they would read through it at home privately. I didn't feel that it was possible for an actor to impose, to insist, his ideas on the work. That's not to say that he doesn't have his ideas about what he's saying, his interpretation, his emotions, his feeling, but it was a formal approach with holding back somewhat, indicating an idea, a feeling to the situation. Shakespeare couldn't possibly understand completely what he wrote. I don't think so because it's cosmic—that's what made it a masterpiece, a great work that is still with us. We can read it one night this way, and the next night we can read through it another way, and still another night find another way to read through it. I wanted to present the text in that way, that it would be possible for each person in the public to find his own way in reading through this text, and the actor was there to help the public read through the text the way they would do privately at home. I had almost no set—it was just a vast space. Sometimes it was darker or lighter, very similar to *Parsifal*. The text was so rich in pictures that I found it very difficult to make pictures, and I wanted a mental space, a blank canvas, so to speak, where one could visualize the words. With Chekhov, this was a very small play that he wrote very quickly; and I think he had said at one time that it shouldn't be longer than thirty or forty minutes. My production was about two-and-a-half hours. But it is a play about an actor who wakes up in the middle of the night and he is on-stage. To me one needed a lot of space around the words. It's a play of interior reflecting, and it was different from Shakespeare. My Shakespeare production was very formal. I'd never really directed a work in a naturalistic way, and my challenge was to see if I could do something in a more naturalistic manner. I couldn't really see doing Shakespeare in a naturalistic way, as I did with Chekhov; it seemed to be of another nature.

Boyd: Did you find yourself encouraging a kind of psychological impersonation by the actors in the Chekhov—more so than what you spoke about in the Shakespeare?

Wilson: More so than Shakespeare but not a lot.

Albee: I'm not surprised that Bob mentioned that this thirty-minute play took two-and-a-half hours, for the simple reason that one of the many interesting things that Bob Wilson has been doing over the years is altering our sense of time in the theatre. He changes for me when I see some of his work—he sets me adrift and I lose contact with real time, and real time becomes the stage time that he creates, and it could be quite exciting. Sorry I didn't see that one of Chekhov's!

Wilson: Well, it's similar, also, in Wagner and, say, the *King Lear*; I know that one of the assistants in lighting said to me the other day, "You know, this is supposed to be early morning and he's made the stage so bright!" But, one has a line of time that can be running, in, say, a sense of natural time and then this line is interrupted by this other line of supernatural time; and both of those ways of thinking about time were in my direction of the *Parsifal* and *Lear*.

Boyd: I think you all equally share in your work an intent focus on each moment of the play. In dealing with *new work* or making new productions of "classic pieces," we're in a difficult state in American theatre these days, as I'm sure you're all aware. Because so much of what we think of as American theatre is darkened by the increasing shadows of consumerism, apathy, economics, television, boring theatre, it is incumbent on us to encourage, cultivate, and create new work all the time. Yet it becomes increasingly difficult as one balances the axe to confront an audience with challenging material at a time when the economics encourage the need to make "box office." How do we approach making new work these days? How do we balance the need of the box office with the need to investigate new directions, new things, new writing, new playwrights?

Albee: . . . I'm convinced that if for a period of ten years, maybe even five, no commercial, bad, empty work were permitted on any of our stages, and only exciting, vigorous, difficult, tough, wonderful plays were permitted on our stages, I don't think the theatre would go away; I think that would become our standard. I just don't think that our theatre-going audiences are being offered any choice. They are being offered the lowest common denominator in the commercial theatre because everybody assumes that they don't want much. A regional theatre that, with sufficient financial support, for example, does first-rate work all the time will become a beacon, a place where people will come. They say, "Never underestimate the taste of the American public." I'm not so sure I totally agree with that. As it is in politics, we are not offered choices anymore in our elections. We are offered the choice between mediocrities. For example, we are offered tiny little choices; we are not offered the fundamental choices that we need. I'm convinced that if our audiences were exposed to only that which is the most provocative, done most provocatively and interestingly, I think most of the "junk" would leave our theatres and probably never come back. . . .

[The closing words of panelists Robert Wilson, Edward Albee, and Gregory Boyd:]

Wilson: . . . Our responsibility is . . . to maintain a balance of interest "in protecting the art of the past and in creating art of our time; in protecting the art of our homeland, our community, our nation; and in protecting the art of all nations." [Wilson paraphrases a quote by Andre Malraux explaining his philosophy as cultural minister of France under President de Gaulle.]

Albee: . . . Art is useful; it is not ephemeral, it is not decorative. It is there to instruct us, to clarify our minds. . . . I'm convinced that a society that listens to its string quartets, looks at its abstract paintings, and goes to see its Beckett plays— and Bob Wilson's work and a lot of other things—is probably a lot better capable of governing itself. The arts are essential to our understanding what we are as sentient human beings. The resistance to the arts strikes me as having a good deal to do with our growing unwillingness to participate completely in our own lives, our turning our backs on a particular kind of instruction and clarity and order that the arts can bring to our lives. We fear them because they shed too much light; and that's such a shame in a democracy.

Boyd: It's one of the few things that lasts throughout time. We go back to any of the ancient cultures; we always go and look at what the artists have done.

4

Robert Anderson, Playwright

Robert Anderson's plays have been produced professionally and in community and college theatres all over the world. In 1980 he was elected to the Theatre Hall of Fame. His most famous plays include *All Summer Long* (1952), *Tea and Sympathy* (1953), *You Know I Can't Hear You When the Water's Running* (1967), *I Never Sang for My Father* (1968), and *Solitaire/Double Solitaire* (1971). In 1991 two of Anderson's works were shown on television: *The Last Act Is Solo* and *Absolute Strangers*. He has been nominated for the Academy Award and the Writer's Guild Award, and has won the Screenwriter's Guild Award, the ACE Award, and the William Inge Award.

Anderson responded to my queries in a letter dated April 2, 1992, forwarded to me through Dr. Therese Jones, University of Colorado.

I want to make some general remarks about the playwright-director relationship before I take your questions one by one. By *contract*, the playwright has control of his script: nobody can change a word of it without his permission. Directors or actors can suggest changes, places where they are uncomfortable, don't feel a line is "right," but then it's up to the writer to say "Yes" or "No" and, if he wishes, to write the new line. For example, Henry Fonda starred in a play of mine . . . *Silent Night, Lonely Night*. On our way into New York, Hank came to me and said he was having difficulty with a long speech, wasn't comfortable with it. I told him he was not supposed to be comfortable with it. He told me he'd been a "good fellow" and would I try to loosen it up for him. I did, and he played it that way one night. He came back and said, "You were right. It should be difficult!"

Robert Anderson, playwright. Courtesy of Robert Anderson.

Another example of a different kind: with my play, *I Never Sang for My Father,* we were nearing the end of rehearsals when Alan Schneider, the director, Hal Holbrook, the star, and Gil Cates, the producer, said to me that the ending didn't pay off. They did not suggest that the story be changed, but that the scene in which the son breaks away from the father should be somehow more dramatic. After seeing a run-through, I went home, agreeing with them. And I sat at my desk and said, "Okay, Dad, let's have the scene we never had." [The rewritten scene] in effect saved the play. This is the only time that anything like this has happened to me . . . the complete rewrite of an important scene! I'm glad I was not a horse's ass, glad I did not insist on keeping my original version. I don't think I would or could ever change the *story*—that is too basic in the whole concept of the play. But to change the dramatization of the story—what happens to make it come out—*that* can be changed, though I don't want to have to come up with a scene like that ever again.

The playwright casts in company with the director. I wanted Deborah Kerr to star in *Tea and Sympathy.* This was my first Broadway play, I was thirty-six, and I did not know that you did not send a play to an actor without the approval of the director. I had worked with Deborah on a radio show, and felt she was perfect for the part (though I had not written it for her; I never write for a specific actor). I sent the play to her; she liked it but felt it was not the play in which she wanted to make her Broadway debut. I did not tell Kazan that I had sent it to her, but told him I would like her to play the part. He said he wanted this play to be the "discovery" of *me,* not of a Hollywood star. He was not commenting on her ability. So we went along seeing other stars. Naturally I did not tell Deborah. And I didn't tell Kazan that Deborah didn't want to do the play. Finally he said, "What are we going to do?" I asked him to go to California to meet Deborah, and I asked Deborah to meet him. They met and he wired me, "You're absolutely right . . . and she's going to do the play." You rarely find such perfect casting as Deborah in that play.

When I taught playwriting, I told my students that half the job was learning how to write a play; half was learning how to get along with other people. Kazan, of course, is a miracle: he believed he was serving the playwright, helping the writer realize his play. He had me read the play aloud to him several times, asked me questions about this or that, *never* suggested that this or that should happen. We did do some work here and there, but he never wrote or suggested a line—just made comments and asked questions. Later, when I wrote two novels, I found that's what a good editor does, too. Asks questions.

It is important that the playwright and director are doing the same play. Sounds strange? It often happens if the play hasn't been talked out beforehand that they are *not* doing the same play. Kazan and I talked about *Tea* a lot. "What does Laura feel toward Tom at this moment?" When I read aloud, he'd stop me. "Why did you read that line that way?" [All my directors] have been good—Alan Schneider, Arvin Brown, Peter Glenville—but with Kazan I felt assured that he knew my play, knew all my feelings about it, what I would like, before we went into rehearsal.

I see my plays rather clearly in terms of action and activity while I'm writing them. This makes it difficult sometimes to accept a director's version. But usually a director is more or less open to query and suggestion. However, Kazan said something very important to me. He asked me to stay away from rehearsals at certain times. "I didn't watch you make your mistakes. I'd rather you didn't watch me make mine." It saves wear and tear on both.

The playwright never talks directly to the actor except to say, "You're wonderful." A director builds up a different channel with each actor—very personal and distinct. A playwright could ruin it all by intruding. He talks to the director, gives him his reactions and suggestions. Also, the actor who is uncomfortable with something talks to the director, not the playwright. I know what I want, but I am not a director; I don't know how to get an actor to do what I want. I talk in *results,* but the director talks in *process.*

Specifically about Bill Inge: he gave me *Picnic* in its early drafts to read, and I made suggestions. Later, he gave me the script and said, "I like the suggestions you've made. Would you collaborate with me on it?" I declined, telling Bill we didn't write the same kind of play. But Bill obviously needed and wanted someone to give him a hand with *Picnic.* Anyway, Josh Logan—or Josh and Bill—did change the ending, and the play was an enormous success! A Pulitzer, a big movies sale—and yet Bill would sit in our house and bitch about the change. One day I stopped him and confronted him, told him that by Dramatists' Guild contract he had had the right not to change the ending; but he had agreed to it, the play had been a great success, made a lot of money, and so on, and that he should shut up about it. Of course, as you know, he later rewrote the play with his original ending, and called it *Summer Brave*.

A few years later I had a play, *Silent Night, Lonely Night*, and I sent it to Josh, with the history of Bill's *Picnic* in mind. Josh called me and laughed, "I love it except for the last two minutes, and I know you won't change them." Those minutes contained the *meaning* of the play.

Some points: some directors foolishly cross out all the author's stage directions. Kazan finds them very important. They can be important in telling the story—as important as the words. In *Tea and Sympathy*, there is a scene where Laura is trying to keep a student (who is in love with her) from dashing out into a rainy night to go to the town prostitute to prove to everyone he is a man. She manages to get him to come into her cozy and charming living room (the house-master's living room). He keeps saying he must go. She walks up behind him and says, "Won't you let me take your raincoat," and she *peels* it off him in slow motion. His reaction of cringing emphasizes how he is so in love with this woman that he can't stand her touch. When the play was done in London, I was not present for rehearsals, but when Laura took off the coat, she *stripped* it from the boy in one movement—and there was no response from the boy! I don't necessarily want the director to use my stage directions; but when they are essential to telling the story, he has to use them, or come up with his own equivalent.

Now, for your questions:

1. Who suggests and controls rewrites; and at what stage in the play's development does the rewriting end?

Answer: At a dinner-theatre production of my play *You Know I Can't Hear You When the Water's Running*, they changed the sex of a male playwright who wants a nude man on stage to a woman. I called the producer; he said since the play had been written twenty years ago, his director felt that making the playwright a woman made it more contemporary. I told him I would close his show.

As for rewrites, for me they usually occur before rehearsals begin. When the lines are read at rehearsal, some things do crop up, and as you go along, you hope there is not too much to do in the way of rewriting; but the collaboration ends with the opening. I have never touched the text of a play after opening; usually the director leaves for another show, and does not return to check on performances—which can sometimes ebb and flow over a long run.

2. Is the script merely cerebral, a textual entity into which the director must help the actors pump emotion to create the meaning of the play?

Answer: God no! A script is the heart of the production . . . written with passion . . . and visualized by the playwright. The details of course can be changed—placements of sets and the like. But the meaning is there, the emotion is there! The director helps the actor convey the emotion, helps the play convey its meaning, but he does *not* invent either!

3. Must the result of direction be a "glossy" (photograph) of the script, or can it be a less mimetic reflection?

Answer: No! Not a "glossy." The direction and the actors, and the sets and lights and all, should be a "realization" of the script. That is why director and playwright should be doing the same script! I had an interesting incident with *All Summer Long*. The extraordinary scene-designer, Jo Mielziner, who did four of my plays, came to me after dress rehearsal in Washington and said, "I think I've ruined your play with my set." (The play was a small one about a small house threatened by a rising river, and Jo had built it up all out of proportion.) I would not say he had "ruined" the play, but the set was not right.

Sometimes people will say to me about a performance, "Weren't you thrilled by the way she played it?" The answer is, of course, "Yes." But writers usually see their plays in their minds as being brilliantly played, so it is hard to exceed their expectations.

As Maxwell Anderson wrote so well in his volume *Off Broadway*, most theatrical production is usually a compromise of some sort. Not always. You can't always get the director you want, the actors; but with whomever you get, you are always working to realize your vision. You may find different ways to achieve that vision, but that vision made you write the play and is important to keep in mind during the production.

4. Can the director alter the ending to get a more theatrical or commercial finish?

Answer: A director cannot alter the ending without the author's consent and co-operation. Nobody can "insure" a commercial success. If we could, we'd all be millionaires. I did alter the means of achieving the *same* story ending I always had in *I Never Sang for My Father*. But it's important to note that nobody made a "suggestion" as to *how* it should be changed. They simply said they felt it was not the right scene to bring about the ending that I intended—son leaves father. He leaves him in my finished version for the same reason as in my first version, but in the second this reason is dramatized and theatricalized more fully.

5. What is the director's principal function? Is it to observe, explain, and implement the author's text?

Answer: Directors have various functions with different playwrights. One of the functions often overlooked is to help the playwright keep excited about his script. Often by the time the play goes into production, the author has lost enthusiasm for his play. If he knows the play is admired, he is more likely to take fire and keep the creative forces going as needed. So a director should keep "high" on a play for the playwright *and* the actors. . . .

There is no principal function of a director, except perhaps in general terms to "realize" the play. When my dear friend Elia Kazan left the theatre to do movies, I asked him why. He finally said words to the effect that, "In the theatre I am realizing *you* and *your* work—that is my job. In the movies it is more *my* vision that I am realizing." That is why he was meticulous in spending months to find out what was in my play—why this, why that. He was famous then for sometimes imposing a certain style on a play, vigorous, physical. At one rehearsal he said to me, "If you find me up to my old tricks, give me a nudge."

Directors help the actors discover a play. The actors have to find the play, find their parts. I remember once with Kazan, I was impatient with how slow some of the actors were. He shut me up. "They're discovering your play." The director helps them discover it, helps them find what is behind the lines. He once told me, "You may not agree with what I and the actor arrive at to motivate your line or action, but you'll get what you want!" With each actor it was a different approach. That was Kazan's genius. I don't think "explain" or "implement" are the right words. I don't think the play should need "explaining." The director answers questions. Kazan talks with actors around a table the first days, examines. He doesn't sit down and say, "This is what the play is about." "Implement," though a mechanical word, might mean getting the best out of everyone. Actors trusted Kazan—they'd do risky things knowing he would bring it down a notch, or temper it. And he achieved a great deal by affection. That made opening night and thereafter especially difficult. Because after the "love affair" he was gone. And everyone missed him.

These are things I have written and spoken about before in lectures. Perhaps they go some way to answering your questions.

Sidney Berger, Director

Dr. Sidney Berger, director of the School of Theatre, University of Houston, Texas, has been a member of that faculty for twenty-three years. During his tenure, Berger's activities have included founding and directing the Houston Shakespeare Festival and the Children's Theatre Festival. He further unifies educational and professional theatre by serving as associate artist at the Alley Theatre and artistic director of Stages Repertory Theatre.

The following interview was conducted by me on April 10, 1992.

Luere: Shakespeare, Beckett, and others have borrowed plots, characters, themes from earlier playwrights. If in theory, an author's text and intent are sacrosanct, isn't the intent of the original author the one a director should follow?

Berger: No, no, I don't think so. . . . That's no different from saying that the director of Shakespeare's *Hamlet* has to go back to the Thomas Kyd *Hamlet*. No. They're separate works.

Luere: But let's say the second author, Shakespeare, has changed the intent of Kyd's. Shakespeare's is *not* the original intent to honor!

Berger: But these are different texts. Let me put it another way. I think you must divorce one text from another; they may have the same characters, perhaps the same plot—Shakespeare stole virtually every plot he ever used—but the point is that he made it all his own; it became *his*. And for me, as its director, my job is this: I consider myself a director who serves to continue the evolution of that play. I

Sidney Berger, director. Courtesy of Sidney Berger.

don't think theoretically the play is finished until it's alive on stage; and I think the next artist who takes the play and moves it forward is the director. The great Russian director Meyerhold had an extraordinary theory. He suggested that developing a play was much like the stages of a rocket: you start with a playwright, then the playwright falls off and the director takes the play with the actors; then the director falls off, and the actors must take the play away from the director and make it their own; and finally in a sense the actors fall off and it belongs to the audience. Now those stages I think are correct, that after a given period of time the director's usefulness is gone; after a given period of time the playwright can no longer serve the play because there are different personalities evolving the work, making that play move into a different sphere that belongs to their personalities—the personalities of the actors.

Luere: Does the process go backwards, ever?

Berger: It never goes backwards, not in my mind. I don't see how it could!

Luere: I ask because your department's distinguished university professor, Edward Albee, is directing his new work, *The Lorca Play*, "evolving" it, as you like to say; the student actor playing Lorca, Wade Mylius, said to me that he loves Mr. Albee's directing because he gets to go ahead and do things on his own; he's responsible for evolving his character; but sometimes the two, Mr. Albee and Wade, disagree. Last night Mr. Albee had him change the delivery of a scene that Wade had worked out. So, in your theory of how a play progresses—as I follow it— the staging develops from the play, and Mr. Albee's directing, and then the actor takes over, thinks it through and decides what he wants; but here, with Wade's delivery of Lorca, Mr. Albee took him back. . . .

Berger: Well, you see, that's looping, that's different.

Luere: *Not* retrogressing?

Berger: It doesn't have to be retrogressing! In other words if the director is looking at a play, sees what the actor is doing even in accordance with his direction, and discovers that the road taken by the actor and the director is the wrong road, then I think it's necessary to go back to the beginning and start over. We do it all the time—because you are choosing roadways and sometimes you get lost and sometimes you reach dead ends. Actors certainly do it all the time, as I do. An actor will come to me and say, "Let me try something," and it doesn't go anywhere. Or he'll try it and I as a director make a discovery because of the actor's success. So it is a collaboration. The collaboration of the playwright must be with the director, must be with the actors, and must be, ultimately, with the audience.

Luere: Better to have a playwright direct his own, then. With a playwright and a separate director, it could be chaos?

Berger: It could be chaos, but that's why people like Grotowski and others who are really auteur-directors take old texts and then in a sense redo them; Robert Wilson to a degree does the same thing. Then it becomes essentially the director's work.

Luere: But is that good or bad for the original script?

Berger: If the director is brilliant and is capable of creating this piece called a "play" through his directing ability and his playwriting or adapting ability at the same time, then it could be wonderful. I think it's a rare thing.

Luere: Even were it so and the "evolved" play should come alive on stage, that collaborative "involvement" of Meyerhold's that you cited a few minutes ago—that sounds to me as though the playwright fell off in the rocket-stages—not because he was ready but because he was *dead*. That's fair??—he'd thought it *up*!

Berger: But then, let's say, if I do *Virginia Woolf* and I decide as some people have that it is really about four men—so I stage it that way because Edward is gone or doesn't know or whatever, I'm no longer doing Edward's play. I'm doing my distorted version of Edward's play. I was asked to be a guest critic at a play festival once, and a director did a production of Williams' *Glass Menagerie*; and if you remember the last stage direction of the published play, when Tom says, "Blow out your candles, Laura," she does and the stage goes dark. But in this production, Tom said, "Blow out your candles, Laura" and she didn't; she walked off-stage and the candles were still lit.

Luere: The director's idea?

Berger: Yes. And afterwards I said to the director, "Why did you deliberately change a direction that the playwright gave you, one which had to do with the end of the play?" And he said, "Because I didn't feel that the play was about what he wanted it to be about." In that case he totally changed the play as it is written. This is not "Laura goes to the sink and takes a glass of water"! We're talking about a substantive direction that the playwright is giving the actors and the director, one that has to do with what the end of the play *is*. In changing it, he completely destroyed the playwright's intent.

Luere: And it's too late to sue him!

Berger: Well, it happens all the time—it happens all over the country in places that nobody discovers.

Luere: Do you know David Levine—the head of the Dramatists' Guild?

Berger: Yes. Certainly.

Luere: I met him several years ago. He gave me a copy of the legal rights and guarantees that the Dramatists' Guild protects. . . .

Berger: Yes, but no one can go around to every small school or theatre or whatever throughout the country. They can't; it's impossible. They can do it on major productions of course. But the point is that there is a principle involved, and that is, if you want to direct a playwright's play, then you are accepting the work that has been given to you. If you want to *adapt* the playwright's play, then you had best deal with the playwright first—and that's why Grotowski said, "I'm going to take a play of Calderon's and I'm going to adapt it!" Well, Calderon's dead and it's public domain and Grotowski can do whatever he wants to with it.

Luere: So we hear "The best playwright is a dead one"?

Berger: Yes. It often goes, "Death to the author, and long live the interpreter." But, you see, I think that's an extreme position. I don't think that 98.8 percent of directors feel that they need to distort the play in order to make it be viable. I think there are some directors who are led primarily by their own vision. Robert Wilson is led by a vision that is peculiarly his own and has the genius to back that vision. The result may not be the play as the playwright wrote it; it is the play as Mr. Wilson has brilliantly conceived it.

Luere: Speaking of "adapting," how much leeway does a director have in dramatic development of a character? Can the director and the actor change the author's intent—the script's characterization—even though they do keep to the dialogue? By laughs, or suggestive body movements, can a director let the actor change the subtext—which might alter the whole aura of the play, say, from comedy to farce, or tragedy to melodrama?

Berger: Any human being with any kind of perversity might try.

Luere: With Edward Albee's *Lolita*, I thought Donald Sutherland did just that—or tried to—and changed the nature of the script's Humbert Humbert.

Berger: What we're talking about here is an actor's development of a character in a way *not* justified by the text.

Luere: Well, I liked Nabokov's novel and didn't see why the staged main character seemed more despicable than the book's—or than Albee's—published version.

Berger: It's the development of the character by the director and the actor, however supportive or distortive of the text.

Luere: But a playwright could try a law suit *only* if the director or actor had altered the actual words spoken? Wasn't it the director's role to stay true to the script? The Broadway Humbert Humbert was *not* like the published Dramatists' Service script.

Berger: Albee was adapting a novel, but he had a concept of who that character was, which I think he honestly derived from the novel. And the living playwright in this case can certainly say, "No! Your interpretation is not justified by my text." He could say, "What I saw on the stage was *not* my character." I think when you talk about realizing a character, sometimes you succeed, sometimes you fail. Clearly that production failed, for whatever reason, I don't know. But when you're the director, the task is the realization through you, through you and the actors, of the material of the play; and you have to bring that creation and living solution onto the stage. A director to my mind is not a "stage-er," not someone who makes pictures; a director is someone who takes the play (as I said at the outset) to another stage of its evolution. He takes the print off the page and helps translate it into living terms. That's what I think a director does.

Luere: But still being careful about unscripted movements and facial expressions and tone of voice?

Berger: The director is the controlling element, the one who has to guide the production. There is one governing eye; that in my mind has got to be the director.

Sometimes the playwright gets mistreated because the director is not a good director or is very heavy-handed. There are a thousand reasons. For example, Alan Schneider did such a great job with Edward's plays in the 1960s because he was a brilliant director, and ably complemented a brilliant playwright.

Luere: Alan Schneider gave up on Broadway. Did you read his *Entrances*?

Berger: Yes . . .

Luere: Didn't he leave Broadway midcareer because he was frustrated by the low level of drama getting rave reviews there? He went to university and repertory theatres. And you left, too.

Berger: Well, I found the environment in New York to be counterproductive to working in theatre; I found that I spent most of my time doing the wrong things, getting the job instead of doing the job. I knew I had a certain amount of life and I could not invest it in the wrong thing.

Luere: And here at the university, is directing beset with the same author/director strife you might have had there? Or are your plays by *missing* authors?

Berger: Most of the time I would say. Not dead authors—but authors who are not present. In other words if I do a [David] Mamet or a [Sam] Shepherd play here at the university, they're simply not going to appear at rehearsals. When I did Harold Pinter's *Betrayal* last year at a professional theatre in the city, I felt my job in producing that play in the absence of the author was to be as scrupulously honest to what that playwright wrote as I could be, given the circumstances I was in. Pinter was not there to say, "Well, I don't like the space that you are working in" or "I don't like that actor."

Luere: Can you give a more specific example of that phrase you mentioned before—your phrase "given the circumstances"?

Berger: Yes. You've got to remember that when a director sets to work, he has a very specific set of circumstances. (Don't mind me for using "he" interchangeably—it's a generic word.) The actors' personalities are radically different no matter where the director works. The space I work in, the budget of that theatre, the philosophy of that theatre, the producer, all of that has to do with the nature of my production. When I go to the Alley and direct a play, it's another set of circumstances. Even the audience complexion changes. But I don't, I can't, direct *for* the audience.

Luere: You can't?

Berger: I can't, I don't, direct *for* them, because they are total strangers to me. I adjust to them. But I cannot in a rehearsal for six weeks create an audience that is going to be my partner. As the great Guthrie put it, I am the audience of one. I can work with the play and I can work with the actors as my collaborators and partners. Ultimately the audience comes into the theatre and *then* they become my collaborators. Because when they are there and reacting to that play, I have got to alter my work depending on what I sense from that, and they become the last stage.

Luere: And *then* you might alter your staging?

Berger: Not "might"—I do. Let me make something clear: when I say "alter," I don't mean "pander." I mean I can hopefully sense from an audience in previews whether something is not clear, is not clear enough, is obscure, whether the actor is missing moments and the audience is reacting and telling him—or me—that. I have to take into account all of these things. But the difference is that I don't have a whole lot of time to do that in most normal academic runs. Most university productions play five or six performances. Now when I'm directing at the Alley it's different; and it's interesting, because I go back a lot when I have a long run. I remember when I was working with Theatre under the Stars—the producer's a good friend—and he said, "Why do you keep coming back? You're not getting paid for it!" And I said "Because I can make it better"—meaning that as I'm watching the audience, as I'm watching the actors, I can make adjustments.

Luere: I often see Mr. Albee standing at the back of the theatre, watching the people.

Berger: That's telling you something, and to ignore that is foolhardy. But there's a thin line between hearing what they're telling you and pandering to an audience and therefore to yourself by saying, "If they're restless right here, I've got to do a stage trick!"—even if the director does that unconsciously. I'll never forget what Michael Bennett, the great choreographer/director, once said to me! We were at a meeting, and he said that in *Follies*—he directed *Follies* on Broadway—there was this wonderful thing of chorus girls floating from Stage Right to Left, or Left to Right, and he said, "One of the reasons I did that was because I knew the eye would follow a moving object, and when I had a problem down Left that I could not solve, I floated a girl Stage Right so that the eye would move away from the problem and watch *that*!" Now that's a trick! Well, for Bennett it was an act of desperation, but nevertheless it was a directorial deception. But I'm saying that when you, the director, "hear" the audience, hopefully you can solve the problem! And to do it, you try to adjust whatever is going on, on stage, to the fact that the audience is telling you,"This moment is not working." That's a directorial and actor "difficulty" in the process of solution.

Luere: In what you are calling "sensible" altering or adjusting for clarity, would a director have leeway to "adjust" the author's actual staging—say, for an audience's unique circumstances, its idiosyncrasies? In London, Sir Laurence Olivier adjusted sexual scenes for Tennessee Williams' *Streetcar*—partly to comply with Britain's censoring. *Or* he *might* have done so anyway, knowing his audience's moral or religious taboos? Now, here, with Albee's *Lorca Play* in rehearsal for Houston's International Festival audience, aren't you afraid some patrons may take offense at the Roman Catholic cardinal who enters buttoning his pants and robes, obviously caught and interrupted during an intimacy with his attendant?

Berger: Clearly some people in the audience are going to be offended by it, as some might by an obscenity.

Luere: Having a quickly summoned, obviously interrupted *cardinal* and his aide come on-stage with their flies open is *not* an obscenity?

Berger: To some, certainly, but I think there has been a real demystification of the church in the last thirty to forty years, and, I don't think that's as much of a problem as one would guess. Look at *Tiny Alice*.

Luere: And how long did *Tiny Alice* last?

Berger: But that's not the point. The point is that the audience did not get up and walk out on *Tiny Alice because* of that; and the play was not judged deficient because of it.

Luere: I'll bet Laurence Olivier would have put up a curtain! And some *did* walk out at Edinburgh on Albee's slurs at Catholic priests in *The Man Who Had Three Arms*.

Berger: But that production succeeded. We did Tennessee Williams here and audience members were very upset about certain things sexually that happened in it. There's a masturbation scene in *The Confessional*, and a lot of people find that material highly offensive. But the point is that the playwright here is using it in a way that is not designed deliberately to insult or to offend. It is used to make a point. Sexuality is certainly expressive of who we are as much as our emotional or rational process.

Luere: So the point of lampooning the Spanish cardinal here? It's the author's "argumentum ad hominem"—his tool for satirizing the church's stand against the homosexual Lorca?

Berger: Well, it's more than that. I think what the playwright is trying to do is to indicate that these great icons are *put* there, and are in uniform in a sense, but it's really the uniform that's being respected, not what's in it. What's in it is very blatantly human and very fallible. Boccaccio wrote about it in the fourteenth century. These are human beings within the garb of an authoritative office.

Luere: So that we'd know it was *that* cardinal and not cardinals in general.

Berger: Well, I would hope.

Luere: And a director's *not* to "adjust" a script to cater to any moral or religious scruples of its probable audience. That would be censorship—and not what you meant by an audience being "the last stage" of your "collaborative process" where you'd "modify" an author's script under a "very specific set of circumstances."

Ah, but what about a circumstance having to do with your cast's abilities? What if the director—you—chose a play with lovely language, poetry—Shakespeare's, or, here, Garcia-Lorca—but you had to pick your cast from students without polished voices, without rounded vowels, without standard American speech? Would the director have license to "adjust"—to cut the playwright's text back from oratory to daily discourse for the actors?

Berger: You're asking a *very* complicated question! Let's say that I am a director, and let's use another example, okay? Let's say I'm a director doing Shakespeare here at U of H, and for another production, doing Shakespeare in the park, professionally. When I do it in the park, I have very high expectations because I have a much larger pool of trained professional talent to draw from. So that when I do Shakespeare *there*, I can work far more with the poetry because I've got people who are trained—hopefully—and experienced in its use. But when I decide to do Shakespeare here, I should realize at the outset that I am going to deal with students who are of varying ability and experience. That's what a university is. That's what any school is.

Luere: But they're good actors.

Berger: Of course. They may be wonderful actors but they vary in experience; they vary in training. Well, I have *two* chores then: Alan Schneider once said when he was at San Diego that he did not want to be a teacher while he was directing. Okay? My role when I'm directing here at U of H *is* to be a teacher while I'm directing. My responsibility when I'm directing at the Alley or at any professional theatre is *not* to be a teacher. When you're in an academic or conservatory environment, you are constantly teaching *as* you're directing. Now that does not mean that you are less a director than you are a teacher. It means that you have two jobs you are doing, and that you have to do both equally well. If I have young men or women who are not handling the verse competently because they have not been trained well enough, I can't go out to the audience and say, "Excuse me, ladies and gentlemen, but Actor L or V is just not very well trained yet, so please be nice to them." If I expect people to pay $1 or $50 to come into the theatre to see the play, they deserve to see the play performed as well as possible. My job is to teach those actors in the rehearsal period as much as I can humanly teach them, and to direct the play as well as I can humanly direct it. Or else not to do Shakespeare at all!

Luere: But not choose and then *cut*? Not adjust the script to "circumstances"—as some directors do?

Berger: Well, I don't. I don't do *King Lear* here; I *do* do *Comedy of Errors* or *Midsummer Night's Dream*; I do those plays I think the actors are capable of within their limitations. Sometimes those limitations can be extended. You never know what's going to happen. I saw [a student-actor], for example, in *Comedy of Errors*, do a superb job in that play. I never expected her to reach such heights, but she *did*. She's very talented but had a limited amount of training. So we did a lot of heavy teaching during that period of time, and it paid off, because ultimately she ended up with a performance of substantial quality.

My point, though, is that it is not going to be the same process that I might go through in a professional venue; but at the same time it's got to be good enough in expectation that an audience can *see* the play and still see the *play*.

Luere: As a director of Albee's *The Lorca Play*, for example, you would *not* cut or adjust the amount of poetry in its script?

Berger: I might in Shakespeare for purposes of eliminating or substituting for archaic language, or, in extreme circumstances, because of an actor's inability. I *do* cut because sixteenth-century audiences were different from those in our time, and there are other exigencies as well. The canon is not to be worshiped but realistically and creatively produced. When Franco Zeffirelli did *Romeo and Juliet* (the film), he cut the potion scene: there is no potion scene in that film. And at a meeting with him I heard a scholar take him to task for having done that; and he listened very carefully, and then in his own sweet voice he said, "Lady, I cut it because she couldn't do it."

Luere: A choice instance there of directorial modification?

Berger: Of course! For if an actor cannot handle something because he/she is unable to for whatever the reasons, the director has some choices he must make: with a play in public domain he can cut; the better option is to work with the actor until it becomes viable. Those are the choices we have to make every day in rehearsal. What is at risk, however, particularly in cutting, is the play itself. I'm very wary of simply saying, "Let's cut that scene because she can't do it." Zeffirelli had a fourteen-year-old Olivia Hussey do Juliet. A fourteen-year-old in Shakespeare's time was radically different from a fourteen-year-old in our time—and he knew that he was buying one thing and was going to have to give up another. When I'm doing a Shakespeare here, as I said earlier, I'm not going to do a play that I know the students simply are incapable of handling at their level of experience and training. Now there is a theory, academically, that has been thrown at me a number of times, and that is, "You *should* do *King Lear*! They are students and they should know what it is like to play it." My answer is that I'm training students to perform before an audience. They are being trained to be actors or directors or designers. I'm not going to train them to be unable to function in a professional world because what I was doing was totally unreal. I'm opposed to that way of teaching. I will not do things that are so far out of students' abilities that they end up failing and thinking, "Oh, failure is good for me." Failure is good for them in terms of extending their reach, not by denying them any reach at all.

Luere: In your workshops, here, I notice you emphasize these same directorial issues: adherence to script or cutting it at will. In fact, your Albee Workshop productions last week staged two versions of each student play, each with a different cast and director: one cast was directed in complete compliance with the author's script, and the second staging, which followed at once, showed the same play with a different director following his own will in deviating from the original script.

Berger: Well, it's an idea Professor Albee and I talked about initially. I remember us saying at one point, "Wouldn't it be great if we saw the play done two different ways, just to see what the differences would be?"—because it *is* a workshop.

Luere: Let's take a play whose staging has already become established—Williams' *Streetcar*, for example. In London, director Laurence Olivier had to deal with the famous play's prior staging by Kazan and Williams on Broadway. Isn't that situation—the script of an already-lauded play—harder for a director to deviate from, to approach, to modify, to envision freely and creatively?

Berger: No, it's not. If I were doing a well-known play—let's take *The Glass Menagerie* again—what I find happens to me when I direct it is this: once I walk into the rehearsal hall and the door closes, I am in a completely different world, and that world emanates to a degree from me. Everything I am, everything I have experienced, the manner in which I've grown—all affect how I start developing the play with the actors. The same thing, I might add, happens from the actors' perspective: I can't do Eddie Dowling's production because I'm not Eddie Dowling. So when I start, all those models just vanish—they go away because there is no way I can put myself into those bodies.

Luere: Or would even *want* to! With *Streetcar*, Olivier said he didn't want to "warm up somebody else's cake"!

Berger: He was correct! He had to do the play from his own perspective! Now, that may be good, bad, indifferent, shallow, or deep; but finally, it is a singular production that evolves from the talents and personalities rehearsing it.

Luere: And your phrase "from his own perspective"—the director's—he keeps his own *perspective* without distorting the author's *intention*.

Berger: Yes. He should. But in the case I cited previously from *Glass Menagerie*, if the director doesn't have the actress blow out the candles, then he is quite consciously distorting the author's play!

Luere: So, what's an example of perspective—of what a director *can* do that's "perspective," but not "distortion" of intention?

Berger: Let's use a classic as an example. When Olivier directed a *Richard III* or a *Hamlet*, it was *his* production. That was *his* view of that play; it comes from *who he is*. It is *not* distortion since there is a basic loyalty to the text.

Luere: Can you give me an example of what comes from the director's perspective, from "who he is," and therefore is *not* directorial playwriting?

Berger: All right. Yes. Let me give you a better example. The ghost of Hamlet's father appears, invariably done with great lighting effects and clouds of fog and smoke. It never worked for me, and I didn't understand why! I did *Hamlet* several times, and the moment failed for me even though I copied everybody else's way of doing it. The last time I did it I stopped and thought to myself, *"Why* is it not working? Why has it never worked for me whether Olivier or anyone else did it successfully?" And then I remembered a friend of mine in LA, whose mother was living with her at the time. She told me of an incident. Her mother, widowed, was in the bathroom, and she saw what seemed to be the ghost of her dead husband standing in the doorway; and she said she was terrified because it was so absolutely simple and real! He was as real to her as—as you are sitting on that sofa. And it was as if you were dead but you're just sitting the way you are. She said for weeks she couldn't sleep because of that! And, for whatever the reason, that came back to my memory and I thought, "Well, of course, that is the whole answer. The whole answer is related to the way Shakespeare must have done it originally—which was that the father's figure was seen in full daylight at three in the afternoon: there were no smoky effects or strange strobe lights or anything else." And so when I did it, when it happened with just an actor walking out on stage with no effects at all, everyone knew that the old king was *dead*, and it became an extraordinary and very frightening moment. But I had to discover that. It came out of an experience that I had, and out of my understanding of the play and of Shakespeare's own time; it came out of a lot of things that melded together and produced that way of doing that moment. Other directors have done that moment differently.

Luere: From their own perspective—and it isn't reauthoring the play?

Berger: I'd not changed one word.

Luere: Well, you're off the hook! That was a fantastic example.

Berger: It is the one that stays in my memory longest.

6

Danny Mann, Director, and Edward Albee, Playwright

Danny Mann, New York theatre, film, and television director, is remembered for Broadway successes like *The Rose Tattoo, Come Back Little Sheba*, and the film versions of these plays, plus other films such as *The Teahouse of the August Moon* and *I'll Cry Tomorrow*. Mann was a member of the Actors Studio and the American Theatre Wing and was associated with New York City's Neighborhood Playhouse.

The following remarks between Mann and Edward Albee, playwright/director, were recorded and transcribed by me in April 1992, at a discussion at the Inge Festival, Independence, Kansas, on the relationship between playwrights and directors. A news column by Leslie Stair, staff writer for the *ICC Buccaneer*, Independence, Kansas, is appended for its additional recall of the discussion.

Albee: Theatre is not merely the furnishing of pleasure or fun. It's engagement of thought, of self, of mind.

Mann: But it has to have emotion. The play *has* to have emotion. And the director has to add it, handle it; he has to help actors to deliver emotion. The director determines and defines what emotions should be included in the play. When you direct, you want the audience's participation—which has to do with emotion, not just with cerebration, not just thought or idea!

Albee: [Strenuously objecting] A first-rate play's text has *not* just cerebral ideas; it has *all* the emotions right there! In a great play, the playwright does *not* need the director's "help." The *good* director translates what is already there in the play; he does not have to *create* it in a first-rate play. It's in the subtext.

Mann: Okay. He should follow the emotional idea of the text. But he can use selectivity. If the stage direction reads, "He laughed uproariously," what does the director have to do? Follow it?

Albee: He can change it if he keeps the emotional coloring. There are two kinds of stage directions: explicit and implicit. Explicit—they're an indication of what the author *felt* and *saw* and *heard* when he wrote the play. And these are *useful* to a director. The implicit ones—they're contained within the essence and nature of the character. A good director directs these—the implicit directions. In *Krapp's Last Tape* Beckett indicates that again (third time) Krapp walks off. In my production [at the Alley Theatre, 1991] Krapp starts to walk off, then returns, does not go all the way the third time. My intuition was that three was too many. Later I found that Beckett had [modified] the exits himself in his directing of Krapp. What separates a good director from a poor one is his ability to follow the implicit stage directions.

Mann: Some directors *never* read the stage directions!

Albee: Let's say the stage directions read: "Banquet table. Lots of food. Actor runs up and gorges himself." But this actor is puzzled. So he runs to a bar next door to the theatre to ask the author, "What am I supposed to do? What does this represent?" The author, lying on the floor, says, "Famine." Now, "famine" can't be acted. The actor runs, next, to the director and asks him, and the director says: "Hunger!" And the actor *does* the scene *well*! The director translates (the text) into terms that the actor can understand.

Mann: I knew a director who got a letter from Bill Inge during production of one play; said the letter's contents were better than the play itself, and he wished he could have included it in the production.

Albee: I like to think that one creative intelligence has an insight into another creative intelligence. And what emerges need not *be* a photo-image of his intention, but it should be the *reflection* of his intention.

Some playwrights should not be allowed into the theatre: they're hysterics. But if a playwright can learn the considerable craft of direction, if he can overcome the actors' being taught to mistrust the author, and if he can be objective about his own writing—*no* other person than the author can give as accurate a translation of what the playwright saw and heard when he wrote the play—no more accurate representation of the author's intent.

"Playwright-Director Panel Focuses on Roles"

By Leslie Stair, Staff Writer
[Reprinted from *The ICC Buccaneer*, May 10, 1991, 9.]

The playwright/director relationship: should a playwright direct his own play? On April 26, in the William Inge Theatre, during the 10th Inge Festival, a seminar was held to discuss the controversy.

Members of the panel were playwrights Edward Albee, Robert Anderson, Jerome Lawrence, and directors Daniel Mann, Marshall Mason, and George Keathley. Moderator for the discussion was David LeVine, executive director of the Dramatists' Guild.

Playwright/Director Albee said a director should understand the author's language and show a willingness to translate the words accurately.

"Authors talk only to the director; that's the reason I became a director, so that I could talk directly to the actors," Albee said.

According to Albee, some playwrights should not be in the theatre during rehearsals because they cannot control themselves and seem to dissolve into hysterics.

Playwright Jerome Lawrence said, "You have to let the director be the captain during the rehearsal of your play. We as writers direct our plays at the typewriter or word processor."

Director Danny Mann said, "The author attempts the impossible and the director does the possible."

According to Albee, playwrights can be first-rate directors if they can be objective about their own work; no one can be more accurate in understanding their own material.

David LeVine said, "If you sell a play to be made into a movie, the writer loses control of his work. In films the writer becomes almost anonymous."

According to Lawrence, some directors unfortunately never seem to read stage directions, but they are in [the script] for a reason.

Director Mann left the audience with this thought: "Where the writer ends, the director starts; where the director stops, the actors begin; and where the actors stop, the audience begins."

7

Lanford Wilson, Playwright

Since the mid-1960s, Lanford Wilson has been an active figure in the Off-Off-Broadway movement. Among his early plays, usually directed by Marshall Mason, were *Balm in Gilead* (1965), *Lemon Sky* (1970), and the Obie Award winner *Hot l Baltimore* (1973). Wilson co-founded the Circle Repertory Company in 1969, where most of his work now opens. His collaboration with the company's co-founder, director Marshall Mason, has been long and harmonious. Wilson's later plays include *Angels Fall* (1982), *Burn This* (1986), the "Talley Trilogy" consisting of *Fifth of July* (1978), the Pulitzer Prize–winning *Talley's Folly* (1980), and *Talley and Son* (1985). He has received the Brandeis University Creative Arts Award, the New York Drama Critics Circle Award, a Vernon Rice Award, and both Rockefeller and Guggenheim fellowships. His most recent work, *Redwood Curtain,* premiered at Seattle Repertory Theatre, Seattle, Washington, January 13, 1992.

This interview, conducted at Circle Repertory Offices, New York City, is excerpted herewith from *In Their Own Words* (1989), Theatre Communications Group, with permission of the author, David Savran.

How long have you worked with Marshall Mason?
'65, I think, was the first time we worked together.

What is your working relationship?
It's great. He'll say, "I'll take care of this and you take care of that." It's like two heads instead of one. It's especially terrific on the large-cast plays. He'll say, "I'll

never get that girl to do that." So I say, "I'll talk to *her*, if you can get *him* to do what he's supposed to do." He has seen a play at least fifteen times over the year I've been working on it. We've seen readings of it. He has read scenes. I've read scenes to him. He knows more or less what the play is, so we both know exactly what we want. And then in casting we find ourselves very, very close every time. And since we both know what we want, we trust either to get it. And so if I'm talking to someone over in the corner, he knows I'm not telling them something that is going to undermine his purpose. He says, "Good, that's taken care of." I don't do that too much, but it gives him maybe a quarter more time than he would normally have.

Do you normally go to all of the rehearsals?

All except for the first two or three when they're improvising. They need to do that for scenes like "the first time she met Burt." And that's very nice because if they improvise it, they'll always have that experience in their minds when they're playing, to fall back on. I would rather die than see them improvise. I always think it's better than the scene I wrote. But when they start saying my words, I'm there. Because they may need me. Or I may need them.

Do you rewrite a lot before the first rehearsal?

I did a lot more on *Angels Fall* and on *Talley and Son* than I did on *Burn This*, which is a good sign. I also did very little on *Hot l Baltimore*. *Burn This* has taken forever because I wanted John Malkovich, and he couldn't do it for the longest time. I finished it in December and we got him for a reading in August. So I rewrote it some for the first reading we had here, and some for August, and some for California for December. But not a whole lot. We'll probably be paring it down during rehearsals—it's a little wordy—and clarifying and changing some things. I've rewritten the first scene about five times. It's only the first half of the first act that keeps changing and will keep changing. The rest stays exactly the same.

Do you do much writing in rehearsals?

Clarification. If someone says something for the fourth time and isn't making sense out of it, I'll say, "Do you know what that means?" He'll say no. I'll ask, "Who knows what that means?" And the other three people will say what they think it means and if they're right, the first person will say, "Oh, of course, what an asshole I am." If no one quite knows I say, "That means this, in other words." And they all go, "Why didn't you say that?" Then I usually go back to the typewriter to clarify because I don't think there's a point in being misunderstood. I hate not understanding something—unless it's the sort of play you're not supposed to understand, which is a whole different thing. But I'm not writing *Last Year at Marienbad* and neither is anyone else I know.

And do you rewrite often after a first production?

I wish I didn't, but I do. I keep writing. The trade edition of *Fifth of July* is quite different from the last rewrite of the play, published by Dramatists' Play Service. I have a horror of anyone doing the hardback version instwad of the actors' version.

What production are you particularly happy with?

There are about six or seven. We've done some very good work. We did *Hot l Baltimore* here and then we did it in California, and I came back from California thinking I had seen the ultimate production. But the production here was forty times better and I didn't know it until we came back to it. I was hyperventilating. I completely forgot that I had written it. I just had not seen anything like that on the American stage before. . . . I thought Malkovich's production of *Balm in Gilead* was absolutely stunning. . . . Both *Lemon Sky*s have been terrific. *Serenading Louis* at Second Stage was the most difficult rehearsal period I ever went through. . . . I rewrote a couple of scenes and I think I improved them but I couldn't really tell. . . .

Who directed?

John Tillinger. It looked like shit all during rehearsals but the first preview was pretty damn good and the second preview was pretty damn amazing and after that it was just astonishing. But the play has always been difficult for me. I hyperventilate for all the wrong reasons. I like the play, but I don't like my experience of the play.

What direction do you see the American theatre going in now? It seems that both Broadway and Off-Broadway are changing.

Have they? How?

Broadway is no longer a forum for serious drama, with a few exceptions.

Name one.

Glengarry Glen Ross.

And *Hurlyburly*. That's about it. Even *Benefactors* didn't do it for me. *Glengarry*, *'night, Mother*, and *Hurlyburly*. Especially *Hurlyburly*. What do you know? A good play on Broadway. Good Lord, it's enough to put you in a time warp. . . . We're building a strong theatre literature that is being done across the country— it's not being done in New York except for about two weeks or sometimes all of three or four months—but it's being done in a 700-seat theatre in Pittsburgh as it did in a 70-seat theatre in New York. So I don't feel particularly good about New York theatre—the finances are totally f___. But I feel very good about the theatre across the country. After all, that's what we're talking about. We can't be bothered about New York theatre.

What are your plans for the future?

I would hope to write a decent play. I've been getting involved with these damn actors who can't move with a play for an extended life. It happens time and again. I'd like to stop doing that, write for unknowns. The next play will be for unknown actors or else I'm going to sign them to a two-year contract. When you work on something very hard and do it correctly with no compromises, you want it to be seen that way by as many people as possible. Only in one case, with Richard Thomas coming into *Fifth of July* and Joe Bottom who followed him, have I had a production with replacements as good or better than the original. Both guys were not only dynamite, they fit into the ensemble. But that almost never happens when you're doing an ensemble piece.

Do you have a favorite among your plays?

I don't really. It depends on my mood. Until I see it on its feet in front of an audience, I'll like *Burn This* the best. I might even like *Hot l Baltimore* if I read it. I've not read it since it closed Off-Broadway, twelve years ago or whatever, so I don't know what that play is anymore. But really, whichever one I'm going to do next is my favorite.

8

Robert Wilson, Performer, Director, Writer

A controversial figure in English-speaking theatre at this time, Robert Wilson has distinguished himself as a performer, writer, producer, and director. Abroad, Wilson has mounted productions at the Deutsche Opera, Berlin; the Frankfurt Opera; the Centre Pompidou and the Opera Bastille, Paris; the Zurich Opera; and other productions in Vienna, The Hague, Rotterdam, and the Musee d'Orsay. In America, Wilson is most famous for *Einstein on the Beach*, a collaboration with Phillip Glass. Wilson's production of Ibsen's *When We Dead Awaken* opened in 1991 at the Wortham Center in Houston, Texas; in February 1992 he produced Wagner's opera *Parsifal* at the Houston Grand Opera; and in October 1992 he directed his adaptation of George Buchner's *Danton's Death* at Houston's Alley Repertory Theatre. In 1993, Wilson's opera *The Black Rider* premiered in New York City at the Brooklyn Academy of Music.

Excerpts here come from an unpublished interview by Elizabeth McBride, art critic and creative writer, Houston, Texas, February 8, 1992.

McBride: Should directors working with a text think themselves creators, interpreters, or guides?

Wilson: I think we are guides—performers, directors, designers. We indicate ideas. But we don't impose our ideas on the audience—to impose them on the public is too fascistic.

McBride: Can you comment on the difference between directors taking a text and stripping it versus choosing instead to write their own?

Robert Wilson, performer-director-writer. Copyright © 1992 by Jim Caldwell. Courtesy
of the Alley Theatre.

Wilson: Well, I do write my own texts. I wrote my own *Parsifal* and performed it
with Christopher Knowles for over a year. I've written other performances. And I'm
doing a piece called *The White Dove* with Phillip Glass. But I'm also interested in
doing something like *Danton's Death*. I like the idea that it's so inconclusive. I like
the idea of a man speaking forever, and then, suddenly, another man speaking forever, and at the end there's no conclusion. So I'm cutting a lot of things that I think
are unnecessary. But the bones and structure are interesting. I was interested in the
Ibsen play because its female is dead, which is strange—I couldn't do it in a naturalistic way. *Parsifal* interested me because of the idea of looking at the piece
through the character Parsifal. I don't particularly agree with Wagner in the text. I
looked to the original Essenbach for the story. I like the music.

McBride: Some critics consider your work an example of the deconstructive
process. Do you agree?

Wilson: An artist can create a new language; and once this language becomes dis-
cernible, he can destroy his codes. And in this deconstructive process he can then
reconstruct another language. And in society we're not allowed to do that. We're
taught grammar and speech, and how one is supposed to speak and write. In an
opera like [*Parsifal*], the gestures are not conventional; they're gestures you've
never seen on a stage before because they're made for this work. This work is
choreographed. And once this language becomes understandable, I try to change

Mario Arrambide as Ulfheim and Stephanie Roth as Maya in Act I
of Henrik Ibsen's *When We Dead Awaken*. Adapted and directed
by Robert Wilson from an English version by Robert Brustein.
Courtesy of Dan Nutu.

it. I think that's what Mozart did; he wrote music with themes and variations. In the
ballet, that's what George Balanchine does, creating steps. So in that sense it is a
deconstruction. I try not to impose the meaning. This production was radical in
Germany, criticized, although now many people are coming to its defense, starting
with the Wagner family (actually, the great-great granddaughter of Richard Wagner, the widow of Wieland Wagner), who are saying that of all the productions of
Parsifal since the beginning, this one has gone the furthest in making the opera
more universal.

I had a letter from one of the family saying that Wagner wrote to a lady friend
shortly before *Parsifal* was first put on and said that the work would probably be
misunderstood as a celebration of Christianity and it's really not. It's about strug-

gle and strife. It's a work that I don't understand and that I don't think one can completely understand. If one could, one shouldn't do it. It's something one wants to think about. You present things on stage in a clear way but with a distance. It gives you time to reflect. I don't like to make interpretations for the audience. Also when I'm the author I don't like to interpret.

McBride: Why did you take the grail scene out?

Wilson: I didn't take it out really. I just didn't want to see one hundred knights standing on stage passing a grail cup and eating a cracker pretending it was a religious service for music that is supposed to be religious. To me that is sacrilegious. When it is portrayed in such a way, the story is the mystery—the beauty of the work. I took all the knights off the stage. I wanted a singing temple of light.

McBride: Does your work help clarify for you the difference between religiosity and spirituality?

Wilson: Well, I think it opens it up. It doesn't limit it or narrow it. The work is presented with a question, not an answer. If you have the answer, don't do it. If you know why you're doing something, don't do it. It's because we don't know what we're doing that we work as artists. It's interesting, the subject matter [of *Parsifal*] is this innocent fool; and if we can approach it through the eyes of Parsifal, to know what he is experiencing, then when we leave there's a continuation, something that we continue thinking.

McBride: What do you see as the function of a critic?

Wilson: The good critic is not an interpreter. The good critic is like a good actor who poses questions. The bad critic goes home and writes an interpretation in a matter of hours. To go home and write a good review takes time. That's for philosophers. They take time to think and to draw various connections. But the critic—no.

McBride: Do you have an interest in what the press or public say about your work?

Wilson: Some years they love you and some years they don't. Some years you're in, some years you're out. You really can't worry about it. You just have to keep working.

McBride: Some critics speak of the formality of your work. Is this formality a technique of aesthetic distancing?

Wilson: My work in general is very cold. And most things I've seen in the theatre are too sentimental or too emotional. I prefer a distance with the emotions. You must never fill the theatre with your emotions; you must always leave room for the audience to participate and fill in the spaces. My work is interior. But it's not more interior than exterior—there's a balance between the two. Most theatre is superficial. The deep emotions must not come from here [waves his arms] but from here [points to his heart].

9

Jose Quintero, Director

Jose Quintero is credited with founding Off-Broadway in the 1950s with his Circle in the Square Repertory Company. Since 1956 Quintero has staged eleven of Eugene O'Neill's plays in New York City. He currently holds the Wortham Chair in Theatre at the University of Houston, Texas. In these passages he recalls the "struggle" he waged with the spirit of playwright Eugene O'Neill during the staging of *Long Day's Journey into Night* in 1956—"the terrifying struggle which [O'Neill] won," forcing Quintero "to direct his play with deep pity and understanding and forgiveness" (Quintero, 215).

The following is excerpted from Quintero, *If You Don't Dance They Beat You* (Boston: Little, Brown, 1974: 215–64).

If there is anything such as the traffic of souls in the hereafter, mine will go running after his, as in life I unknowingly did. . . .

Sometimes when I am in the middle of directing one of his plays I've cried out in the empty, ghost-ridden theatre, "God damn you, O'Neill." And to myself: "You willed me here . . . you had a key to me. . . ."

[Envisioning O'Neill's Plays]

Every time I have done any of his plays I have had a sense of existing in two entirely different kinds of realities: the commonplace, photographic reality and the interior reality of fantasy. I think the struggle of these two realities—where the impossible can happen among the commonplace, where the figures become regal,

Jose Quintero, director. Courtesy of the Alley Theatre.

monumental and totally equipped for tragedy—gives that unbelievable tension to his works. O'Neill just happens to have double vision, that's all.

I am so tired of hearing that *Long Day's Journey into Night* is an autobiograph-ical play. For Christ's sakes, what great work of art is not? . . . O'Neill had a mother and a father, like all people. But only one person could write a masterpiece about them. . . . So our research has to follow his design. Not the outward one of appear-ances, but the inward one of feeling.

[Blocking the Play]

I have never blocked a play in the usual sense. As a matter of fact, I don't think there have been any kinds of markings in the script of any play I've ever done. I've never taken the script at home and arbitrarily written a certain line, "Moves to the table," or "Goes to the window," or "Opens the door," or "Lifts a glass."

[Planning the Set]

The title [*Long Day's Journey into Night*] itself implies immediately a moving thing. I'm well aware that it's the characters in the play that make the journey, but the journey must be accompanied and intensified by the various speeds and moves that the sun experiences as it makes its long voyage across the sky, because we're going to have to personalize the sun, tear into his chest a multicolored pallet in the shape of a heart, which corresponds to the pallet of the human heart and mind. So, in some way, you have to bring nature into the set. . . . Which room, do you think, of all the rooms in the house, is the room where a family spends most of its time in the summertime? You realize . . . these are just questions for you to think about, to translate into your own language.

> Quintero describes his work with actors on entrances: Fredric March as James Tyrone; Florence Eldridge as Mary Tyrone; Jason Robards as their son Jamie; and Bradford Dillman as the younger son, Edmund. Quintero addresses his cast by the roles they play or by their own names.

To Mary and James Tyrone:

Now, Florence and Freddy, you're coming from the dining room. That's the up-stage entrance. (Freddy asks Quintero: Do you want us to enter together, or one a little behind the other?) I'll let you answer that yourself. What is it that you are try-ing desperately to do in this scene, the total scene? (Freddy: I want to keep her happy and give her all the love I have so she won't go back to taking those terrible drugs that made us send her to a sanitarium. She has just come home and we don't want her to worry.) Well, how then should you enter? (Freddy: With my arms around her of course.) You're right, Freddy. Now, do you mind starting the first line off-stage, for you have been talking to each other since you left the dining room? All right let's try that. Just hold it for a minute until I get down into the house.

[Developing O'Neill's Characters]

To Mary Tyrone:

Florence, darling, you don't have to go and see how drug addicts act or what their outward behavior is. You are an actress, not a doctor. Drugs make you forget, take you far away to a tolerable world. Why? This is where all of our energies and talent and sweat are going to go. That's going to be the same for you, Freddy, and for you, Jason, and harder for you, Brad, for you'll also have to be the one who in-vented the long, *Long Day's Journey into Night.*

To Edmund:

Brad, you don't understand what stammering means to a writer? Particularly one who would be a poet above all things? Do you understand how unbelievably painful it is to you to admit it? First of all, to yourself, then to your father, then to the whole God damned world? . . .

To Mary Tyrone:

Now remember, Florence, we have to smile and laugh just like any ordinary housewife who is delighted, who has just come back to her happy home after being away at a hospital for some minor illness. You have to forget all the horror and humiliation and madness which caused them to have you committed. How did it begin, Florence? Did a couple of nurses have to come here and drag you into an ambulance while you were screaming insults at them? . . . You have to forget that, have to be so careful. So speak, darling, as softly, as coquettishly as you can with your next line—"I've gotten too fat, you mean, dear, I really ought to reduce." Continue Freddy. (Freddy to Quintero: I feel like hugging her here.) That's right. Do so. Don't ask me to. Just do what you feel, if it's wrong, I'll tell you. After all, if you embrace her, the thing you're going to tell her will go right into her little ear. . . .

To Edmund:

(As Edmund talks back to his father) Edmund, raise your glass and make a toast. . . . Remind him, Edmund. Go on, remind him. . . . Go on, Edmund, scream it at him! . . . He's been a miser with your mother, he's been a miser with Jamie, and he's been a miser to you. . . . Edmund, if you call him a miser now, I really and truly will believe you, but you'll have to excuse me, boy, because I'll agree with you with tears running down my face. Tears for the joy lost. . . .

To James:

James, you can come in now. She's still moving upstairs. (Now to them all:) So why don't you all do like Jamie? Sleep will come. You can't take anymore. Go on, sleep for a little while. [Then] . . . Suddenly you're awakened by a distorted melody played on the hall piano. . . . She's come downstairs. . . . She's looking for something she's lost, and she's dragging her wedding gown behind her. . . . She keeps on walking. . . . Now, with surety, yes right there. . . . She drops her wedding dress. James, get up and bring to your hands all the deep and now and forever love you have for her and pick up the empty gown and hold your gone-away bride close to your chest, and ever so gently.

. . . And it was with that feeling of deep pity and understanding and forgiveness that I directed *Long Day's Journey into Night*.

PART THREE

Tiers of Director/Playwright Interchange: Five Case Studies

At this point, a definitive view of what a playwright does and what a director does still defies definition and demarcation. Postmodernists echo early challenges to the "tyranny" of playwrights, quoting Antonin Artaud's position that the director is not merely "an artisan, an adapter, a kind of translator . . . [one who is] forced to play second fiddle to the author" (118). Extremists relish Artaud's claim that "No one has the right to call himself author, that is to say creator, except the person who controls the direct handling of the stage" (117). The classic view of text and script as worthy of total deference may be losing out during frequent and noisy clashes with postmodernism. It is a waiting game to see if conflicts over control will soar, deconstruct, or ultimately settle down to a nice polyphony on stage.

In the interim, sorting through the quirks and variations of theatre teamwork, one easily perceives the beauty of the artistic result or the failure of the staging. With effort, one finds the key to why the director/playwright team succeeded or failed. Some sets functioned well, communicated, if only for a time. Few typify this sort better than Tennessee Williams and two of his directors, Elia Kazan and Sir Laurence Olivier. Though Kazan was a director's director, the collaboration with Williams worked for five plays; and Olivier's strong need to modify and interpret Williams' text caused no rifts. Another author, Arthur Miller, also worked smoothly with Elia Kazan, producing high-level drama. British playwright Caryl Churchill purposely chooses to develop scripts side by side with directors.

But other teams did not function well. Years after Arthur Miller and Elia Kazan's steady teamwork, Miller and a new director, Elizabeth LeCompte, handled diversities less well. Upon occasion, a heavy-handed director may have exploited power and robbed playwrights of their ego: William Inge, for one, gave in to director Josh Logan's drive, but rued his decision the rest of his life. In contrast, Edward Albee, as a director, strengthened the general position of playwrights by his determination to protect his plays from undue directorial modification. (In later years, when William Inge was asked about positive trends in contemporary theatre, he applauded Edward Albee, who, he said, stayed freer of directors than "some of us" and "had always kept directors at bay."[1]) Yet Caryl Churchill for decades has kept directors close to her muse, even before a page of a script materializes.

The problem for the future is to find theatrical solutions acceptable to directors and also artistically satisfying to playwrights. Perhaps all playwrights should direct their own plays. But the talents to direct and to write seem quite separable and rarely found within one man or woman. Moreover, how many authors are able or eager to handle a one-person show with today's critics leaping to label any who try "auto-erotic" and "self-possessed"? Perhaps the workshop method is the answer—if its co-authoring style suits any and all types of drama.

Fortunate and grateful playwrights acknowledge the lift a talented director gives to a text. Is it sensible to concede that serious directors have taste, sensitivity, and their dramatists' hearts on their batons? What we may need is the balance suggested in precept whereby a director is presumed to interpret the implicit if not the explicit directions in a script. What else will help? With living playwrights and their directors, qualities like mutual candor, respect, and willingness to bend are paramount. With a legacy from the past, a straightforward staging will require qualities of the intellect and imagination. Whatever the nature of a team, respect for creative genius can keep our theatres legitimate.

Five productions from midcentury to the present—Tennessee Williams' *A Streetcar Named Desire* (1947), William Inge's *Picnic* (1953), Arthur Miller's *The Crucible* (1983), Samuel Beckett's *Ohio Impromptu* (1991 staging by Edward Albee), and Caryl Churchill's *Mad Forest* (1992)—bear witness to our culture's progressively altering point of view toward text and performance. Interestingly, a study of their directors and playwrights' collaboration as they were staged suggests a range in their profit from—or lack of support by—our culture's existing legal contracts.

NOTE

1. In a 1964 taped interview at the University of Southern California, William Inge spoke of Albee's unfailing autonomy in staging, citing *Who's Afraid of Virginia Woolf?* as a text that was produced "as is."

10

A "Director's Director": Tennessee Williams and *A Streetcar Named Desire*

In 1971 Elia Kazan reflected on his direction of four of Tennessee Williams' plays before his definitive split with the playwright in the late 1950s. "Well, these plays were all different problems," but he quickly added, "*Streetcar* had no problem, all you had to do was cast it right, and anybody could have directed it" (quoted in Ciment, 81).

Williams collaborated with Kazan during the staging of *A Streetcar Named Desire* in 1947, and with a second director, Sir Laurence Olivier, the next year in London. The collaborations brought the playwright joys and trials. To follow in turn Kazan's and Olivier's discourses with Williams and to observe the playwright's reaction as the two directors interpreted and altered his text delineates what helps a writer of genius turn a script into a performance.

Williams knew the value of direction. "I can't direct my way out of a paper bag," he stated in 1958 (quoted in Donahue, 127). The wry remark sprang from his decision to "try his hand at directing" after the aforesaid split with Kazan; but Williams gave it up after one "frustrating experience," though for one play he kept the credit line "Co-directed by the author and Owen Phillips" (127).

With the loss of Kazan, Williams regretted that without the director's "inspired and vital" help, at least one of his plays (*Summer and Smoke*) was not converted at its premiere "into the exciting theatre that the best direction could have made it" (Windham, 225).[1] The play's failed premiere had shaken Williams: "I always believed that it was a play that could live in production (though utterly dead on paper)" (225). In his *Memoirs*, Williams recalled directors mangling his scripts; he

Tennessee Williams, playwright. Copyright © Cunard White Star by
W. A. Probst, The Cunard Steam-ship Company Ltd. Courtesy of the
Photography Collection, Harry Ransom Humanities Research Center,
The University of Texas at Austin.

confessed his bitterness toward "the autocratic behavior" of at least one director
and disagreed with several whose casting choices, he said, "did not fit my play's
very special requirements" (Williams, 295).

   With *Streetcar*, no court battles or headlines of "Play Closed after Dispute" or of
"Who's to Say Whether Playwright Is Wronged?" eventuated—though neither
Kazan's nor Olivier's relationship with Williams was without anguish (Freedman,
E6). While shaping *Streetcar,* each director made cuts, altered dialogue, changed
focus, recast the text (three acts in place of two). Of the technical nature of their
changes, factual accounts have been compiled by scholars like David Richard Jones
in *Great Directors at Work* and Philip C. Kolin in "Olivier to Williams." While

Jessica Tandy, Kim Hunter, and Marlon Brando in *A Streetcar Named Desire*, original production, Barrymore Theatre, New York City, 1947. Courtesy of the Photography Collection, Harry Ransom Humanities Research Center, The University of Texas at Austin.

these accounts focus on details of the modifications, they are less relevant to the tenor of the playwright/director relationship itself. For example, Jones qualifies his observations thus: "In the discussion that follows, I repeatedly give (Kazan) credit for ideas and changes that may really have originated with Williams . . . my decision to say that 'Kazan did' something to the script makes for easier reading and reflects the credit that is conventionally given to the director" (Jones, 183).

Both directors appear to have believed, like theorists and linguists today, that fictive discourse, whether poem, play, or story, is ethically open to directorial interpretation (Smith, 133–34). Typical of Kazan's stance on closed versus open texts was his answer to two authors of another play who were upset that he ignored their explicit stage directions: "That chicken shit? I never read that. What do you think my business is in being here? I'm the director . . . I never read that kind of thing!" (quoted in Jones, 183).

Kazan and Olivier each drew on his own artistic vision of *Streetcar*'s script to make the play work as theatre. Of Kazan's effort, the playwright freely acknowledged in 1960 that "Kazan tried to interpret honestly what I have to say. He has helped me reach my audience, which is my aim in life—the bigger the audience, the better" (Donahue, 126). Of Olivier's direction of Williams, the following media praise is of consequence to playwrights or purists: "Olivier's production lifts *Streetcar* at times far above the intrinsic value of the playwriting" (Hayes, 2).

Whether Kazan and Olivier remained within their prerogatives as directors or overstepped authorial rights while shaping Williams' play depends on one's view of text. Theorist David Richard Jones feels that a director should be involved in "editing, molding, handling, orchestrating—controlling the material's immediate and consecutive values by adjusting rhythm, emotion, and texture, by changing mood, speed, brightness, and loudness—in an attempt to render the subject true or well" (182). But if the artist's view is that text is inviolable, then its director becomes nothing but a producer of the author's play (182).

My focus in this case study is less on each change Kazan or Olivier initiated with *Streetcar* than on the measure of communication between playwright and director and the tenor of their collaboration as the ultimate performance took shape. Evidence of the directors' search of Williams' text for emergent meanings and of the exchange of their findings with Williams appears in Kazan's production notebook and in Olivier's letters of appeal to the playwright to allow his cuts and changes.[2]

The collaboration between Tennessee Williams and Elia Kazan began in 1947 with *Streetcar* and lasted through *Camino Real, Cat on a Hot Tin Roof, Baby Doll,* and *Sweet Bird of Youth*—until the rupture in their relationship in 1960 by the "fiery director's walk-out" (Donahue, 125). The ambiance that pervaded their teamwork is incarnate in Williams' statement to Kazan at the outset: "I have written all this out in case you were . . . troubled over my intentions in the play. Please don't regard this as 'pressure' " (Pauly, 79). During their years together, their success was engendered in part by "a shared wish to move beyond the limitations of their theatrical proclivities" (78). Williams' penchant was for plays that lay in "the murky depth of the subconscious" (77). Kazan liked "tightly knit plot-lines and well-focused social commentary," above all, "those that dealt with experience I knew well in my own life" (Ciment, 32). Hence Kazan admitted, "The playwright I found myself furthest away from in material . . . was Tennessee Williams" (32). And Williams depicted Kazan as one "whose nature was so opposite to mine" (Williams, 169). With such disparity, Kazan needed to be "a skillful mediator," a role that he "had assiduously cultivated before he came to Williams" (Pauly, 78).[3]

In contrast, the collaboration between Williams and Olivier was short—just the span of the London production (August 12, 1949 through August 19, 1950). Little has been documented about the ambiance surrounding their work on *Streetcar*. But the playwright's *Memoirs* and his letters to friends anticipate trips to confer with Olivier, just as the director's cables, notes, and letters show Olivier painstakingly informing Williams of his revisions of the text. Olivier, seeking Williams' consent to his anticipated changes, vowed that Kazan's violation of text had been bloodier than his own. "God damn it, Colonel, I don't understand you; how you can jab at a single thing I've done when you submitted (I suppose you submitted) to this vandalism in NY [*sic*] I can't fathom" (Kolin, "Olivier to Williams," 152). Presumably Olivier rejected the adage that "In the theater, as in the Bible, everything begins with the word" (Freedman, E3) or, phrased more colloquially, "If it ain't on the page, it ain't on the stage." Thus London's *Streetcar* was distinctly Olivier's yet as well-directed as Broadway's (Miller, 47). Like Kazan, Olivier was a mediator. Producing *Streetcar* with a government subsidy, he tactfully "answered questions that were raised in the British Commons" about the play's plethora of sexuality (Jones, 175). Moreover, Olivier had a "touchy rhetorical job" to persuade Williams to allow alterations in a work already acclaimed (Kolin, "Olivier to Williams," 148). Olivier even managed good feelings between himself and Kazan on the latter's visits to London (144).

In moving the script to the stage, each director needed to experience the inner workings of the script. Kazan's method was to say to himself, "I'm now speaking for this author. . . . I'm doing a play by Tennessee Williams: I must see life like he sees it" (Ciment, 35). The director wanted the play to have the scale, mood, tempo, and feeling of Williams (35). When he first agreed to direct the play, Kazan said to Williams that the author was "the great artist" and that he, the director, was "the constructionist—or trying to be" (74). Still, Kazan felt that his own search to infer meanings in Williams' text was proper even though Williams was a workman as well as an artist, one who put everything into his script. Brooks Atkinson wrote that Williams "not only imagined the whole drama but set it down on paper where it can be read" (34). Williams' playscript was "a remarkably finished job," one that delineated the characters "at full length" and foresaw "the performance, the impact of the various people on each other, the contrasts in tone of their temperaments and motives" (34). Notwithstanding this available, definitive material, Kazan's notebook for *Streetcar* shows him inferring and supplying meanings. Yet in the view of literary theorists, Kazan's work is legitimate if one maintains that meanings are not set and preestablished by the author, but are by nature indeterminate in a piece of fictive discourse such as drama (Smith, 134).

Olivier's exploration of *Streetcar* required a sensitive collation of more magnitude than Kazan's. Olivier had to contend not only with Williams' prerehearsal script but also with his final official promptbook for Broadway with its textual changes and remarked blocking. His assiduous study of them shows his wish to stay within Williams' intent, and led to cables and letters across the Atlantic: "I have taken from the (prerehearsal script) a good deal as I feel that this text is nearer to *first thoughts* . . . (than to) second or third thoughts inspired by persuasion or anxiety to accommodate some interpretation" (Kolin, "Olivier to Williams," 152).

Moreover, Olivier's discernment of what was in Williams' play sprang from his particular culture. Unlike Kazan's, Olivier's vision was "something an Englishman would see from a distance" (Ciment, 70); the director was removed from the play's tension between Blanche's southern "aristocracy" and the new uncultivated society of Stanley and his friends (Miller, 48). Olivier did not want to repeat what Kazan had done, "warming up somebody else's cake," as he called it; he wanted his staging to express his own sensibilities about the text (Kolin, "Olivier to Williams," 156). Nonetheless, his pleas for his own reading are politic, "filled with cordiality, high praise . . . and acknowledgement" that *Streetcar* is a masterwork (148).

When casting began for *Streetcar*, each director had a voice in the choice and a share in the credit. It was Kazan who encouraged Williams to sign Marlon Brando to play Stanley on Broadway (Pauly, 82). Later, Kazan said, "I think one of the best things I did for the play was to cast Brando in it" (Ciment, 71). In 1946, on *Truckline Cafe*, Kazan had worked with Brando. His audition for *Streetcar* was attended by Williams' friend and colleague Margo Jones, who exclaimed, "This is the greatest reading I've ever heard" (Williams, 165). Williams felt that "Brando had a charisma on the stage that corresponded to the charisma of Laurette Taylor in its luminous power" (165). For Broadway's Blanche, Kazan and the play's producer, Irene Mayer Selznick, dissuaded Williams from his choice of Tallulah Bankhead. Together, the three decided on Jessica Tandy. Satisfied, Williams writes, "I told Kazan that he should cast the rest of the parts as he wished and I returned to Rancho Santo on the Cape" (166).

In London's casting, Olivier selected Vivien Leigh, his then wife, for Blanche. Williams had at first been leery of the choice, but in May 1949 he wrote to his friend, Donald Windham, "I have a feeling now that (Vivien) might make a good Blanche, more from her off-stage personality than what she does in the repertory. . . . She has great charm" (Windham, 239). The casting of Blanche produced an interpretation of the character by Vivien Leigh that London acclaimed. The *London Times'* reviewer thought that "[t]he best thing I saw in America was Miss Uta Hagen's performance as Blanche: [but] Miss Vivien Leigh's is finer" (Hobson, 2). Even critics who found the play "garrulous, perilously near to soliloquy with rare interludes of action" and of "otherwise limited appeal" applauded Leigh's superior performance; more than one said she gave Olivier's production a highly theatrical quality and made Williams' play outstanding (Miller, 18).

During subsequent blocking of the play, Kazan's and Olivier's attitudes toward the author were deferential and respectful, if at times harsh. Kazan considered Williams' presence in New York an asset, and invited the playwright to rehearsals, "even those at which he was blocking out the action" (Williams, 169). Williams was part of the staging. "I always had fun working with Kazan," Williams wrote in his *Memoirs* (169). Kazan asked the author's advice on how certain bits should be played, a practice that Williams suspected "was only to flatter me, for he never had the least uncertainty in his work once he had started upon it" (Williams, 169). Williams writes that "once in a while he would call me up on stage. . . . I remember his asking me to demonstrate my conception of the old Mexican woman who passed along the street . . . chanting" (169).

Williams' letters tell of his frequent conferences with Kazan on *Streetcar* during its development (Windham, 267). Kazan admitted to having a fiery temper and gratefully acknowledged Williams' patience with it in their daily encounters. As the acting developed, the director moved from the stage back into the orchestra, and "finally by the end of this second week . . . to the back of the house" (Jones, 160). The two sat side by side, with Williams "passing notes, answering questions, demonstrating such movements as the flower-seller's entrance, and filching dialogue from an earlier one-act play to supply some incidental dialogue between Stella and Eunice" (160). Ciment's *Kazan on Kazan* notes that "If (Williams) saw something funny, he'd laugh very loud. If he didn't like something, he'd say 'NO!' out loud, and I'd say, 'Shut up!' . . . and once I told him, 'Don't come to rehearsals any more. *NEVER* speak to an actress again!' . . . And he never did again, after that, speak to an actress" (82). Still, Kazan found that Williams was "very generous with his praise when he liked something" (82). Williams liked much, and told a friend during these weeks, "This man hasn't made one single mistake in judgment since these rehearsals started" (Maxwell, 116).

Unlike Kazan with Broadway's *Streetcar*, Olivier was geographically removed from Williams, and collaborated through cables, letters, and an occasional meeting. Of Williams' prerehearsal trips to London we learn from his letter early in April 1949, four months prior to the London opening, "I have to be in London on the 25th for a conference with the Oliviers and Irene" (Windham, 239). His reference is to Irene Selznick, producer of both stagings of the play. Communications from director to playwright reveal that Olivier "cajoles, corrects, admonishes, pleads, flatters, and reasons" to be able to direct the play according to his own vision (Kolin, "Olivier to Williams," 148).

As the play approached Broadway and then London, each director perceived the play's length and looseness of structure as a looming concern, a common contention in mounting a play. During Kazan's development of *Streetcar*, critical assessments of its early tryouts deemed the play tediously long. Typical was Robert J. Leeney's in New Haven: "(The play) in its present form suffers from too many long and frequently wearisome speeches" and needed to be "tightened" (Kolin, "First Critical Assessments," 48). But Kazan's shaping soon lessened the effect of length through his redivision of the text into three acts rather than two. The first act as scripted had lasted ninety minutes, but the rearrangement reduced it to sixty-two, with the second act having twenty-nine and the third, forty-eight; hence the audience perceived the play as shorter (Jones, 163). Williams also approved actual cuts in the text's final scene, agreed to drop scripted blackouts between scenes, and allowed the use of curtains so the stage could be changed more quickly. Analysis of the original playscript and the revised one shows that Kazan reworded speeches; he also rewrote parts of scenes and almost all of scenes 5 and 9; he "inserted new dialogue for minor players, but did not alter the central events or the number or order of scenes . . . he changed characters' names (Boisseau became Du Bois)" (183). The total effect was that of "a gardener cleaning the soil . . . aside from removing extraneous objects he changes nothing" (183). In all, Kazan sought audience interest, of equal concern to Williams, who had said his honest aim in life was "to reach my audience—the bigger the audience, the better" (Donahue, 126).

In London the length of the play also gave Olivier pause as he prepared its staging. He wrote Williams that the play was too long "even *with* all my cuts" (Kolin, "Olivier to Williams," 151). Two scenes in particular, Olivier felt, were "dangerously loaded with length" and "strained the audience" (151). In the scene Olivier calls the "Mitch-Blanche," he had found the preview audience restless: "You can *feel* them feeling that a long speech is upon them," that they "won't be rapt anymore [and are] within a few inches of getting rebellious" (154). Indeed, London reviewers at opening still called the play "garrulous," with "a tide of words many thousands strong" (Miller, 18). In another scene, whose function Williams had designed "to give Blanche dimensions as a character," Olivier thought that "Blanche is not needed" to describe the situation because "the audience has been conscious of (it) for an hour" (Kolin, "Olivier to Williams," 154). Olivier respectfully but humorously cabled Williams: "I don't want you to force me to bake the cake so rich that the audience can't taste it anymore" (154). Harold Hobson of London's *Sunday Times*, seeing *Streetcar* a month after Olivier's letter to Williams, thought it needed still more tightening: "From the point of view of construction the play has too many short scenes" (Miller, 48). Throughout previews, Olivier had pleaded with Williams for cuts: "Forgive me please. . . . I am your servant but I wouldn't be keeping faith with you or my office if I didn't tell you the things that I feel so strongly" (Kolin, "Olivier to Williams," 156). Williams acquiesced and "Olivier got his way," for the play, which had run three hours in tryouts, was cut to just over two hours in London (145).

Helpful as these resumes of near rifts may be in studying playwright/director relationships, a more idiosyncratic element, characterization, gives deeper insight. Nuances in the directors' perceptions of the psyches of Stella and Blanche, and of their interaction with Stanley, were at the outset afield of Williams' original intent both on Broadway and in London. As Kazan grappled with each character's psyche, then transferred appropriate behavior to the stage, he reflected his early period with the Group Theatre in New York. Kazan used Stanislavsky's terminology— "spine" and "through line"—to prepare. He searched for "behavior that's truly social, significantly typical, at each moment" (Kazan, "Notebook," 21). His meticulous work with each character's spine must have pleased Williams, who had said, "My chief aim in playwriting is the creation of character" (Pauly, 78).

However, Kazan's staging of Stella brought about a temporary impasse with Williams. From the start, Kazan's reading of Stella had distressed Williams. As the playwright observed the actress at rehearsals, he thought Kazan was afield of his true intent, was visualizing Stella as lively and spirited rather than doomed and lethargic. Kazan's notes show that he was interpreting Stella's superobjective as a desperate determination to "Hold onto Stanley" (Kazan, "Notebook," 24). She was decidedly like Blanche, "would have been Blanche except for Stanley" (24). She wants "just to live for Stanley's pleasures" (25). Kazan had felt that "She cannot live narcotized forever. . . . She begins to feel . . . and needs more variety" (25). Kenneth Brown wrote that Stella "delights in her view of herself as an altar on which Stanley can vent his rage . . . she embraces the role for what she understands to be love" (Kolin, "A Playwright's Forum," 179). However, Kazan's "Notebook" records in full the playwright's written admonishment to him on the fourth day of rehearsals, revealing Williams' concern over Kazan's handling of Stella in scene 1. "It seems to me that she has too much vivacity [sic], at times she is bouncing around in a way that suggests a co-ed" (quoted in Kazan, "Notebook," 25). Williams' stage directions had advised that Stella was to act with "narcotized tranquillity," but Kazan felt this was not making a big enough contrast between Stella's demeanor and her sister Blanche's "feverish excitability" (25). Williams explained further that his text's phrase ("narcotized tranquillity") was "a difficult one to be literal about, but I do think there is an important value in suggesting it" (26).

Whether Kazan heeded Williams' objection is conjecturable, since Broadway reviewers still called Stella vital—at least joyous. C.W.E. Bigsby, perceiving her the "real hero of the play," wrote that Stella "revels" in her husband's "sensuality" (106). Other critics call her "sex-happy" (Falk, 81). In fact, the sight of her uninhibited bliss is what so enrages Blanche (81). Stella "still throws herself in defiant, exuberant joy" on stage (Bigsby, 13). Later, the London media's negative criticism of one aspect of the role is significant: they recorded that "the attenuation of Stella's role is a major factor in the play's unresolved conclusion" (Miller, 89).

Happily, Kazan's ultimate analysis of "Stanley" agreed more precisely with Williams' early remarks to the director on the character's nature. In an April 19, 1947, letter to the director, Williams stressed that Stanley "was not a black-dyed villain" and that "the audience should respond favorably to Stanley's initial aversion to Blanche" (Pauly, 80). Kazan's notes reflect his agreement: "Stanley has the vulgarity, the cruelty, the sadism, and at the same time he has something terribly attractive about him" (Ciment, 71).

With Blanche, Kazan's notes show his struggle to follow the playwright's intent. After Kazan thought he had Blanche in hand, Williams' injunction that "Blanche must have the understanding and compassion of the audience. . . Certainly pity" (Pauly, 80) must have brought him to a standstill. Years later, during interviews with Michel Ciment for *Kazan on Kazan,* the director remembered that "Harold Clurman directed the road version of the play . . . and he saw Blanche as a heroine! I didn't" (Ciment, 71). During the play's preparation, Kazan's "Notebook" labels her "a misfit, a liar," and says that "the audience at the beginning should see her bad effect on Stella, want Stanley to tell her off" (22). But though Kazan saw her at the outset as a "heavy," the "Notebook" soon demonstrates his search for more boundaries of her character: "The more I work on Blanche, the less insane she seems" (23).

Kazan delved into Blanche's psyche to explain her to himself, "to justify the way she behaved"; he wanted to "recreate the experience out of which that behavior came" (Ciment, 71). After his exhaustive work, Williams stalled him for a time by warning him that "There should always be an area in a dramatic character that you don't understand . . . an area of mystery in human characters" (Ciment, 71). Mentally, Kazan translated Williams' word "mystery" into "ambivalence" and rethought his analysis; almost immediately he came to perceive Blanche as a copy of her creator, Williams, "an ambivalent figure who is attracted to the harshness and vulgarity around him" though he also fears it "because it threatens his life" (Ciment, 71). The analogy appeared to help, for without untoward incident, Blanche emerged. The ultimate result of Kazan's work on each character's super-objective led critics to rejoice that "Williams created the characters and Kazan brought them to life" (Pauly, 86).

From records of the following year in London, we find insights into the inner workings of the Williams-Olivier relationship. Like Kazan's, the new director's perception of the characters' natures differed from Williams' scripted injunctions. This divergence led Olivier to rush earnest entreaties to Williams to permit him to alter both dialogue and focus in selected beats of the play. Olivier's protestations to Williams mirror the director's theory of open versus closed text in theatre. "Unless new readings are in order, a play is not going to live," he wrote. But he added hopefully and judiciously, "This (play) of yours, like other masterpieces, will continue to live and be fortified by new readings all the time" (Kolin, "Olivier to Williams," 155).

The essence of the director's conflict with Williams over his play's characterization appears at the beginning of Olivier's eighteen-page letter to Williams asking for his "Order of Release." Olivier confesses that "I cannot understand at all . . . the whole nature and character of Blanche" (152). Prior to the letter, Olivier had cabled Williams that Blanche's lines as they appear in the "Ape Scene," while they are moving in the printed text, become laughable when the actress recites them on stage. Hence audiences were considering Blanche's dilemma neither poignant nor tragic, but a highly mirthful one. "Our adult friends . . . *laugh* at it" and at its "overwritten smack" (156).

Interestingly, the London *Sunday Times* made a purely incidental comparison between Blanche's behavior and that of girls in popular farces who are "common enough" and are "glamorized by bright lights . . . and catchy songs" (Hobson, 2). Inauspiciously for Williams and Olivier, the review concludes that "Blanche's character is not the stuff out of which great tragedy is made" (2).

As Olivier sought clarification and freedom to modify the text, his diplomatic phrases bespeak the ambivalence of his relationship with Williams.

Would you please try to reconsider this? I truly think you are underestimating the audience's powers of apprehension a little. (Kolin, "Olivier to Williams," 154)

There isn't honestly quite enough in the text to support this and I have done my best about it as follows. (151)

If you and I had been together on the original production, I would counsel your deliberation on the scene. (155)

Can you not reconsider this? (154)

Whatever troubles there have been . . . there is nothing but joy in my heart for the thing's success (which is certain). (157)

Olivier concludes his long entreaty to the author about Blanche and other problems with tact and respect. Though he will be "praying all the time" that Williams' "Order of Release will come" before the next rehearsal, he pledges that, should it not come, "I shall go into rehearsal on Monday trying to get the things back that you want back to your satisfaction" (157).

Did London's director have his way with Blanche any more readily than Broadway's director with Stella? Did Williams' cable or "Order of Release" reach London in time, letting Olivier do with Blanche as he wished? Williams-buffs know the answer from the playwright's oft-published comment to Philip Oakes quoted in the *Sunday Times*, March 1974: "I had an 18-page letter from Olivier explaining and justifying the cuts. I can't say that I liked it. But I thought if a man takes the trouble to write me an 18-page letter then I should go along with him" (35).

In sum, Tennessee Williams in midcentury let Kazan and Olivier search his text for emergent meanings on which to act in their ultimate stagings; and he acknowledged that artistic direction can elevate a script in performance. Nearly half a century later, directors have even more leeway; they do not make "performance" solely an animated glossy of the text. And though neither Kazan nor Olivier indulged in blunt overriding of authorial intention, today's directors may be overshooting the margins of text and the normal rights of interpretation. The president of the Dramatists' Guild, David LeVine, warned in 1984 that "the issue is not always straightforward" (Freedman, E6). A *Sunday Times* reviewer guessed that "To some innovative directors, the best playwright is a dead one" (E6). A cry today of "Death to the author" and "Long live the interpreter" may be a sneer at the supposed Biblical inference, "Everything begins with the Word" (E3).

Tennessee Williams was alive and kicking when Kazan and Olivier approached *Streetcar*; yet he placed few walls around his text. He reminisced in 1974: "There were extensive cuts—partly on the grounds of [the play's] length, partly because of the prudery of the time. . . . I can't say that I liked it" (Oakes, 35).

But he allowed it.

Did Williams allow his directors leeway because they conveyed clearly that their innovations were to bring scenes on quickly, to match audiences' attention levels? Did his approval flow from the directors' friendliness and courtesy? In 1974, at age sixty-three, the playwright recalled to a *Sunday Times* writer that Olivier's brilliant production of *Streetcar* had not been "altogether the play that he wrote"

(Oakes, 35). Could Williams have sensed, wisely, that a director's awe of genius would inspire him to elevate a script?

Or perhaps Williams' easy concession came from a more arcane consideration. Only five years after *Streetcar*, and long before the parting with Kazan, a regional director of one of Williams' plays asked him how he would feel if the play failed. The playwright said, "I've begun to develop a sort of insulation about my feelings so I won't suffer too much" (Windham, 307). The regional director had warned, "What a dangerous thing for a writer," to which Williams conceded, "Once the heart is thoroughly insulated, it's also dead. At least for my kind of writer. My problem is to live with it, and to keep it alive" (307). Was the playwright masochistically trying to keep his heart vulnerable by gambling with directors and failures in later collaborations? Notwithstanding his drive to draw audiences (Donahue, 126), maybe Williams' insulation from failure was already nascent with *Streetcar*. One guesses that the rationale for Williams' easy interaction first with Kazan and then with Olivier belies rules of thumb about authorial rights or directorial privileges.

But why, then, the ultimate break between Kazan and Williams? Assessing their relationship during *Streetcar*, we saw no misrepresentation of the spirit of a play, no autocratic assumption of directorial prerogative; and we know that their engagement continued for three more plays. Some reports blamed Kazan's pressure for rewrites in the years after *Streetcar*—once for an entire act (the overpublicized third act of *Cat on a Hot Tin Roof*). "You find yourself doing more revisions for him than for any other director," Williams wrote (Donahue, 37). But in retrospect, Williams himself denied this claim: "The charge that Kazan has forced me to rewrite my plays is ridiculous. Nobody can budge me an inch" (125). Moreover, Williams liked rewriting, and wrote of dissension between himself and directors who refused his voluntary rewrites.[4] Williams had "an addiction to working over the acting version of a play," adding characters, revising scenes "for hoped-for productions sometimes seven years off, as with *Camino Real*" (66).

However, Williams' version of the definitive split was not that the two differed, nor that they bickered, nor that Kazan himself reauthored the extra third act of *Cat*; rather, Williams sensed that Kazan wished to direct plays with more audience-draw than Williams' were by that time eliciting (125). *Camino Real*, a box-office debacle, admittedly had been problematic, and Kazan issued "a carefully worded statement to the press . . . relinquishing his directorship due to a conflict in commitments" (125). Later, Williams summarized the walkout for the *New York Times* as "due to a misunderstanding related to complaints directed at Kazan for his supposed interest in looking for popular successes" (125). In fairness, theatre history reveals that Williams' plays at the time of the rupture were not drawing the audiences of earlier periods.

In this respect, a friend tried to dissuade Kazan from his concentrated direction of a run of commercial successes, "Look—for the rest of your life you can do that type of show . . . but you have to do something which is much less safe, but much more satisfying. Something which also has a very good chance of failing" (Pauly, 224). Without Kazan's proclivity for commercial theatre, a contemporary director,

Alan Schneider, was in despair at "the grosser tastes of the commercial theatre's audiences" (Schneider, 376); but Schneider dropped his career on Broadway to move to not-for-profit regional theatre a decade after Kazan split from Williams.

One can look elsewhere for the cause of the Williams-Kazan rupture. Granted that Williams held Kazan to be "a brilliant director whose forte is his perceptiveness and his awareness" (Donahue, 81); yet one can assume that for a director/playwright relationship to survive and persist, its partners of necessity must be more parallel than Williams and Kazan in the sort of drama to which they incline. Kazan had a penchant for sociological drama; Williams, for psychological fare. By the late 1950s their diverse proclivities may eventually have defeated their 1947 resolve to share their years in drama. In *An American Odyssey*, Thomas H. Pauly proposes that "In pointed contrast to *A Streetcar Named Desire*, Kazan's search for sociological relevance never got together with Williams' lyric introspection" in the playwright's later works (168). To validate this theory would demand specific research on what type of drama Kazan chose to direct after he parted from Williams and his introspective bent.

Meanwhile, the collaboration between Williams and his directors for a time was a launch toward a galaxy where play and performance are one.

NOTES

1. A later, very successful production of *Summer and Smoke* was directed by Jose Quintero.

2. Kazan's "Notebook for *Streetcar*" was published in 1963, edited by Ruby Cole and Helen Krich Cinoy (Indianapolis: Bobbs-Merrill). Selections have been widely republished. Olivier's letter to Tennessee Williams is a valuable "found-text" located by Philip C. Kolin and published in *The Missouri Review*.

3. Pauly describes Kazan's methodology with plays. "Shrewdly he would evaluate the tenor of the times and assess the prospective audience appeal of the proffered assignment. Once he agreed, he would carefully work out what the play was saying" (78).

4. In his *Memoirs*, Williams recalled that in 1970, with his play *Out Cry* at New York's Lyceum, dissension arose between him and the director. Williams had submitted rewrites in Washington to try to improve the opening monologue of the play, but the director had refused them (295).

11

A Tyrant Director? William Inge
and Joshua Logan

The amount of subjectivity observable in the end product of creativity varies. Theorists favor artists who, though they utter their own secrets, can achieve universal-
ity (Arendt, 174, 186). Theatre critics in particular often censure art that is too
solipsistic. In the production process, subjectivity or inner necessity (30) poses a
problem because play and performance entail both an author and a director. Whose
subjectivity, if any, is to be honored?

A playwright of the 1950s, William Inge, said that subjectivity soars in scripts
because a writer's "first need is always to please himself"; he must have "a selfish
purpose" since he writes "because he has some feeling about life, some awareness
or concept that he must find expression for" (Inge, "More on the Playwright's Mission," 19). And since "a writer's basic need is to communicate," Inge continued,
"his work [will] expose his thoughts and feelings, and even his prejudices and
worst limitations" (19). Yet, Inge added wryly, an author must not arbitrarily pretend to "righteousness"; that would make us "a little wary" (19). Among the playwrights whom Inge admired was Edward Albee, who today both writes and directs
his own works. At a theatre forum, Albee recently conceded that as an author he
sometimes overwrites, gets "infatuated with the sound" of his own voice, and puts
in "all sorts of scenes and speeches" that he, as his own director, must prune from
performance.[1]

English director Peter Brook expects to be subjective when he approaches a
staging. Brook observes that a director "brings to [the work] and always has and
always will his subjectivity" (Berry, 114). He compares a playscript to a piece of

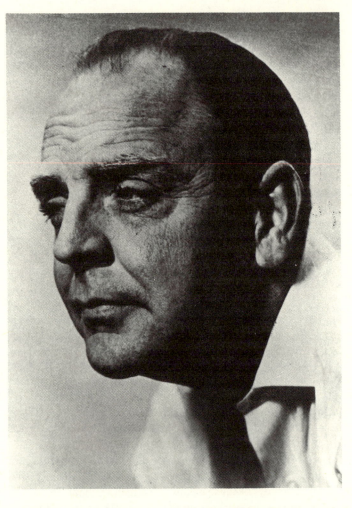

William Inge, playwright. Courtesy of The William Inge Festival.

fabric: "this fabric reaches us . . . not as a series of messages, which is what authorship almost always produces, [but as] a series of impulses that can produce
many understandings" (114). Hence a director is not constrained to find one message from the fabric's creator; rather, he is free to make an individual choice from
many viable "understandings."

Yet overblown shares of subjectivity brought to interpretations of a playscript can
enhance or diminish an author's intent and/or the play itself. In 1953 Joshua Logan's
direction of William Inge's *Picnic* showed positive commercial results at the Theatre Guild's production in New York's Music Box Theatre. The play "ranked high
among the top grossers of all time" (Brustein, 52). But during its run, *Theatre Arts*
critic George Jean Nathan, who usually praised Inge plays, objected that while

Logan's production of *Picnic* "was a tip-top one by Broadway standards . . . operating with a vengeance in behalf of the popular box-office," it was not "the honest piece of work" that Inge's previous efforts had seemed (Nathan, "Director's *Picnic*," 15). The critic concluded: "What now meets the eye in the [Music Box] production presided over by Joshua Logan [is] a field day, in short, for everyone but the playwright, whose pole-vaulting stick has been lost in the shuffle" (14). The playwright seemed to be "shoved into the background by way of allowing the director to make a name for himself" (15). The experience may have prolonged the "sickness of mood and temper" (Voss, 326) that had plagued the author since his youth.

The collaboration between Inge and Logan seems a paradigm of what can happen to authorial intention and to aesthetic merit of a script when an obliging author already insecure about his identity (Wood, 227; Williams, 208) too readily surrenders to directorial subjectivity. "That Inge and Logan did not agree on many key issues is well known" (Reilingh, 194), and the trickle-down from their troubled teamwork seems germane to what historians call Inge's undeveloped potential during his subsequent years (Brockett, 656). A definitive assessment of Inge's work lies beyond the intent of the present study; however, to what extent *Picnic*'s commercial success or artistic status in the early 1950s rested on Inge and Logan's give-and-take is a provocative point for study.

AUTHOR AND DIRECTOR COLLABORATION ON *PICNIC*

Pivotal controversy during and after Inge's lifetime has touched upon how much Logan's vision for *Picnic*'s physicalization on stage differed from its author's. Yet theatre researchers today say that "the creative processes" behind Inge's writing and rewriting of his plays in production "have not been thoroughly treated" (Reilingh, 204). A fuller analysis of Inge's pattern of writing seems requisite to assessing the Logan-Inge teamwork on *Picnic*.

Before submitting a play to a director, Inge's creative process entailed compulsive rewriting—often a complete rewrite a week. It was a kind of busywork to remove his own private tensions that otherwise led the writer, an alcoholic, to "resort to the bottle" (Wood, 226). Friends described Inge as "filled with fears he could not articulate" but "tranquilized under liquor's influence" (227). His friend and agent, bored with rereading, once wired him "NOW JUST STOP. I CAN'T BEGIN TO READ YOUR PLAY EVERY WEEK" (Wood, 227).

By the playwright's own admission, he had not fully completed his manuscript when *Picnic* went into rehearsal (Inge, *Summer Brave,* 4). As Inge's director readied the script for performance, he both augmented and modified the playwright's original creation. At Logan's behest, Inge reenvisioned and rewrote his play to fit the director's master design; and Logan himself rewrote and inserted dialogue to round out Inge's characterization of *Picnic*'s "hero" (Logan, 355). Each of the two figures has preserved the experience in letters, essays, articles, or memoirs.

From the director's point of view, details of the collaboration appear in *JOSH: My Up and Down, In and Out Life*. In that 1976 memoir, Logan divulges his early opposition to Inge's title, focus, and setting, as well as to the playwright's dramatization of rising action and resolution of conflict. Even the title Inge had inscribed on the script, *Front Porch*, displeased Logan. Before casting began, he immediately renamed the play *Picnic* because "it was a town Labor Day picnic that motivated much of the play" (Logan, 349). Its subtitle became "A Summer Romance in Three Acts" since Logan was visualizing a sexual intrigue with a single plot, action, conflict, and locale.

But the playwright himself had thought hard before settling on his preferred title for a work whose theme he envisioned differently from that which his director would later see in its pages. In a column for the *New York Times*, before the play's opening, Inge discussed his rationale for several titles he had contemplated. "One [that] I considered for my new play was *Women in Summer* . . . because it recalled something to me: a memory of women, all sorts of women—beautiful, bitter, harsh, loving, young, old, frustrated, happy . . . a little fortress of women" (Inge, "*Picnic*," 3). After more thought, Inge sought a title more indicative of his focus on women's plight in their culturally constrained porch fortresses. He commiserated with those who in the 1950s still lived in a male-dominated world where the front porch was their realm. "I was fascinated to find . . . how the women seemed to have created a world of their own, a world in which they seemed to be pretending men did not exist" (Inge, "From *Front Porch* to Broadway," 33). In the play, "none of the women—Flo Owens and her two daughters, Madge and Millie; Rosemary Sydney, a schoolteacher who lives in the Owens' home; and Helen Potts, who lives next door—has a strong relationship with a man" (Voss, 329). In Inge's script, "the force is generated by the women" (329). Thus, before turning his script over to Logan, Inge had settled on *Front Porch* to focus on women as a group—in his play, sisters Madge and Millie, their mother Flo, and schoolteacher Rosemary, who lives with the family. Inge's script, from title to conflicts, crises, and aftermath, demonstrated his resolve to dramatize the lot of women in his day.

The playwright's concern for the feminist dilemma in what he had entitled *Front Porch* was known to his peers in the 1950s. Robert Brustein and others had already stereotyped Inge as matriarchal, as one who "follows Williams in writing she-dramas, in giving to women if not the leading then certainly the pivotal (and insightfully created) role in his work," and concentrating "on the pathos of the woman's suffering" (Brustein, 53). Lampooning Inge's caricatures of brawny men, Brustein quotes Herb Gold's epithet for an Inge-man as a "male impersonator" (54). Brustein categorized Inge's plot-lines as melodramatic, revolving around "a heroine threatened either with violence or sexual aggression by a rambunctious male . . . equipped with bulging biceps and enormous sexual potency . . . but the woman is able to domesticate him without difficulty" (54). He saw *Picnic*, like other Inge plays, as depicting "the situation of the helpless child-man and the comforting mother-woman in progressively disguised form" (54). Brustein sums up such examples of Inge's work as "preachy" (54).

Didactic or not, Inge's care in selecting his play's title, *Front Porch*, affirms that he had plotted structure and action to make his "handsome, muscular, bragging hoodlum" hero, Hal, attract, shock, and repel the ensemble of females on stage: "Their reactions to him are the substance of the play," wrote Inge (Inge, *"Picnic,"* 3). And the playwright's self-chosen title, *Front Porch*, aptly symbolized the fortress Inge's males approached.

But Logan's title would point elsewhere, not to the "series of impulses" in the fabric of Inge's script; in line with Peter Brook's philosophy of directing, Logan found other viable "understandings" from the fabric's creator (Berry, 114). In this instance, Logan's concept of the play's content and his demand for a change of title caused a subtle but decisive shift. With Inge's *Front Porch*, his emphasis had been on the plight of his whole assembly of women in the wake of societal mores; but Logan's title would narrow both critical and popular attention to a sole romantic liaison—that between the play's Hal and Madge. Nonetheless, with the director's determination plain, Inge sanctioned the change, inviting further and more drastic demands by the play's director. A decade later, after *Picnic*'s Broadway success, Inge, for his own satisfaction, again rewrote, revised, and restored the play. The final title, *Summer Brave*, today appears on the cover of Inge's preferred rendition, which stands on library and university shelves quite near the Logan version of *Picnic*.

Notwithstanding this easy victory with the title change, director Logan, vexed at the need for more extensive restyling—and frustrated by the whole project— chose to leave the production at once, though he had seen beauty and potential in the script. "I was so discouraged with the first draft that I gave it up," Logan confessed (Logan, 349). But the play's producer, the Theatre Guild's Lawrence Langner, was sufficiently interested in the work's potential to try to bring Logan back. Langner was sure that when rehearsals began, Inge would be aware of "how bad it is" and would give them "something else" (349). Logan came back, and Inge tried to oblige, tried to lift the mood of his play. However, when rehearsals began, Langner was still protesting, "It's a promising script . . . but it certainly needs changing" (Nathan, "William Inge," 72).

Among specific facets Langner found objectionable were Inge's dialogue— which critics of his other plays had applauded—and the implausible actions of his characters. "For one thing the girl falls for the young man at first sight and promptly gives herself to him. That certainly won't do. . . . You just can't have that in theatre. You have to prepare an audience for the girl's surrender with convincing dialogue" (Nathan, "William Inge," 72). A drama critic, present as producer and director, studied the text, recorded the conversation along with his own comment that "From that moment on it was evident that Inge's play was going to be subjected to arbitrary and groundless alterations" (71). While critics have lauded Inge's "faithful observance of life, sharp appreciation of character, and gift for beautifully accurate dialogue" (Nathan, "Director's *Picnic*," 15), Logan thought Langner's judgment "quick and accurate," and later wrote that "Without Lawrence Langner there could have been no *Picnic*" (Logan, 349).

Such wholesale criticism of the script as Langner and Logan continued its staging soon narrowed to Inge's setting, tone, and resolution. In their professional view, a structural fault lay in Inge's six-set staging. Logan considered the author's physical organization sprawling and unfocused, and he urged the playwright to reorganize his whole script. At his insistence, Inge rewrote at length, condensing the entire action of the play into a single set. Now all of the play's scenes would be played in the backyards of two adjacent houses, and the effect of overstretching to which the director and producer had objected was erased. The play continued, and, luckily, what Peter Brook, discussing staging in a similar context, called "the fine content" and the "many levels of meaning," were not "steam-rolled out of existence" in *Picnic* (Berry, 116).

Years after the play's run on Broadway, Inge's aforementioned edition, *Summer Brave*, retained the Logan-inspired, streamlined setting:

ACT ONE: The action of the play takes place on the front porch and lawn of a small frame house in a small Kansas town. (Inge, *Summer Brave*, 7)

ACT TWO: When the curtain goes up, Millie is on the stage alone. . . . Dance music issues from the radio, kept on the porch during the summer. . . . Madge comes onto the porch. . . . (31)

ACT THREE: After a few moments, the motor of Howard's Chevrolet is heard chugging to a stop at the side of the house. Rosemary . . . stumbles [on the porch steps] almost blindly and drops to the doorstep. (57)

Inge's retention for *Summer Brave* of the revised, one-set format suggests that he agreed with his director and producer, at least in the matter of setting; its appearance in the preferred version explains in part Inge's later, expressed indebtedness for the "efficacy of [Logan's] manipulations" (Reilingh, 194).

A far less taxing problem developed in casting the two main masculine roles, Alan and Hal, leading the director to ask for more rewrites by Inge. As rehearsals began, Logan felt that Inge's scripted part for Alan did not suit the actor playing the role. Inge had conceived Alan, Madge's local suitor, as older than Hal, the play's principal—the stranger who initiates the plot's movement and suspense. In Inge's script, Hal was a college freshman who had been a young buddy of the senior, Alan, but who had dropped out after football season. The actor playing Hal, Ralph Meeker, was very well-cast as the young freshman, had "the qualities the role needed," and was "succeeding well" with his scripted part (Logan, 349). But the actor playing Alan, both director and producer agreed, had been miscast. Logan recalls that he had cast the part with his eyes shut and quickly rued his haste (351).

The company already had Paul Newman, then an unknown, in a minor role where all, including Inge, felt he was doing well. The role was that of Joker, the young garage attendant who had only a one-liner to deliver when he makes a pass at Madge. Shrewdly, Logan realized that the young Paul Newman could easily take over the larger role of Alan, and asked Inge for a rewrite that would switch Hal's and Alan's ages. Hal would then be the older upperclassman—still well-acted by

Meeker—while Alan, a younger freshman, would be a plausible role for the fledgling actor Paul Newman. Inge, with his confidence in Newman's suitability, agreed
to rewrite the roles. He did so quickly, the switch was made, Logan was pleased,
and that problem was solved.

Yet Inge's subsequent and preferred edition, *Summer Brave*, does not retain this
particular change to an older Hal and a younger Alan. Instead, *Summer Brave* returns to Inge's first intent: Alan is once again older, "just out of college . . . cau-
tiously dressed, well-bred" (*Summer Brave,* 10). And special note is given in
Summer Brave's stage directions to Hal's being younger than Alan. Twice this later
text refers to Hal's appearance and actions as those of a youth: "Hal Carter appears
at the edge of the porch. He is an extremely handsome and virile youth . . . dressed
only in dungarees and cowboy boots . . . he is a youth who takes his body for
granted so there is nothing exhibitionistic in his unconscious physical display"
(13). One may wonder at Inge's returning the two characters to their pre-*Picnic*
ages when he had so readily and successfully switched them for Logan.

Far more trying for the author than these early accommodations of his director's
subjective vision was Logan's charge that the play's glum closing action and resolution must be entirely recast. Logan wanted a light, not dark, unraveling of the action. But in Inge's plays, "seldom does he depict love as free and happy" (Voss,
331). Any serious director must put on stage "a direct statement of what he believes the play contains" (Hodge, 10). During Logan's staging of what *he* found in
the text, he was increasingly repulsed by the needless grief in Madge's final action.
In the third act of Inge's original draft, Hal "leaves the small town on the run, de-
serting Madge, [who stayed] to face those wagging tongues that would jeer at her
for the rest of her life" (Wood, 29). The director was convinced that Inge's finale,
with the "fallen" Madge still on the front porch and subjected to her town's con-
descension, "turned the beautiful [heroine] into the 'town pump' "; he protested to
Inge that such a downbeat ending "would leave the audience as unhappy as it did
me" (Logan, 347).

Logan's common sense about the commercial properties of a play was leg-
endary; convinced that audiences would not accept the act's present resolution, he
pressed Inge "to change it, to have Madge go off to follow her man, no matter what
the cost" (Wood, 229). But this time the playwright could not surrender his ending.
Emotionally or mentally, Inge proved unable either to envision or to execute a pivotal change. In playwriting texts, interpretation is defined as "a sincere attempt at
finding an author's ideas in a play and at rendering them honestly and appropriately through theatrical arts" (Hodge, 10). Logan has never been labeled *in*sincere;
and while he saw "tenderness, beauty, comedy" at many spots in the script, he
found its resolution for Madge—whose romance he had now made the play's
focus—too sour and masochistic to accept.

Still Inge hung back from Logan's injunction that he submit the substantially
different closure that the production ultimately featured. If we ask a theatre person
what directors do, we may learn that their role is to form a vision of the script and
then to express it through staging; but their particular vision and expression must

not presume to establish itself as the absolute meaning or sense or interpretation of
the play (Berry, 116). As Logan pressed for the sunnier, less dreary ending that he
thought more likely to succeed with audiences, he discerned that the playwright
was emotionally unable to execute it. Yet Logan insisted he turn it out.

In truth, Logan must have been aware that Inge hated slickness, fell back from
pandering to the public with a happy ending: "he kept writing this endlessly slow
dimout . . . everything was negative: Hal left Madge; Madge's rich suitor, Alan, left
town; . . . Madge, besmirched, walked back to the dime store with local boys cat-
calling" (Logan, 348). Logan feared that this "attenuated rosary of disappoint-
ments" would alienate the audience; he wanted a finish "that would save the play"
(348). The director admits "prevailing upon Bill" unremittingly; each time Inge
protested that "we can't just have a 'corny' happy ending" with Hal and Madge
running off together, Logan would jump in with "It wouldn't be corny or happy,"
then accuse Inge of trying too hard, straining too much "to get an unhappy,
Chekhovian inconclusiveness" (351).

At the close of one of these long pressure sessions during which Logan vehe-
mently urged for the revision he had requested, Inge suddenly flushed and stood
up, waited, and then "went off to try again" to give Logan what he wanted—the up-
beat ending (352). What he brought back Logan still ridiculed as "virtually the
same one I had seen before, only much, much longer and more turgid" (352). Discouraged, Logan pressed him further, whereupon Inge, furious, finally submitted,
saying, "All right, I'll write it, . . . but I want you to know I don't approve" (352).

At that juncture, Inge angrily and nervously exited the room. Legend has it that
the playwright was wholly unnerved at what Logan demanded as he rushed out
(Nathan, "Director's *Picnic*," 15)—yet this time he succeeded in constructing what
Logan wanted: he changed the glum ending with its bleak future for Madge to a
less self-punishing one. In it, Madge does not stay to be "the town pump"; she will
not suffer the haughty contempt of the townsfolk; for at Logan's prodding, Inge
lightened up and released her from bondage to the town:

Madge: It's no use, Mom. I'm going. Don't worry. . . . I've got ten dollars I was saving for a
pair of pumps, and I saw ads in the Tulsa *World*. There's lots of jobs as waitresses. . . .

Flo: [Wailing] Madge . . . Madge . . . [Madge runs off now, Flo still tugging at her, then giving up and standing by the gatepost, watching Madge in the distance.] (Inge, *Picnic*,
167)

Madge's escape—from a future with the town's pointed fingers shaming her—satisfied Logan.

Even with the director's hard-won and pivotal change whereby Madge leaves
town to run after Hal, Logan sought still another to make the play flourish com-
mercially. The play's out-of-town previews were still receiving bad press. Inge's
agent recalls that "even in St. Louis, Bill's own home base, *Picnic* did not get a
warm reception" (Wood, 229). Though viewers approved Madge's escape from
the town's rejection, they still found the end inadequate, and could not accept the

role of Hal as Inge had drawn it. Hal did not have heroic qualities. Hence Logan was convinced that the play needed one final insertion to heighten Inge's characterization.

As he watched audiences, Logan had perceived the seeds of aversion to Inge's hero when two men walked down the aisle objecting, "Some hero!" (Logan, 354). In place of Hal, "a loudmouth, a braggart, almost a bully," they wanted this man, with whom Madge now ran off, to be a "a hero figure with whom they could sympathize" (Wood, 229). Logan was alarmed. He feared that his audience had missed the whole point of his revised finale. Perhaps these reviewers were assuming, as they watched his staging, that the dramatist actually admired his play's slob, Hal, since Inge was rewarding Hal with a conclusion that featured the heroine joining him. To Logan, their mistaken response became a deciding factor. He recalls: "A huge electric bulb had turned on in my head" (Logan, 355). The character of Hal must be modified so that audiences could accept him, could feel that aside from his swaggering exterior, he had an inner core that was not foul and indecent (355). What was necessary was that something be inserted somewhere in the play's dialogue to make audiences more sympathetic to the character of Hal. The director and his producer decided "the most reliable character" to speak up for Hal, to get audience compassion for him, was his friend Alan. Part of the rationale was Logan's shrewd discernment during previews that "All the ladies adored Paul Newman" (355).

Hence, to win audience endorsement of Hal, Logan telephoned Inge to request this critical change. What now seems astonishing is Inge's quiet response to Logan's call. Inge answered, "Josh, if you can think of anything to do, do it. Write it down and I'll okay it. In the meantime, just put it in, if you feel it will help" (355). Dialogue that the director and producer themselves immediately wrote to make Hal more acceptable was inserted into Inge's script with only a few words changed by Inge, at a spot where Alan, Hal's college friend, and Flo, Madge's mother, discuss Hal's boorishness:

Flo: But a fraternity! Don't these boys have a little more . . . more breeding? . . . But how did the other boys feel about him?

Alan: They didn't like him, Mrs. Owens. They were pretty rough on him. Every time he came into a room, the other fellows seemed to *bristle*. I didn't like him either, at first. Then we shared a room and I got to know him better. Hal's really a nice guy. About the best friend I ever had. (Inge, *Picnic*, 57)

The brief insertion gave the needed depth to the portrait of Hal. Audrey Wood, Inge's agent, has upheld Logan's insertion of the passage. "Hal's college friend, Alan—played by Paul Newman—tries to explain to Madge's mother that Hal's overbearing manner is merely a defense mechanism, spawned by his own insecurity; beneath all the bluster and bravado, Hal is truly a decent, likable guy" (Wood, 230). She recalls that with the added passage, the reviews changed. In Wood's opinion, "The missing piece of character exposition" appeased the audiences, and "from that point on, *Picnic* worked, and does to this day" (230). As Logan had anticipated, the impact on the audience was now less alienating than Inge's original design.

But for *Summer Brave*, the author did not stay with Logan's finale. He deleted the director's "decent, likable guy" insertion, and lets Alan make a shocking admission about Hal:

Mrs. Potts: And your fraternity put him *out*?

Alan: Well . . . the other fellows really didn't like Hal.

Flo: Of course they didn't.

Madge: Was he blackballed?

Alan: That's the word they use. (Inge, *Summer Brave*, 37)

Logan's demand for "happy" in place of "glum" in his staging, which Inge saw as manipulation (Reilingh, 193), may have insured the play's sensational and immediate triumph—2 seasons and 477 performances. With *Picnic*, Inge won the Pulitzer Prize in Drama, the Outer Circle Award, and the New York Drama Critics Award. For this and other productions, he was credited with "careful plotting, authentic-sounding dialogue, and sympathy for his characters" (Reilingh, 190). Perhaps Logan's insistence on the happy denouement sprang from "his canniness about the commercial value of comedic reconciliation" (Jones, 37). The American public, in a period of changing sexual values and roles (Reilingh, 203), may have needed a comforting reaffirmation of "gender roles" being tested in the play through characters like Hal, "who [verged] on prettiness" and Millie "who [did] not have the character of a pretty girl" (Jones, 37).

Yet many critics immediately objected to the final product. George Jean Nathan wrote, "We are sufficiently convinced in view of all of this, that the man who wrote the unrestrained, unfrocked, and independently honest *Come Back Little Sheba* is not the man who wrote *Picnic* as we have now got it on the stage of the Music Box" (Nathan, "Director's *Picnic*," 15). Nathan thought the production "a big Broadway show at the expense of a small but doubtless considerably superior play" (15). Harold Clurman, too, disliked the tone and color in the production, which he ascribed directly to its director. His review of *Picnic* chided Logan for turning "a delineation of a milieu seen [by its author] with humor and intelligent sympathy" into "a rather coarse boy-and-girl story with a leeringly sentimental emphasis on naked limbs and 'well-stacked' females" (Clurman, 176). Logan's handprint on the production brought disdain. "What the play was like in its original form I do not know; but judging things from Inge's antecedent, highly meritorious *Come Back Little Sheba*, it is a good guess that [*Picnic*] was a much simpler, much less strained, and altogether more honest piece of work than what now meets the eye in the production presided over by Joshua Logan" (Nathan, 15). Of *Picnic* and other Inge plays, Robert Brustein wrote acidly, "Considering the modesty— one is tempted to say the mediocrity—of his work, it is clear that the excitement over Inge has been inspired by something other than the intrinsic value of his plays" (53).

Whether *Picnic*'s "something other" was the direction of Josh Logan or "the taste of the American mass audience" (Nathan, "Director's *Picnic*," 54) is not clear from Brustein's criticism (Reilingh, 13). The 1950s had been a period of social revolution (Bigsby, 13), but in Inge's plays "the subject is compromise" and his characters, rather than topple the status quo, "[came] to terms with each other and with their ordinary lives" (Reilingh, 190). By the 1960s neither scholars nor audiences seemed interested in Inge's "typically-depicted ordinary people" (190).

After two decades, the *Dictionary of Literary Biography* assesses Inge's achievements as "properly not regarded as equal to those of Eugene O'Neill, Tennessee Williams, and Arthur Miller" (Voss, 327), though a "decade of critical and popular success brought Inge the fame and fortune he had long desired" as well as a Pulitzer Prize, a New York Drama Critics Circle Award, and other recognition (327). Oscar Brockett's *History of the Theatre* assessed William Inge as "not having lived up to [his] initial promise" (656). Though his plays—*Come Back Little Sheba* (1950), *Bus Stop* (1955) and *The Dark at the Top of the Stairs* (1957)—were, like *Picnic*, commercial successes when they were produced, Brockett concluded that the dramatist's work "now seems essentially a more naive version of [Tennessee] Williams's" (656). Brockett's assessment lines up with critics during Inge's career who called his work "largely dominated by Williams' personality" and thought *Picnic*—as Logan produced it—"a satyr play glorifying the phallic male" (Brustein, 53). Ironically, Williams considered his pseudo-rival a powerful playwright whose work was "suffused with the light of humanity at its best" (Williams, 113). In Williams' mind, Inge was the better writer of dialogue: "He loved his characters, he wrote of them with a perfect ear for their homely speech" (113). Today Williams' work draws more critical attention than Inge's, though the annual William Inge Festival and Conference at his birthplace, Independence, Kansas, may be stimulating scholarship by providing a forum for analyzing and performing the author's works (Reilingh, 204).

THE AFTER-YEARS: REGRET AND RESENTMENT

Though until now, Inge "has not attracted the attention of biographers that might be expected for one of America's most successful playwrights of the 1950s" (Reilingh, 198), theatre archives do point straight toward *Picnic*'s buoyed-up ending as the seed of Inge's years of harbored resentment against his director's hand. For his lifetime, Inge's fealty was to his originally plotted finish baring the fate that falls to women who defy their culturally defined roles on the front porches of America. Conversely, Logan remained convinced that what he had sought was wiser: to leave with the audience a bit of hope for Madge in a new environment somewhere, sometime.

Inge's words of dedication on the frontispiece of *Picnic* in 1953 must be acknowledged: "TO JOSH: who gave of himself unsparingly in helping me to realize the play. I shall be always grateful." But the grudge Inge later held over Logan's hand on *Picnic* has been verified by his friend, playwright Robert Anderson, who during his own career collaborated with directors as unlike as Alan Schneider and Elia Kazan.

Anderson recalls that Inge was rancorous about the alterations that Logan had decreed for *Picnic*. "Bill would sit in our house and bitch about the changes."[2] "One day," writes Anderson, "I stopped him and confronted him, told him that by Dramatists' Guild contract, he *had* had the right not to change the ending; but he had agreed to it, the play had been a great success, made a lot of money, [and] he should shut up about it."[3] But Anderson's temperament was not Inge's. Though directorial styles vary, Anderson's premise would seem to be that a director is free to find his own modus operandi rather than be tied "to any one way of doing things" (Hodge, 10). Anderson, who did *Tea and Sympathy* in 1953 with Kazan and *I Never Sang for My Father* in 1968 with Schneider, does grant that "it is difficult sometimes to accept a director's version" of one's intent.[4]

Inge had tried to reject his director's vision, to be independent, but had failed. Legend, again, has it that when Inge was asked about positive trends in contemporary theatre, he applauded Edward Albee, who had stayed freer of directors than "some of us"; Inge envied Albee because "he kept the director in the background," as with *Who's Afraid of Virginia Woolf?*, a play that was produced "as is."[5] Albee kept productions close to his intent by mastering the art of directing and then handling his own stagings. Significantly, at the 1991 Inge Festival in Independence, Kansas, Edward Albee received the Inge Award for Lifetime Achievement in the American Theatre. At the presentation, family, friends, and others close to Inge before his death spoke of the author's envy of Albee's independence and stern control of his creative output. The festival's main seminar addressed a topic appropriate for the playwright-director: "Should a Playwright Direct His Own Play?"

The subtexts of the Festival scholars' papers touched on Logan's direction of Inge's *Picnic*, on Inge's pathological depression and reputed disenchantment with theatre and life after the 1950s. Presentations included "Difference, Defiance, Despair: The Suicide Plays of William Inge," and "An End to This Desperate Struggle: William Inge's Previously Unpublished Play: *The Love Death*." These scholars and guests also watched and analyzed a special revival of *Summer Brave*, which Inge's estate had recopyrighted in 1982. To his former agent, Audrey Wood, it seemed a paradox that Inge, with a long-running play like *Picnic*, had "refused to accept the audience's verdict as to his play's resolution" (Wood, 320). He had never stopped believing "that his original ending, in which Madge remains behind, bereft of Hal, in that small Kansas town, to live out her days as a figure of gossip and a pathetic town character, was truer to his own vision of his characters" (230). Inge's ultimate return to his own intent for the ending in *Summer Brave* was "Bill's way of proving he was right" (230). Wood, however, insists, "Alas, he was wrong. Audiences preferred his play in its original form" (230).

Josh Logan, too, called Inge wrong for publishing his *Summer Brave*. In 1976 Logan recorded his vexation over the author's public insistence on his intent. "To

me, it is one of the saddest moves in a pitiful life. It's as though he killed his favorite child. . . . Perhaps he can be excused—though I can never excuse him—for
going back to his original ending" (Logan, 356). Logan maintained that the altered
ending leaves Inge's "leading lady a lesser person than she started out" (356).

But reading the final page of *Summer Brave* may prove otherwise. There the
strength and will of the heroine emerge in the positive attitudes of Madge and her
mother toward her ability to manage her own future. Madge comments to Mrs.
Potts, her neighbor, and to Flo, who has been mother and father to Madge:

Madge: I am perfectly capable of making up my own mind, thank you.

Flo: Well, I like that!

Mrs. Potts: Let her make up her own mind. You don't have to worry about Madge!

Flo: I just can't *help* worrying!

Mrs. Potts: Madge is a woman now, Flo. She's not a girl anymore! (Inge, *Summer Brave*, 76)

The cumulative effect of the two women's comments may quell Logan's claim that
Summer Brave's ending, with Madge staying on her porch rather than following
Hal, makes her a weaker woman than *Picnic*'s. The opinion is personal and rests
with the reader.

What can be gleaned from Inge's and Logan's interplay on *Picnic* is that the aesthetics of play and performance are hazy and complex. The style of directing for
which Logan was known shares basic assumptions with today's staging theory.
Francis Hodge's 1988 text, *Play Directing*, outlines standard techniques or starting
points for interpretation of a text. "The director is a master designer . . . a critic and
stylist. What the director puts on stage is a direct statement of what he believes the
play contains" (Hodge, 10). But Hodge also cautions that "Interpretation, as presented in this book, is defined as a sincere attempt at finding the author's ideas in
a play and at rendering them honestly and appropriately" (10). Thus a director's
"style" for a particular production is declared by "the kind of individualization
[he] uses in this process, without overriding the play" (10).

Should theatre history declare Josh Logan's "style" for *Picnic* an exercising of
his freedom to choose his own path in interpretation? Or should historians term his
mode an overriding of the author and his play, a failure to uphold his playwright's
basic vision of his small town characters and their lives? A partial answer appears
on William Inge's coverpiece for his *Summer Brave*, which bears the inscription,
"The Rewritten and Final Version of *Picnic* by William Inge." Turning a page to
the playwright's preface, we gather fuller impressions:

It wouldn't be fair to say that *Summer Brave* is the original version of *Picnic*. I have written
before that I never completely fulfilled my original intentions in writing *Picnic* before we
went into production with the play back in 1953, and that I wrote what some considered a
fortuitous ending in order to have a finished play to go into rehearsal. A couple of years
after *Picnic* had closed on Broadway, after the film version had made its success, I got the

early version out of my files and began to rework it, just for my own satisfaction. *Summer Brave* is the result. The title is from a poem of Shakespeare's,

> Age like winter weather,
> Youth like summer brave.

I admit that I prefer it to the version of the play that was produced, but I don't necessarily expect others to agree. *Summer Brave* might not have enjoyed any success on Broadway whatever, nor won any of the prizes that were bestowed on *Picnic*. But I feel that it is more humorously true than *Picnic*, and *it does fulfill my original intentions.*

Today, as Inge perhaps anticipated, "*Summer Brave* has come and gone, but *Picnic* remains, as strong and successful as it was all those years ago when Madge first ran off to follow her lover, Hal, to the applause of satisfied theatergoers" (Wood, 230). What does the success of Logan's direction prove? Whether it documents the gift of Logan's taste and theatre know-how or whether it bespeaks the appetite of America's audiences is but conjecture, coming from either side of the fence that runs through literary criticism.

What a scrutiny of the Inge-Logan collaboration suggests is that a talented director's subjectivity in theatre can on occasion turn a possible failure into a success, though in the process it could bury the vibrations of spirit of an amenable, malleable, and insecure author.

NOTES

1. Albee's remark at the Alley Theatre symposium on playwrights and directors, January 1992.

2. Robert Anderson's comments in a letter dated April 2, 1992.

3. Ibid.

4. Ibid.

5. Inge's respect for playwrights who could maintain control over texts is cited in a taped interview made at USC in 1964 (Inge Collection, Independence Community College, Independence, Kans.).

12

A Director's Distortion of a Modern Classic: Arthur Miller's Shift in Stance

Once upon a century, "the playwright was king of the hill, not the star actor or director, and certainly not the producer or theatre owner, as would later be the case" (Miller, *Timebends*, 181). Directors sang the old tune, "The best playwright is a dead one." But by the mid-twentieth century, Arthur Miller, then a fledgling writer, was freeing directors for flights of fancy with his new plays. The period was often called "The Time of the Director," and traditional theatre hierarchy began to change as directors relished and expanded their powers. One of them, Elia Kazan, boasted, "I've been held partly responsible for this development" (365). With the depriviliging of playwrights, Archibald MacLeish published two versions of his Kazan-directed play, *J.B.*, the original and the Kazan-inspired one, and William Inge wrote separate texts for *Picnic*, the first for director Josh Logan, another restored to Inge's prior intentions.

The nature of Arthur Miller's involvement with his many directors turned upon how responsibly they approached the intent—as much as the language—of his plays. He found Elia Kazan dependable and capable during their many successful collaborations, but his relationship with a later director, Elizabeth LeCompte, was adversarial. The picture of their radically dissimilar connections makes an appropriate backdrop for current issues of authority and interpretation.

In the 1940s and 1950s, as new-wave directors made plays into shows, Elia Kazan recalls that "great productions . . . ventured far past anything literal" (365). Directors could take "a piece of material"—play, novel, folk story—and "trans-

Arthur Miller, playwright. Courtesy of Magnum Photos, Inc.

mute it into another form. Call it Pure Theatre. 'Show' is a good word" (365); and estimable results flowed to playwrights. Pages in Miller's autobiography, *Timebends*, show that often an author's immediate pleasure could be "greatly diminished by the news that [a plot] had been changed [and] characters rewritten" (570). But at the same time, Miller wrote, "there was the theatre audience and its almost prayerful attention, the power of its concentration on the happenings on the stage, and its openhearted joy in greeting me" (570).

Many of Miller's director/playwright collaborations won prestigious awards and became modern classics. The New York Drama Critics Award came to Miller for 1947's *All My Sons*, directed by Elia Kazan; the Pulitzer for 1949's *Death of a Salesman*, also Kazan's. Though *The Crucible*, with Jed Harris as director in 1953,

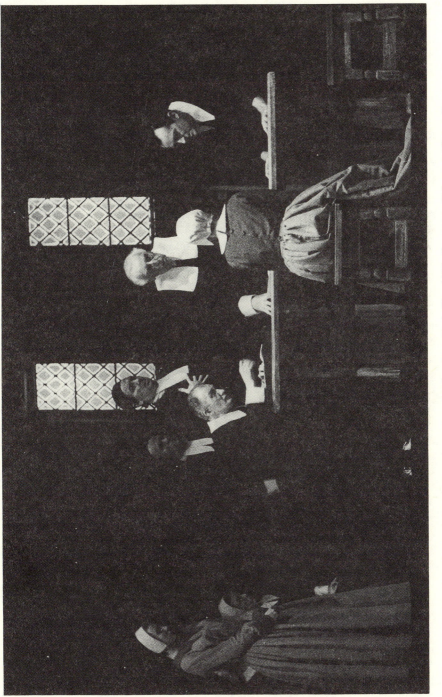

The Crucible by Arthur Miller, original production, New York City, 1953. Courtesy of Magnum Photos, Inc.

was not a commercial success until years later, its initial production won Miller the Antoinette Perry Prize.

But at one point, three decades later, Miller's easy style with directors changed. At the top of the hill and with a plethora of prizes and an international reputation, Miller shifted from his casual, agreeable stance on a director's function; he tightened his control, and even threatened litigation against one director, Elizabeth LeCompte, who attempted to ignore Miller's scripted intent. The playwright's shift from the easy freedom he had given earlier partners to the protective stance he took against LeCompte with *The Crucible* was widely covered by the press. Today a reappraisal is politic—a close look at the contrast between Miller's personal ties to Elia Kazan but distance from Elizabeth LeCompte, and at Miller and LeCompte's lack of accord on staging style and textual intent.

Unfortunately for analysts of Miller's collaborations, the author's tightened stance cannot be studied in conjunction with diverse stagings of *The Crucible* by Kazan and LeCompte since Miller's plan that Kazan, as usual, direct its premiere production did not materialize. Hence insights into reasons for his shift are less obvious than those gained, for example, by scrutinizing mountings of Tennessee Williams' *Streetcar Named Desire* under different directors. Nonetheless, a study of the harmony between Miller and his long-time director Kazan on *Death of a Salesman*, and of the author's total lack of accord later with Elizabeth LeCompte over *The Crucible*, suggests a pivotal pattern in collaborations between authors and their directors.

Whether with new or established plays, the complexities of production teamwork interested Arthur Miller, who wrote in his autobiography, "in making a play, people come together primarily as elements of a creating organism and not out of love or mutual regard" (299). Yet one factor affecting any team's approach to text may be the personal closeness, or in contrast, the distance between the playwright and director. For while the bond between Miller and Kazan was strong, LeCompte and Miller were strangers. Kazan writes in his memoirs that "Art and I were consanguineous . . . by all distinctive features of behavior we were the same fellow, or so it seemed" (366). Kazan and Miller were "best friends, [and] the success of productions had brought us closer. We were in daily contact" (365). Whether or not Kazan concurred with a particular intent of Miller's, "the old bond of many-colored twine" was there (450).

Thirty years later, had Miller and LeCompte been as well acquainted as Miller and Kazan (and their interchange as longstanding), the curious, imaginative use of production that LeCompte envisioned as "a tribute to the playwright" (Massa, 52) might have been approached receptively by Miller rather than rejected angrily. In February 1983 LeCompte's Wooster Group "opened rehearsals to the public of a new work-in-progress entitled *L.S.D.*: a forty-five minute version of *The Crucible* using the final sections of each of its four scenes" (Savran, "The Wooster Group," 100). At the time, a *Village Voice* columnist noted a lack of communication between LeCompte and Miller, stating that the playwright was "deaf to her intentions with his script" (Massa, 52); he seemed to misunderstand her hopes to "put the audience in a position of examining their own relation to [the work] as witnesses to the story of the play" (Savran, "The Wooster Group," 102). He was not aware of— or did not clearly comprehend—her intention to use "irony and distancing" to cut through to the "intellectual and political heart of *The Crucible*" (102). Whether or not her design was valid comes down to "a matter of personal taste" as well as legality (102); and the "taste" of LeCompte seemed not so akin to Miller's as that of his earlier director-friend Kazan. Moreover, the playwright was uninvolved with LeCompte's present or future status as a director—though in midcentury he had fostered Kazan's growth as a theatre figure. Kazan readily and proudly acknowledged that "The professional standing of a director depends on the plays he's able to attract" (321); and he had attracted Miller's output for four successive years from 1947 to 1951. Of their long collaboration, Kazan says, "Our work unit . . . functioned perfectly. Miller and I, the actors . . . jelled" (319).

What had smoothed Kazan and Miller's work besides the friendship was the director's demeanor; for of their years of interchange, Kazan vowed, "I was a hell of a good boy, compliant and respectful with Art Miller" (660). Even during a tentative period of dissociation between Miller and Kazan during the House Un-American Activities Committee's political investigations, the playwright spoke fondly of "Gadge" (Kazan's nickname). Kazan knew that he stayed on in Miller's mind though another director, Jed Harris, staged the first production of Miller's now widely produced work, *The Crucible*, for at the opening night party after that production, Miller "raised a glass of spirits . . . and said in a tone of vindication, 'This one's for Gadge' " (Kazan, *A Life*, 472). Thirty years later, from 1982 to 1985, it was this same *Crucible* that LeCompte unsuccessfully sought Miller's permission to modify. However, LeCompte's behavior throughout her contacts with the by-then-celebrated playwright was totally unlike Kazan's "good old boy" style. Without benefit of prior contacts like Kazan's with Miller, LeCompte wrote to the playwright for production rights to *The Crucible*. When he did not answer, she proceeded with rehearsals anyway. Nor did she acquiesce when Miller, learning of her work, proposed that she cease her unlicensed rehearsals (Massa, 52). Rather, she prepared and forwarded letters to him pressing the advantages of giving her the withheld legal permission; and her persistence was a torch that flamed for many months.

Of course, the granting of production rights unquestionably hinges on far more than friendly ties between principals. In successful theatre teams, a weightier determinant is the author's stance on deconstruction of the text itself. Are the author's words, both stage directions and dialogue, set or adjustable, closed or open? Yet on that count Kazan and LeCompte thought alike: a director must "bring something new to the play" (Freedman, "Play Closed," E21). Thus his directors' stands on modification of script seem not to have been the deciding factor that swayed Miller toward the one at midcentury or away from the other in the later era. Long before LeCompte's innovative approach to the play, evidence points to Miller's early awareness of Kazan's directorial view of text, one as deprivileging as LeCompte's would be in 1983. In Kazan's memoirs, he recalls having asked Miller to alter scripts extensively, a request that Miller honored with no objection, setting a precedent for Kazan's future approaches to his texts (Kazan, 361; Pauly, 78–79). Miller's concessions to Kazan's scenic concepts were quick and total; for example, the spector house in *Death of a Salesman*, instigated by Kazan and the play's scenic designer, was readily written into the script by Miller and has remained an integral fixture of the play's staging throughout its performance history. Miller's pattern of altering text at his director's suggestion continued for this and other plays (Kazan, 361; Pauly, 78–79).

Like Kazan, LeCompte wished to add "something new" to a Miller work. She planned an "abbreviated version" of *The Crucible*'s text and an overlay of its language with portions of other writers' works (Freedman, "Play Closed," E21). But LeCompte seemed to be disregarding the soul of Miller's play through a far less ordinary interpretation than its author had intended. Miller had designed his play to mirror the long-ago religious rites and spirit of the Puritans in Salem, Massachusetts (Miller, *Eight Plays,* xi). But LeCompte conceived its superobjective more broadly; she envisioned it as a work "that examines political repression as much as religious domination" (Freedman, "Play Closed," E21), one fully applicable to the throes of subsequent decades—including her own. Hence she wished to alter its focus through the evocation of an LSD "trip" (Freedman, "Who's to Say," E6). To bring the play to life in the present, she was planning "to use film footage of L.S.D. advocate Timothy Leary debating G. Gordon Liddy of Watergate fame, among other elements" (E6). Miller may have been correct in his recorded fears that to let her alter the spirit of *The Crucible* "might discourage a major revival of the play later" (Freedman, "Play Closed," E21). Such reluctance is understandable for an author of established classics.

Moreover, the presentation style LeCompte was planning would significantly alter the aura of the play. In her intended staging at an Off-Off-Broadway site, the Performing Garage in SoHo, she would pantomime Miller's script (E21). Conceptualizing his play as "an icon, a piece of culture," she wanted to use it "like a piece of the American flag in a mosaic" (Freedman, "Who's to Say," E6). To enhance its symbolistic possibilities, she had settled on a surreal staging by her Wooster Group. She hoped this particular style would broaden Miller's themes to include current instances of "hallucination and interrogation" that she perceived in "clashes between counterculture and government" (Massa, 52). And though LeCompte waited, Miller did not wish her to produce what he perceived as a "blatant parody of his work"—though parodies normally lie beyond the protection of the Dramatists' Guild (Massa, 52).

Still LeCompte, refusing to withdraw, issued invitations to Miller to attend rehearsals of the project. At one point, after an unlicensed opening night, Miller did visit the theatre but found it a "speeded-up production" (52) whose fanciful intent he could not approve for his text so easily as he had welcomed other works' alterations in the 1950s (Kazan, 361). LeCompte told reporters, "We've written several letters . . . and we're still hopeful he'll change his mind" (Massa, 52). She received no replies—perhaps since the letters were sent, not to Miller directly, but to his agent, Louis Sanhero (Freedman, "Play Closed," E21). "When she did not hear from Mr. Miller . . . she took it as a tacit approval from the playwright" and went on with the show (E21), using "parts of *The Crucible* even though Mr. Miller had denied it the rights" (Freedman, "Who's to Say," E6). For a year without cease, the playwright/director clash reechoed and intensified as Miller remained distressed by LeCompte's disregard for the general spirit of his play.

Before more specific points of LeCompte's disregard for Miller's script are approached, it is expedient to wonder how Kazan would have conceived the emotional spirit of *The Crucible* had *he*, not Jed Harris, directed it in the 1950s as Miller had planned (Kazan, 450). For Kazan, like LeCompte later, perceived its spirit far differently from Miller's professed intention as he had written it. The author's stated purpose was for his play "to deal literally with the Salem witch trials" (Freedman, "Play Closed," E21) but not to suggest ties to his own life or culture. Conversely, Kazan recalls that he immediately espied a link between the script's Puritan guilt and hysteria and Miller's own personal and political throes while he was creating the play (Kazan, 450). Kazan wanted and needed to understand such links if, as Miller was planning, he were to direct *The Crucible* (450).

Determining Miller's thematic intent to have been either personal or impersonal is difficult when one reads Kazan's and Miller's separate recalls in their subsequent memoirs. Though both Miller and Kazan had been to some degree involved in early Communist party meetings as Miller was working on his manuscript, he rebuffed friends who thought his play would link or compare early Puritan witch-hunts and current Communist baitings. He recalls that Kazan's wife had objected angrily to what she suspected Miller might be including in his *Crucible*. She confronted Miller directly: "You're not going to equate witches with this!" (Miller, *Timebends*, 335). Years later, in 1981, Miller still insisted that he had constructed his script "with strict time reference" (Miller, *Eight Plays*, xi) to the Puritan period's self-professed or self-denying sinners and the consequence of their behavior—and had *not* allegorized present national or personal guilts or errors (xi).

But the author's explicit recollections in his 1987 autobiography may cast a shadow on this insistence. "A living connection between myself and Salem, and between Salem and Washington, was made in my mind" (Miller, *Timebends*, 331). Puritan "acts of contrition, done in the public air rather than in solemn privacy," were distressing him: "I was researching *The Crucible* . . . and I suddenly felt a familiar inner connection with witchcraft and the Puritan cult . . . something more mysteriously personal" (42). His autobiography lingers on sexual anecdotes that startled Miller as he researched the Puritans' lives. "Here was guilt, the guilt of illicit sexuality. . . . Night was the usual time to be subverted . . . a spectral visitor floated in and lay upon [the women] or provoked them to some filthy act like kissing . . . they were encouraged in open court to talk about their sharing a bed with someone they weren't married to" (341). Miller's pages recall his anxiety as he read the records and wrote his play: "I knew that my own life was speaking here in many disguises, not merely my time. . . . I knew instantly what the connection was: the moral intensity of the Jews. . . . Yes, I understood Salem in that flash; it was suddenly my own inheritance" (338). From his Jewish nature, Miller would be as helpless before guilt as were his play's Puritans.

In fact, critics have stated that to reveal the Puritans' "scrupulosity of conscience" was Miller's obsession with his play (Rovere, 14). Kazan, too, perceived Miller's impetus in writing the play to be conscience-oriented; and assuming he would direct *The Crucible*, Kazan formulated a firm concept of its author's intent. He disclaimed Miller's statement that the work "should not be read for 'contemporary significance' " as dishonest (Kazan, 450); and when Miller asked him to read the finished play, Kazan considered its content to be a divulgence of the author's current personal experiences (450). When the play was produced, author Clifford Odets denigrated it as "just a story about a bad marriage" (Miller, *Timebends*, 236). Kazan writes, "If we are to judge solely from *The Crucible*, we would have to say that Art did think of himself as a sinner: the central character in it expresses contrition for a single act of infidelity" (Kazan, 367). The play's John Proctor hangs his head and weeps before the Puritan court, "God help me, I lusted, and there is a promise in such sweat" (Miller, *The Crucible*, 69). From Kazan's involvement with Miller's life outside the theatre, he felt conversant with his friend's remorse over alleged peccadillos a less sensitive person might have put aside as a normal blemish in conduct (Kazan, 367). The play's Elizabeth Proctor begged her husband, "Will you forgive yourself? It is your soul, John. . . . Whatever you will do, it is a good man who does it" (Miller, *The Crucible*, 87). Intimately aware of his friend's fixations, Kazan had tried to dissuade Miller from finishing *The Crucible* (Kazan, 367), had encouraged him to leave off his obsession with the Puritan material and dramatize instead the happy years of his marriage to the popular film star of the period, Marilyn Monroe (368).

Hence if Kazan, not Jed Harris, had directed the premiere staging of *The Crucible*, surely his alleged insight into Miller's personal qualms would have belied the author's declared Puritan-only focus as completely as LeCompte's stylization of it was to do later. For Kazan has written, "I am a mediocre director except when a play . . . touches a part of my life's experience; [otherwise] I rely on mechanics [and] do only what a good stage manager should be able to do" (363). With the author's personal anxieties touching Kazan's "life experience," the director might have shaped the actors' on-stage behavior in line with his own less guilt-driven perspective. At the close of the curtain, as John Proctor protects his name but loses his life, Kazan's actors might have delivered key phrases like the following with a condescending or haughty emotional tone: "Pray God it speak some goodness for me" (Miller, *The Crucible*, 90). Proctor's counsel to Elizabeth as the two are to be executed—"Give them no tear . . . show them a heart of stone and sink them with it!" (90)—could have been voiced with belligerence, or with humility, depending on whether Kazan's intent was to line them up with his own or with Miller's attitudes toward guilt and contrition. If nothing else, the result— had fate not determined that Jed Harris, not Kazan, direct *The Crucible*—would have linked the play to Miller's life and time, lessening its focus on our fundamentalist beginnings. Moreover, had Kazan actually staged his idiosyncratic vision, he might have exceeded Miller's amazing tolerance level in the 1950s and ended the pair's friendly relationship.

Decades later, LeCompte's view of *The Crucible* differed from Miller's as much as Kazan's when the play was being developed by its author. In fact, her attempted experiments with *The Crucible* suggest that over the years since Kazan's era, fixed notions of what constitutes a "performance" had broadened to encompass far more than a single text presented to a director by one author. A performance could incorporate any number of scripts into one grand show. With LeCompte's drive for freer interpretation than directors like Kazan had enjoyed at midcentury, she perceived a script as "one of many kinds of texts," so that the author's pages become "a constant but destabilized element" of production (Rabkin, 146). Her postmodernist goal for *The Crucible*'s text was to make it "an icon . . . to hang in front of a new three-part work" (Massa, 52). Her experimental piece was to be a compilation of texts by Leary, Miller, and others, its characters mere symbols rather than fleshed-out individuals. John Proctor and Abigail Williams were to become "figures on a manuscript, pointers to ideology and attitude rather than 'characters' " around whom a playwright had constructed "a narrative sequence" (Savran, "The Wooster Group," 105). Yet of her textual tampering LeCompte maintained, "We paraphrase, play between the lines, and focus on the girls' hysteria, but we're true to the spirit of the original script" (Massa, 52). Though she vowed, "We love this play" (52), critics at the time wrote that her Wooster Group "not only deprivileges the play while respecting its contribution, it explicitly challenges the identity of text with written text" (Rabkin, 146). For some, her work raised issues of textual interpretation centering upon "ambiguous and subjective notions of artistic freedom" (Savran, "The Wooster Group," 101). As LeCompte continued her fight for legal rights to her creative use of Miller's *The Crucible*, she reduced her illegal incorporation of the play from forty-five to twenty-five minutes, then to twenty minutes of pantomime and/or gibberish. Critics noted that LeCompte's performers "drink, smoke and party while fragments from Act III surface in a fitful rhythm," and that their activity "alternates between the simple act of reading" and a "highly theatricalized mania" (Savran, "The Wooster Group," 105).

Siding with Miller's outraged stance at LeCompte's nontraditional staging plans, his defenders quoted the playwright at length: "I don't want my play produced except in total agreement with the way I wrote it" (Massa, 52). They repeated his disparagement of LeCompte's nonrealistic staging of his play (52). For he had constructed its text with strict time reference, traditionally an accepted determiner of an author's intended style of presentation (Miller, *Eight Plays*, xi). Adamantly, Miller held his drama "bound by natural time," hence pressed toward realism (xi). He had, he insisted, used time "so as to convey a natural passage of hours, days, or months," allowing no true "license for non-realistic style" (xi). What distressed the author's friends, lawyers, and supporters, then, was LeCompte's audacity in continuing the production in a style so inconsistent with Miller's scripted intent. Yet two weeks after Miller's renewed request that her group stop performing *L.S.D.* without his permission, she still persisted (Freed-

man, "Play Closed," E21). For LeCompte hoped she had ended the controversy by
a compromise that cut her use of the play to just twenty minutes of the original
script and also "eliminated dialogue from the sequence, having it performed as
pantomime" (E21).

Headlines during November and December 1984 debated "Who's to Say
Whether a Playwright Is Wronged?" (Freedman, *New York Times*, E6), and repeatedly declared "Arthur Miller Clings to *The Crucible*" (Massa, *Village
Voice*, 52). Six months later, bold print still blared from the New York *Performing Arts Journal*'s article, "Is There a Text on This Stage?" (Rabkin, 142), re-
gretting Miller and LeCompte's lack of communication. Media columns were
also printing mitigating reasons for the problem. A *Village Voice* reviewer suggested that the whole controversy actually bore less on LeCompte's undue license with text than on Miller's fear that LeCompte was reducing his "most
oft-produced work" to the status of a "fossil" (Massa, 52). What all playwrights
must dread more than directors' runaway license with plays is surely their staging them as long-past icons rather than as virile, living masterworks. One column suggested, "Icons are more artifact than art; perhaps the playwright, who
premiered his latest work Off-Off-Broadway, doesn't like to think of his greatest success as a fossil of the '50s" (52). Other sources conjectured that Miller's
aversion to *any* revival of his *Crucible* in the 1980s may have reflected his natural disinclination to reassociate himself with the ticklish 1950s when he created it—a period of his own political imbroglios (Ferres, 3). Memories of old
slurs at him as "a pinko playwright" that had caused his "subsequent difficulties in obtaining a passport to attend the opening of *The Crucible* in Brussels"
(3) could understandably quench any joy of Miller's at LeCompte's proposed revival, one that might under different emotional circumstances have proved an
interesting and vibrant production.

Ultimately, Miller left off his obliging 1950s manner with Kazan's directorial innovations and protested obdurately. He reaffirmed his "artistic reservations" about
LeCompte's unorthodox borrowing from *The Crucible*, explaining, "I thought it
abstracted the play. . . . It abbreviated it" (Freedman, "Play Closed," E21). With the
backing of the Dramatists' Guild, Miller triumphed. "Under the threat of litigation,
the Wooster Group ultimately closed the production" with a colossal loss at the
box office (Freedman, "Who's to Say," E6). The media finally announced "Play
Closed after *Crucible* Dispute" (Freedman, "Play Closed," E21).

In retrospect, Miller's fears for his artistic product are understandable in view of
the pace at which the theatrical world has moved toward deconstruction of authors'
texts. The measure of responsibility any period assigns to a director like Kazan or
LeCompte is seldom uniform or static; thus authors in the 1980s must have stared
apprehensively at the future for play performance if the trend toward directorial
subjectivity should quicken. Though Kazan has proudly termed his 1950s "The
Time of the Director or something of the sort" (Kazan, 364), what might yet
evolve was still beyond expectation. Kazan has written of his freedom with text at
the outset of the 1950s, "I could see no limit to what I might accomplish" (362).

And what Kazan accomplished in those years with Miller was momentous in the opinion of Tennessee Williams, who recalled in a letter to his friend Donald Windham during the 1960s that Miller's play, *Death of a Salesman*, which was "flatly written and lacked dynamics," had been turned into a success "because of the brilliant direction of Kazan" (Windham, 232). And of a production of the same play in England, one that followed Kazan's staging, J. C. Trewin wrote that although the text of the American play *Death of a Salesman* was "otherwise tangled, pretentious, and dull," the production's "vigour and humanity helped to relieve the evening," and made the play "a commercial success" (8).

Perhaps upon successes like these with Miller plays, the veteran directors Kazan and LeCompte were grounding their liberal notions that a script that comes to rehearsals is not the script that emerges in performance. An ultimately published text is not the author's alone but "a document into which the *director*'s stage directions are incorporated, as are some of the contributions of others working on the show—actors' business, designers' solutions, and so on" (Kazan, 362). The script that goes into rehearsal need not be the end product since in Kazan's mental structuring of theatre, a unique categorization appears: "The theatre is not an exclusively literary form. Although the playscript is the essentially important element, after that is finished, actors, designers, directors, technicians 'write' the play together" (362). The playscript was becoming only a component of performance, not its totality, and the full consequences of that evolution were yet to be experienced by playwrights or theatre audiences after the 1950s.

By LeCompte's 1980s, these freer policies of production were increasingly visible on stage; the theatre world was seeing and countenancing presumably "runaway stagings" by what had come to be called, fairly or not, tyrant directors putting on their own "shows" to make "theatre an event of the free fancy . . . less realistic [and] . . . like painting and dance, more of an art" (Kazan, 364–65). But as playwrights like Miller began to rebel, the Dramatists' Guild sought for its members better legal protection against theatre companies' undue license with their texts. Consequently, though "normal rights of interpretation are essential in order to free the full energy and meaning of [a] play" (Freedman, "Who's to Say," E6), undue freedom by a director could more easily be fought in the courts as an infringement on dramatists' rights. As a result, suits against what Kazan praised as "plays turned into shows" (364) had become widespread by the 1980s. Though in midcentury virtually no media criticism had studied Kazan's subjective stagings of Miller's plays like *Death of a Salesman*, many reviewers in the 1980s held LeCompte's work with *The Crucible* to exceed legal bounds by violating the spirit of the play. Her Wooster Group had "conflated [*The Crucible*] into a fifty-minute work in progress, then into a twenty-minute segment of multisegmented work, and finally, in response to Miller's adamant refusal of rights, into a ten minute, largely gibberish strand in a 110-minute collage" (Rabkin, 144). And David Levine, president of the Dramatist group, had conclusively stated, "I consider Arthur Miller's play no different from his car. You wouldn't drive off [in] his car and say, 'Oh, I'll bring it back later' " (Freedman, "Who's to Say," E6).

In sum, biographical and historical data on Arthur Miller's interchange with two different directors verify that the playwright was unprovoked by modifications of his scripts in the 1940s or 1950s. His most frequent director, Elia Kazan, looked forward to each new collaboration, and his imaginative and assertive direction satisfied and pleased his playwright-partner. Sufficient reason for Miller's 1983 switch in stance toward Elizabeth LeCompte may be that without the colleagueship and trust that had melded Miller and his first director, the playwright cursorily assumed from what he saw and heard that LeCompte was parodying his work, mocking his purpose, thus posing for him the risk of forestalling more conventional productions in the future. Moreover, Miller's reluctance to grant authority for free directorial interpretation of scripts could also have surfaced by reason of the author's increased professional status in the 1980s theatre world. Theorist Michel Foucault has perceived a generic difference in performance expectations between a new writer and one who "later acquires some 'importance' " (154). Foucault writes that the latter "governs and commands" more than the former (154). An unknown at the start of his teamwork with Kazan, Miller had become an established figure in theatre when LeCompte approached him for rights of production. And by then *The Crucible* itself, no longer an untried entity, had attained the status of an American classic.

Fairly or not, today's production game lets directors like LeCompte readily surmount traditional walls that once protected classic scripts of deceased and living authors. With Shakespeare, directors "cut and rearrange" and transmogrify characters into "everything from voodoo priestesses to American gangsters" (Freedman, "Who's to Say," E6). And with living playwrights' new works, directors may often have carte-blanche since the absence of prior staging may encourage both author and director to experiment fancy-free. But are today's playwrights obliged to extend full artistic freedom to directors who appproach their already established and celebrated works?

Shortly after *The Crucible* altercation, a journal writer declared: "[W]hile interpretation may indeed be the only game in town, it plays by many rules" (Rabkin, 158). If we have new rules for the game—a pinch of protection for an author's intent—are LeCompte's successors learning them? If not, thwarted authors may start dreaming up fresh lyrics for that old directors' tune, "The Best Playwright Is a Dead One."

13

A Playwright-Director Opens Up a Classic: Albee's Direction of Beckett

With theatre classics, audiences welcome traditional stagings. But popular plays run the risk of becoming stale if enthusiasts cling to long-established stagings and reject freely modified ones out of hand. Equally troublesome is arbitrary altering of a play by an individual director, star, or others who may overshadow each other as they bypass historical continuity, refuting the authority of a text's inherited patterns (Davis, 11).

If indeed the concept of textual purity has validity in theatre—or in any medium—its essence can be lost when an experimental group or its director toys with a classic. Hierarchic squabbles may occur over a work's tone, focus, casting, or even its spoken text. How to define "text" is itself an issue. A director's stance on text may draw critical conjecture if the turn-at-the-top of production falls to an iconoclast like playwright-director Edward Albee, who staged a controversial evening of Samuel Beckett one-act plays at Houston's Alley Theatre in the spring of 1991.[1]

Albee's wish to direct Beckett's works is understandable. Albee scholar Matthew Roudané notes that Albee's plays, like Beckett's, embody "universal psychological experiences" and objectify "unconscious emotions" (15). C.W.E. Bigsby, another Albee critic, says that Albee, like Beckett, prefers to tackle "issues of genuine metaphysical seriousness"; according to Bigsby, Albee develops these themes "in a way that few American dramatists before him have claimed to do, and does so, for the most part, with a command of wit and a controlled humour which has not always characterized the work of O'Neill, Miller, and Williams" (1).

Longtime critic Anne Paolucci agrees; she lauds Albee as a playwright for his re-structuring of the modern stage, "revolutionizing [its] language, extending verbal metaphor into the visual settings of his plays . . . and using epic topography to main-tain allegorical simplicity" (Paolucci, *From Tension to Tonic*, 15). With this innova-tive bent, Albee, though he and Beckett share thematic interests, might be expected to approach a Beckett staging without full adherence to Beckett's scripted strictures. Theatre history shows that in the 1960s, playwright Albee broke accepted patterns to force nontraditional theatre on Broadway audiences. Roudané delves into Albee's penchant as an author for overthrowing drama's established procedures (6–46).

Before the 1960s a play's spoken words plus its author's stage directions tradi-tionally constituted an author's text. Yet directors staging a work today may deem little inviolate but the words to be spoken, with even those fair game for the more liberal directors. Though countless productions have reworked and updated drama with great success, our century's modern classics have not routinely profited from directorial intrusions, any more than have the works of Shakespeare. Director John Gielgud unsuccessfully "freed a 1964 *Hamlet* from the trappings of its time" and so blatantly "contradicted the text" that the production closed quickly (Cronyn, 6). Another nontraditional venture, the film *Prospero's Books*, with Gielgud as actor and Peter Greenaway as director, received mixed reviews of its scenes of an atypi-cal Gielgud, nude among gyrating monsters, his voice electronically manipulated, speaking the dialogue for all the play's roles.[2] One should perhaps note that this was not *The Tempest*—only a show based on it. Many closer interpretations that have attempted to enhance Shakespeare, however, have succeeded with no per-ceived affront to the dramatist's authority.

But directors who too freely alter masterworks of living dramatists have drawn rebukes from author, press, and public. Long before Albee's controversial ap-proach to Beckett at the Alley, Tennessee Williams suffered directorial cuts that Sir Laurence Olivier called "vandalism"; in one instance, ironically, the cuts were made by Olivier himself, who altered Williams' spoken text (with the playwright's later approval) when producing *A Streetcar Named Desire* in London (Kolin, "Olivier to Williams," 152). But the late Samuel Beckett flinched at what he termed "bastardization" of scripts by addition of dialogue and an "omnipresent massacre and abuse of directorial function" in a 1973 production of *Endgame*.[3] So forceful were Beckett's routine protests over tampering that stagings of his work remained almost fixed while he lived. Now Beckett scholars must ask what looms for his legacy, judging from today's ever-increasing leeway to bypass a play-wright's intention (Roof, 106). With Shakespeare and Williams gone this route, can Beckett be far behind?

Albee and other directors, in fact, are being given carte blanche today to find "truth in text" outside the "verbal icon," to interpret text "through the spaces left by the way words operate" (Frye, Baker, and Perkins, 364). Historical accuracy and legitimacy of the dramatic legacy need not be foremost with those who under-take, in Ezra Pound's phrase, "to make it new" (quoted in Abrams, 109). Post-structuralists can "delete the author" and "demote the text" on the basis that "loopholes in language itself" throw into question the certainty of what Beckett and other authors intended in their manuscripts (Frye, Baker, and Perkins, 352). Such theorists concentrate on the reader, who, in theatre, is the director. According to Roland Barthes, a reader is free to experiment with a work, in effect devising new texts for further reading (263). During Beckett's lifetime, changes in notions of what constitutes a text had only begun to confront the two directors whose names are linked historically to his—Roger Blin and Alan Schneider. Each differed fundamentally not only from the other but from the more recent Beckett director, Albee, in the extent of their adherence to the Beckett text.

Roger Blin, Beckett's much-publicized mid-twentieth-century French director, faced what theatre historian Oscar Brockett sees as a basic issue with production teams: whether a serious and inventive director may toy with a script as a full-fledged artist in his own right, or whether he is nothing but a dramatist's interpreter (Brockett, 565). Blin remained conservative: "My pleasure," he said, "is to go in the direction of the author" (quoted in Cohn, *Samuel Beckett*, 151). Chided by modernists for slavish adherence to Beckett's text, Blin replied that "[d]irecting should be invisible" since "movements and words must respect the respiration of the play" (151). Summarizing Blin's refusal to alter Beckett dialogue or staging for easier comprehension by the masses, critic Herbert Blau called Blin "one of the rare French directors who have made no peace with the boulevards" but who "direct where they can the plays they admire and that's all . . . though they are wooed to do elsewise" (Blau, 91).

Coming after Blin, yet still before Albee, director Alan Schneider also weighed what constitutes text and who is in control. During his twenty-five years of association with Beckett, Schneider found "lots to open up" and sought "the best way to do the opening up" (228), insisting that "much remains to be done by the director."[4] Yet Schneider did not alter the text's spoken icon. Schneider has attested, "I stuck strictly to the text" (365). He shepherded Beckett productions, believing that a director should respect the purity of a script when an author's intent is clear and explicit throughout its pages.

But the 1990s urge to reauthor a text has perpetuated Blin's and Schneider's early concerns. Today, Edward Albee holds an ironic position on authorial potency and directorial modification by virtue of his perch on more than one step in the theatre hierarchy. To study the results of what some might consider Albee's liberties with Beckett's legacy during his recent staging of *Ohio Impromptu* and *Krapp's Last Tape* is to delve into the whole, long-standing issue of ever-increasing bastardization of theatre "texts."

In lectures and interviews, Albee has stated his position on theatre hierarchy readily, if at times paradoxically. "Some playwrights should not be allowed into the theatre. They're hysterics," he said at a 1991 Inge Festival seminar. But at the same seminar he stipulated, "If a playwright can learn the considerable craft of direction, if he can overcome the actors' being taught to mistrust the author, and if he can be objective about his own writing, *no* other person than the author can give as accurate a translation of what the playwright saw and heard when he wrote the play—

no more accurate representation of the author's intent." Speaking of directors, Albee contended in February 1991 that "[i]f you respect [a] work, you try to translate it from the page to the stage as clearly and accurately as you can. And if you're directing [a dramatist like Samuel Beckett]—he doesn't need your help" (King, 12). Decades earlier, Albee (still in his playwright shoes) had voiced his perspective strongly: "There is only one true, correct, hard, ideal performance of a play, and that is mine, and I saw it when I was writing" (quoted in Gussow, 52). Albee seemed then to bolster authorial potency.

However, Albee's theoretical position appears equally contemporary and director-oriented if one studies his careful breakdown of the components of text, for he has sharply differentiated between a text's "explicit [and its] implicit stage directions," choosing to follow the latter, which "lie in the subtext, within the essence and nature of the characters" (Albee et al., "Playwright/Director"). At the Inge Festival Albee stressed that the factor "separat[ing] a good director from a poor one is his ability to follow *implicit* stage directions. I like to think that one creative intelligence has an insight into another creative intelligence." He went on to remark that what emerges "need not be a photo-image of the author's intention, but . . . should be the *reflection* of it." Readers of Albee's own texts soon find that he, like Beckett, provides "careful blueprints for a theatrical performance, with detailed indications of how he wishes the play to emerge in performance" (McCarthy, 30). Yet his scripted directions are not blunt authorial demands; rather they are prompts a director *might* follow, often preceded by "perhaps" or followed by a question mark. By 1978 Albee was no longer convinced that a play's ideal performance was "the sole property" of the writer; but he felt dissatisfied "with the sort of direction to be seen in the theater" (29). Since then he has directed his own plays (and those of Lanford Wilson, Harold Pinter, and Beckett) here and abroad. Whether or not Albee, as director, can square his vision with what he perceives to be other authors' intents is of consequence to theatre historians.

To the profit of the theatre, the whole generic issue of theatre hierarchy (and of arbitrary altering of once-impregnable texts) went public straightaway during Albee's 1991 stint as director of the Alley's Beckett bill, for the theatre's artistic director, Gregory Boyd, pluckily held a panel discussion. Boyd entitled it "Beckett on Stage," and held it on a night when the Alley was dark. Albee; Ruby Cohn, preeminent Beckett scholar from California; Alvin Epstein, actor and Beckett director in New York and Europe; Mel Gussow, reviewer for the *New York Times*; and Robert Scanlan, literary director of the American Repertory Theatre, constituted a spirited panel that spoke out on what some saw as Albee's bizarre casting and capricious tampering with one of the bill's two Beckett scripts, *Ohio Impromptu*. (The staging of the other, better-known play, *Krapp's Last Tape*, was less controversial since Albee's production closely reflected Beckett's staging intent.) Challenges and replies, reproach and approval promptly surfaced as director Albee and the four theatre professionals from the East and West interacted. Albee and the panel candidly assessed as legitimate or suspect the innovative turns and thrusts in Albee's handling of Beckett's texts.

In the Alley Theatre's productions, Albee approached the two plays as diverse types of literary documents. The one, *Krapp's Last Tape*, he labeled naturalistic, with an earthy aura filling us with "love, pity, and sadness" for groaning old Krapp ("Director Albee," 32). The other, *Ohio Impromptu*, he called a "stylized dramatic experience that exists in the mind of one of the characters [but] should be accepted as experience on its own terms" (Albee, class session at the University of Houston).

During the Alley panel discussion on Albee directing Beckett, one question prevailed: Had director Albee guarded the esoteric matter in Beckett's text or had he tampered impulsively with it? The question gnawed at the assembled panelists as they recalled Beckett's earlier, fastidious protection of minuscule aspects of production. The dramatist had kept his work unaltered and uncluttered by extraneous props or gestures.[5] Still, Beckett himself allowed for a jot of change, especially in his later works, giving permission to at least one director "to improve upon" a particular script's staging as long as he took care to "keep it cool" (Beckett, letter of June 13, 1965, to Shivaun O'Casey Kenig; quoted in Bair, 578).[6]

Of Albee's "improvements" on Beckett's texts, the Alley panel focused first on the director's tonal approach; Albee's direction gave *Ohio Impromptu*, a late, minimalist Beckett work, the tenor of a Liszt tone-poem, its cadences metaphysical and intriguing. *Krapp's Last Tape*, an earlier Beckett monologue, Albee molded concretely and farcically. In each, a state of ordered tension ensued from light, sound, and rhythm, as Beckett's heroes endured their hellish hours. In discussing

Edward Seamon as Krapp in *Krapp's Last Tape* by Samuel Beckett. Directed by Edward Albee. Copyright © 1991 by Jim Caldwell. Courtesy of the Alley Theatre.

Ohio Impromptu, however, the panelists focused on whether or not Albee had by-passed the printed legacy of both text and casting directions.

Arbitrarily, Albee had opted to scrap Beckett's implicit intent for *Ohio Impromptu*, one of his shortest works, and to run its spoken text three times in succession for each performance. Yet Beckett specifies down to the minute an exact, abbreviated performance time for his minimalist text. The play is a monologue with the first actor, Reader, turning pages in an old volume before him and reading aloud while the second, Listener, sits silent. At the Alley, Albee stayed tentatively with the text's call for a fade-up, a ten-second interval, the turning of a page, and a pause, as Reader begins a tale of which "[l]ittle is left to tell" (Beckett, *Ohio Impromptu*, 28). Reader is absorbed in redrawing a life, reciting a tale of one who now lives with little love, little urge, less fire. As he reads, the music of his language reaches us through the lines' voiced continuants and through the play of vowel against vowel. At intervals, Listener knocks with a hard, dry rap on a long slab of table at which the two actors are seated, to signal Reader to repeat painfully crucial phrases, distinctive Beckett gems of thought.

Indeed, just six pages comprise the script Beckett has consigned to us. But Albee took liberties with Beckett's explicit finish, which appears thus in the text:

Simultaneously [Reader and Listener] lower their right hands to table, raise their heads and look at each other. Unblinking. Expressionless.

Ten Seconds.

Fade Out. (35)

At this point, in lieu of the reading of the text that its author specifies—at most, six minutes of stage time—Albee chose to prolong the eerie aura of *Ohio Impromptu* for eighteen to twenty minutes with a threefold running of the text before allowing it to end. Though Albee's first reading follows Beckett's text, with the actors at opposite ends of the table, for the second reading Albee's actors switch roles and places at the table. For the third reading, again at different spots at the table, each actor speaks some of the lines Beckett originally scripted for Reader.

In effect, both Albee's tripled-text and the single original allow several views of Beckett's intent. One is that Reader tells of a time past when he had come to comfort Listener because a lady whom Listener loves would not see him again. Another—reminiscent of a favorite volume of Beckett's, Dante's *Inferno*—is that Reader recites his own despair over a deceased love called only "dear one," who has sent a shade (Listener) to comfort Reader in his loneliness. Be that as it may, Albee's appropriately slow pacing of Beckett's flow of language lets the mystic shade linger long at each reading. At the end, Beckett's scripted scene lets both comforter and comforted sit stone-like, with no dawn of day, with the text's imagery, "final dawnless day," suggesting that Listener's irrevocable end is upon him. Beckett's comforter, like Dante's Virgil, lacks authority to remain with his charge beyond an allotted span. But at the Alley with Albee, the three repetitions and the

Charles Sanders as the Listener and Lou Ferguson as the Reader in *Ohio Impromptu* by Samuel Beckett. Directed by Edward Albee. Copyright © 1991 by Jim Caldwell. Courtesy of the Alley Theatre.

subsequently thrice-told ending made the shade such an omnipresent image that we felt he, unlike Virgil, was to share the other's ultimate journey—which may or may not have been Albee's intent.

One need not ask if this particular ploy—a tripled exposure to text—leapt unheralded into Albee's mind if one recalls his early fondness as a dramatist for recapitulation in his own plays. Albee's script for *Box and Quotations from Chairman Mao Tse-Tung* exhorts future directors to repeat *Box*'s text three times: "I feel that *Box* will make its points most effectively if played twice (*or even three times*) in a row, without intermission, going to black between each playing" (Albee, *Box*, 4).

At the Alley, panelists differed on the merit of Albee's rerun—or reprise—of the text of *Ohio Impromptu*. Robert Scanlan flinched at Albee's rendition, vowing "I don't think Beckett would be pleased" ("Beckett on Stage"). Scanlan's remark echoed first-night reviews of the play. The *Public News*' Anna Krejci had complained that the three-time reading "only perpetuates the popular opinion that Beckett is repetitive and downright boring" (115). The *Houston Chronicle*'s Everett Evans had felt that Albee's "alternation of lines the third time around dissipates the piece's focus" (E4). In contrast, at the panel discussion, one of the speakers, Mel Gussow, justified Albee's repetition, citing Beckett's text that says, "So from time to time unheralded [the shade] would appear to read the sad tale through again and the long night away" (Beckett, *Ohio Impromptu*, 32). Gussow reasoned that with Beckett's single pass through the text, the audience would have heard the tale but once, whereas the two at the table were privy to it nightly; therefore it was appropriate that with Albee's reprise the audience, too, could be exposed to the tale again and again (and again).

Less a matter of Albee's textual tampering than of expedience, a related directorial antic was caused by the two awkward interstices in this threefold staging. Albee needed a linking or unifying device for these intervals because his preview audience assumed the play complete when the stage darkened after first and second readings.[7] Before the bill's official opening, Albee inserted a series of knocks into the interstices. With stage lights dimmed as the two actors shifted seats, the prerecorded bony knocks kept the Alley audience seated and absorbed in anticipation between the runnings of the text.

More provocatively, Albee toyed with Beckett's casting wishes, though critics hold the choice of actors crucial to director/author accord. For *Ohio Impromptu*, Beckett's script explicitly states that its two characters must be "as alike in appearance as possible" and must have long white hair (27), perhaps so that we interpret them metaphysically as two parts of one soul—as shades of each other. Nonetheless Albee dismissed Beckett's scripted preference. For the roles of Reader and Listener he cast two actors totally dissimilar in mein, size, voice, and manner: Lou Ferguson, a Caribbean native whose honeyed voice and distinctive accent added a second melodic line to the music of the text; and Charles Sanders, an Alley regular who delivered Beckett's dialogue in standard American tones.

As for the hair that Beckett's text explicitly specifies, Albee thought the effect inappropriate for Ferguson, the white too stark against his rich skin color, rendering his appearance grotesque. Hence Albee experimented with substitutes and chose a wig with dark, Rastafarian dreadlocks, equally distinctive and far more natural for this particular actor.

On matters of casting, however, Barney Rosset, Beckett's Grove Press publisher in the 1970s, recalls that Beckett, though never provincial, protested an "all-black production" of one of his plays in the United States because "it was not in keeping with his intention and detracted from the audience's concentration on the play itself" (quoted in Bair, 632). Beckett's aim was that actors be unobtrusive. Once he vowed that "[t]he best possible play is one in which there are no actors, only the text. I'm trying to find a way to write one" (quoted in Bair, 513). In any event, Alley panelist Alvin Epstein, who had worked professionally in the United States and abroad with Beckett, countered that the playwright, though admittedly favoring certain actors for specific roles, was usually less concerned with casting choices than with running of his dialogue. Epstein thought Albee's selection of Ferguson, seasoned by roles in *Raisin in the Sun*, *Master Harold and the Boys*, *Sizwe Bansi Is Dead*, and New York's Shakespeare Festival, gave style and resonance to the spoken text (Albright, E5).

A further circumvention of authorial intent appeared in Albee's innovative lighting for the play. Few authors in theatre history have been so fastidious with light engineering as Beckett, who once delayed an early Paris production of *Play* because the director had not satisfactorily handled this element (Bair, 569). Beckett's script for *Ohio Impromptu* indicates simply and starkly: "Light on table midstage. Rest of stage in darkness" (27). For his own plays, Albee has been equally meticulous with lighting; indeed, he seems leery of it, refusing to play with daring effects and criticizing directors who flood drama with lighting spectacle (Albee, Class session). Still, in *Ohio Impromptu*, perhaps because the play's aura so strongly suggests the metaphysical, Albee has improvised with chiaroscuro. For each of the three passes through the text of *Ohio Impromptu*, Albee tinted the stage with soft hues—pink, then violet, then green. Before the play's opening, Albee told his students at the University of Houston of having read about someone in theatre using "snot green" effectively (Albee, Class session); curious about its properties, he experimented with the mottled tone during rehearsals at the Alley, and, liking its effect, alternated this hue with pink and violet to spot the dark-clothed figures bent at the long white table on-stage. The spectacle recalled an earlier departure by Albee from his characteristic stance against flamboyant lighting: in *Box and Quotations from Chairman Mao Tse-Tung*, he had conceded, "[T]he overall lighting might change—from light blue to deep blue; from red to green; at any rate, from one color-sense to another" (4).

Less a turn from Beckett tradition yet a point of contention with the panelists at the Alley Colloquium was Albee's choice of a nonhistrionic, controlled delivery of the play's spoken text. One review of *Ohio Impromptu* praised Albee for the performance's "seamless flow of sound" that, while mellifluously appealing, never distracted viewers from the "visual imagery" of Beckett's language (Spence, 26). But another, apparently discounting the melodic tones in the voice of actor Lou Ferguson, called the result "dead"—two emotionless voices with no variation in range or tone, with the actors reciting their lines "word by word like androids, giving the words no meaning and therefore communicating no meaning to their audience" (Krejci, 15). This particular censure could belie Albee's celebrated care with the sound and rhythm of language. Typical of Albee's precision with phrasing is his earlier, solemn counsel, from a script of his own, advising: "I have indicated quite precisely the speech rhythms. Please observe them carefully, for they were not thrown in, like herbs on a salad, to be mixed about" (Albee, *Box*, 6). Reportedly, Beckett preferred a "completely straight undramatized reading" such as the one Albee used with *Ohio Impromptu* to the histrionic renditions of his text by many directors (Bair, 578); for Beckett wanted nothing on stage to detract from the rhythms and moods that express his thought (Schneider, 365). What some critics disliked about the Houston production, then, could have been something Beckett himself preferred; for under Albee's hand, the Alley actors spoke evenly, without vocal embellishments or gestures, the only movement being the occasional turning of a page or the knocking of knuckles on the table (Spence).

After the Alley's panel of guest critics had weighed Albee's staging of Beckett's text, a quintessential question lingered: Were Albee's "improvements" gratuitous? Were they in part a bowing to the masses, an imperative necessitated by the reputed obscurity of the late playwright's minimalist language? Director Alan

Schneider has said that "Beckett's metaphors reach into my subconscious soul" (xiv), but as for their meanings or implications, "Beckett would not—and would never—go into larger or symbolic meanings, preferring his work to speak for itself and letting the supposed 'meanings' fall where they might" (224). Panelist Ruby Cohn deemed Beckett's text so obscure in spots that it demands concentration and study by audiences. (In "Explosive Cocktails," she had written that Albee's own language provokes the perplexity of the audience [8, 9, 12].) Panelists Alvin Epstein and Robert Scanlan supported Cohn's view of Beckett's exacting text, recalling that in the 1950s one Beckett director, Herbert Berghof, had advertised for seven thousand intellectuals to volunteer as a properly constituted American audience for *Waiting for Godot*: "This is a play for the thoughtful and discriminating theatergoer. . . . I respectfully suggest that those who come to the theater for casual entertainment do not buy a ticket to this attraction" (Schumach, 41).[8]

To the Alley's panelists, however, Albee himself denied Beckett's reputed obscurity as grounds for his arbitrary repetition of the playwright's text; he saw no need to clarify Beckett nor to make him palatable to a mass audience. "Why is Beckett such an anathema? Is he difficult? Obscure? Impenetrable? None of the above" (Albee, "Some Thoughts," 9). Albee stressed that "Beckett is the least obscure playwright I know" and that he himself finds "not a word in any of his writing that I don't understand, or that anyone else wouldn't understand" (Albee, "Director Albee Says," 32). Albee insisted that "Beckett's plays are models of clarity; he writes with great precision and simplicity" ("Some Thoughts," 9).

In any case, many critics and creative artists have regarded a lack of clarity as an acceptable quality in works of art. One critic, for example, insists that unless a creative artist "intentionally assumes the role of critic, historian, or philosopher, his is *not* the responsibility of formulation" (Seitz, 132).[9] The German-born American artist Hans Hofmann decreed: "No explanations for those who don't understand; some day the philistines will see" (quoted in Seitz, 145). And Albee in 1966, upon publishing *Tiny Alice*, refused to bow to the "expressed hopes" of his public that he might "write a preface . . . clarifying obscure points in the play—explaining my intention, in other words." (Albee, "Author's Note," 5).[10]

Equally long-standing, though, have been viewers' protests that dramatized thought such as Albee's or Beckett's, obscure or not, is less than instantaneously graspable since viewers, unlike novel readers, cannot retrace words or phrases by flipping back through the pages. But Albee contended from the start that the sole intent of his intrusion into Beckett's text to repeat its words three times had been to reemphasize rather than to clarify what Reader calls "profounds of mind" (34).

No one reminded Albee that in 1964 it was Albee and his fellow-producers of Beckett's *Play* (directed by Alan Schneider) who had refused to follow Beckett's express wish that his text be performed twice without interruption. Beckett's plan was that "whatever references the audience didn't get the first time—most of them—would be absorbed the second time around" (Schneider, 341–42). Albee, Richard Barr, and Clinton Wilder "objected strongly to Sam's ideas" for

Play as perhaps right for "less sophisticated audiences" but as eliciting from preview audiences rude remarks "that Mr. Beckett was insulting their intelligence" (341). At the close of *Ohio Impromptu*'s opening night at the Alley, an echo resounded when I heard a viewer smirk as he exited his aisle, "Did Albee want us to *memorize* it?" Mixed comments also filled reviews during the Alley's run of the plays, varying from "loose" to "tasteful." One critic wrote that while the results do show "the hand of a director with his own vision of Beckett's world," Albee had been "true to Beckett" and had "allowed [Beckett's texts] to dictate the shape of the productions" (King, 12). Though one reviewer's title read "Albee's Ego Overpowers Beckett" (Krejci, 10), others read "True to the Words" (King) and "Albee Ensures Beckett Plays Are Accessible" (Albright).[11] A few voiced dismay at Albee's boldness with Beckett, but others praised his instinctive choices of style and spectacle.

What resolution can be made to the generic question of modification of script? Postmodernists may feel that directors today should have total leeway with our theatre classics; perhaps anything goes—as long as the director is of good repute and intention. Even conservative theorists may sanction a bit of directorial license by someone sensitive and creative who maintains a basic reverence for the original work. Albee's buttressing of Beckett's work seems reasonable and defensible (if controversial), for its result properly demonstrates the bleakness that Beckett saw and tolerated in life. On Albee's stage, somber and staid Reader and Listener, clad in black, are true to their Beckett roots: neither actor is brightened by red or orange rays. Beckett characters do not relish life as a highly colored experience. Albee's sporadic and atypical use of light stops at soft pinks and violets. For Reader and Listener do not exult; they endure. Beckett's script and Albee's staging give them meager measure of cheer.

Moreover, though Albee takes a circuitous route to arrive at Beckett's ending by running the text three times, he has not changed the story's ultimate outcome, for two immobile characters in Albee's production approach their end just as Beckett's original Reader and Listener do—trying to believe in a soul's visit from beyond. They may succeed. After all, Albee makes each endure again and again the cryptic tale read from a journal by a mystic visitor. And thrice Reader and Listener sit on in dawnless days. If the end of their route should be a nonexistence where two souls, one dark, one light, can listen to each other for longer than a few minutes, one comforting the other, then Albee's use of repetition may be a metaphor for his or Beckett's intent.

Who minds a smile now at the chance that Albee's threefold rendition of *Ohio Impromptu* might have been sparked by a wish to compensate for denying Beckett's plea to repeat the text of *Play* in the 1960s? Who minds that this "turn at the top" with Beckett's *Ohio Impromptu* is provocative? The evening bears witness to the insight and discernment of a playwright-director. An apostle of authorial intent like early Beckett directors Blin and Schneider, Albee has found "lots to open up" and "the best way to do the opening up" (Schneider, 228), while staying true in spririt to the playwright who had a major influence on him as a writer.

NOTES

This article is reprinted from *South Atlantic Review*, November 1993, with permission of editor Robert Bell, South Atlantic Modern Language Association.

Ralph Voss, of the University of Alabama, who also attended the Inge Festival, graciously read my manuscript; I am grateful for his key contributions. I want to thank Thomas A. Esterfield, of the University of Northern Iowa, too, for his insights into the complexities of Albee's role as a director and playwright.

1. Albee discussed at length his view of who's on top in play production at two seminars: the first, "Beckett on Stage," in March 1991 at the Alley Theatre, Houston, Tex., where he staged two Beckett one-act plays; the second, in April 1991, "Playwright/Director," at the Tenth Annual William Inge Festival, Independence, Kans., during a week-long event titled "Celebration of the American Theatre."

2. National Public Radio's reviewers analyzed audience reaction to the film in segments of "Morning Edition" on November 3 and November 29, 1991. Critics varied in their opinions, some feeling Greenaway had extended Shakespeare's imaginative scope, others finding his product obscure and bereft of Shakespearean semblance.

3. Beckett wrote in a letter of July 11, 1973, to editor-friend Barney Rosset of his concerns over arbitrary entries into the text of *Endgame* by director Andre Gregory, who had added "all sorts of additional dialogue to the script" and had cluttered the setting with "a chicken-wire cage" (quoted in Bair, 633).

4. Schneider's 1960 staging of *Krapp's Last Tape* has been credited by columnist Jerry Tallmer in the *Village Voice* as "inspired, inspirited, perfect: the first full realization in America of a work by Samuel Beckett" (quoted in Schneider, 276).

5. Beckett's drive for exacting control at rehearsals reached to "all technical aspects of the production" including vocal shading, nuance, gesture, and may have caused "barely veiled animosity in almost everyone" (Bair, 627). Yet Philippe Staib, the director of a Paris production of *Fin de Partie* in the 1960s, wrote, "The strength of the man is that he imposes his will without it ever being felt and without ever needing to insist" (Staib, 90).

6. Beckett's letter expressed his confidence that Kenig could satisfactorily expand the few staging concepts Beckett suggested to him.

7. I base this statement on remarks Albee made to me during the Alley previews of his production of *Ohio Impromptu*, February 15, 1991.

8. Yet Scanlan and Epstein admitted to the Alley panel and audience that *Waiting for Godot* was subsequently performed at a prison where the convicts—with no time nor text to tackle—caught both the poignancy and the humor of Beckett, wildly applauding.

9. Referring to the issue of clarity versus obscurity, William Seitz emphatically denies the need for an artist to "comfort the viewer" with explanations of a work's meaning: "Oscillations between the self and the world, abstraction and image, geometry and organicism are symbolically, but incompletely resolved only outside the self, on canvas. To the artist the picture must be the conclusion. I do not think of art in general as a situation of comfort" (132).

10. Albee justified his decision not to write a "preface" explaining his play as follows: "I have decided against creating such a guide because I find—after reading the play over—that I share the view of even more people: that the play is quite clear"; but Albee then qualified his statement thus: "I will confess, though, that *Tiny Alice* is less opaque in reading than it would be in any single viewing" (5).

11. Less well-received than Albee's staging of Beckett was that of Michael Myerberg, an early Beckett director-producer. Myerberg lamented his intrusion into a Beckett text in 1956

when "with extreme measures" he attempted to render Beckett's *Waiting for Godot* attractive to American audiences at Miami's Cocoanut Grove Playhouse. He wrote, "I went too far in my effort to give the play a base of popular acceptance," trying to "illuminate some of the thoughts I felt were left in shadow in the London production" (quoted in Lahr, 303). See also columnist Murray Schumach's *New York Times* note that the production of *Godot* "nearly died on the doorstep . . . failed dismally," with "more than half the opening-night audience [failing] to return after the intermission" (42).

14

Director, Playwright, and Cast:
Caryl Churchill's Approach to Text

In the old days of theatre production, stern maxims ruled. Playwrights' and directors' tasks were relatively disengaged. It was assumed that a playright's script would be ready *before* rehearsals. (If scripts were *not* polished and in hand, trouble could brew for director, cast, and crew.) Directors were known to fume at playwrights wanting "in on" rehearsals: "Don't talk to the actors!" But by the latter third of our century, these maxims were about to be buried with other old saws. In the contemporary theatre, full communication among playwright, director, and performers has become the name of the game, and "the workshop"—a communal method of developing and staging a script—may change the rules and the old lines of power.

Under this relaxed and flexible system, authors like England's Caryl Churchill can share with directors the evolution of script from an idea for a play into a full dramatic action and, eventually, co-determine with the actors the script's actual dialogue; what emerges is both a text and a performance (Klaus et al., 1097). Antonin Artaud—who once called out "Death to the Playwright!" and "No More Masterpieces!"—would be heartened (112).

A veteran of workshop theory, England's Caryl Churchill, and her director, Mark Wing-Davey, have recently developed *Mad Forest*, which played to full houses in December 1991 at the Perry Street Theatre Off-Broadway; the play, remounted in 1992 at the Manhattan Theater Club, had premiered in 1990 on the Royal Court Theatre's Main Stage in London. The growing prominence of the workshop style that generated *Mad Forest* bears up director Peter Brook's adage on cyclical rhythms in theatre history: "Truth in the theater is always on the move" (Klaus et al., 925).

Caryl Churchill, playwright. Courtesy of Martha Swope Photography, Inc.

Caryl Churchill herself has been on the move—the "most frequently produced and most consistently admired among women writing for the theatre in this decade" (Randall, ix). The author of over thirty-two plays for radio, television, and stage, her success with the workshop method may stifle perennial rows over playwrights' control and directors' disregard thereof. Churchill has been using the on-location approach to co-creating dramatic text with directors and with a Joint Stock group of actors since the 1970s. At one of her first workshops (in 1976, in a church hall), the playwright appeared "as thrilled as a child at a pantomime" with the ease and openness of the technique (17). She appears to love the interaction, which encourages a playwright to communicate with her director and with those who will perform a script—and to communicate not only during rehearsals, but long before they begin.

    Among the works that Churchill and various directors have co-developed in workshops, three in particular lend themselves well to a study of collaboration:

Light Shining in Buckinghamshire (1976), *Cloud Nine* (1979), and *Mad Forest* (1992). Each is unique in the amount of time the playwright spent in and out of workshop to turn a conception into a finished performance. Each of the three differs from the others, too, in the type of interchange between playwright and director—and between the two and their cast—before and during rehearsals.

LIGHT SHINING IN BUCKINGHAMSHIRE

The evolution of *Light Shining in Buckinghamshire* from start to finish shows a characteristic Churchill pattern. As far back as 1976, its author was bringing raw, fragmented scripts to rehearsals with her early director Max Stafford-Clark. In a recent interview she recalled an example: "With *Light Shining*, I'd come with a very unfinished script, because I'd written a version which didn't work at all. So then I wrote another version in the ten days before rehearsals began, but it wasn't finished" (Hayman, 27).

What would have preceded Churchill's writing of words on paper was a series of conferences with Stafford-Clark on a likely topic for a projected play. In customary workshop style, Churchill and her director would have agreed on what might be the play's specific subject and setting. Churchill writes, "Max Stafford-Clark and I read and talked till we had found a subject in the millennial movement in the [English] civil war" (CHURCHILL, 184). *Light Shining* would dramatize a similar search for freedom made by "historical and fictional persons" moving through the middle of the seventeenth century (Mairowitz, 24). The plot eventually involved twenty-five characters played by six actors—"a highly suggestive mode of acting" often imposed "by financial controls" of the group sponsoring the production (Klaus et al., 1098).

The play's action is part of a citizens' revolt against their leadership during the English civil war, driven by their belief that if they fought against the king, "Christ would come and establish heaven on earth" and would rule a universal community for a thousand years (CHURCHILL, 183). Churchill recalls, "I worked very closely with Max, and though I (ultimately) wrote the text, the play is something we both imagined" (184).

Pivotal to Churchill and her director's creative processes before any dialogue was put on paper, the playwright has said, were the three weeks she and the director spent with the Joint Stock actors after the two had settled on both idea and setting for the play. During these weeks with the actors, "through talk, reading, games, and improvisation, we tried to get closer to the issues and the people" (Klaus et al., 1097). Discussions with the players dealt with treatment of vagrants and squatters in the period, with butchers and cleavers and shops and fairs, to acquaint the cast with the local color of characters to be developed later (Fitzsimmons, 30). Other background came through readings on religious beliefs about the second coming of Christ and on Oliver Cromwell's span as the nation's leader (CHURCHILL, 184). Then, for a full nine weeks after this group session, Churchill worked up a tentative script with rudimentary dialogue.

During the next six weeks, she and her director again interacted with the cast, refining dialogue with their collaboration, finding appropriate and convincing phrases for the characters. Churchill acknowledges that "while the actors did not write the lines, many characters and scenes were based on ideas that came from improvisation at the workshop and during rehearsal" (184). She has given "endless examples of how something said or done by one of the actors is directly connected to something in the text, [and] just as important . . . was the effect on the writing of the way the actors worked" (184).

At the play's premiere, a critic described the language as "spare, uncluttered, colorful when it needs to be, usually low-keyed and neutral," then added, "Whether this is a feature of the play or the company, I could not say, but it is a delight to listen to nevertheless" (Campbell, 20–21). Another critic called the dialogue "sermonizing" and "heavy going" and thought the play long and slow—though admittedly it made for "truthful reportage" (quoted in Fitzsimmons, 30). Some found the play magnificent, the Joint Stock company's collective playing brilliant, the style "palatable, and finally correct and necessary," and ranked it "one of the finest pieces of English playwriting" (Mairowitz, 24). It may be noted that Churchill's lack of a prepared and polished script to hand a director before the onset of rehearsals had not failed the play.

CLOUD NINE

Four years later, Churchill's workshop-developed *Cloud Nine* (1979), set half in Victorian Africa and half in present-day London, again drew mixed critical response, though for different reasons. A successful workshop will serve two interrelated functions: "to establish a good working relationship among members of the company," and "to provide the mass of 'raw material' which [the author] will draw on to write a play" (Wandor, "Free Collective Bargaining," 14). Still, not all workshops will carve in stone the final written text or its staging. Churchill has said, "I no longer know what's the final version [of *Cloud Nine*] except by looking at the text" (CHURCHILL, 250).

Understandable! Countless changes had occurred in *Cloud Nine* from its first publication before the end of its rehearsals by Pluto/Joint Stock (1979); and then, after rehearsals, came more cuts and alterations, these appearing in the 1983 Pluto Plays edition, one that also includes a few changes from the American production; and, finally, other modifications arose from Churchill's polishing the text in 1984 for the Fireside Bookclub and Methuen, Inc., editions (CHURCHILL, 250).

Though the initial process and the interaction of playwright with director and cast were similar to those of *Shining Light*, one observer of *Cloud Nine*'s ongoing workshops thought the author's final product seemed less than true to the embryo that had developed during the group interaction (Sher, 139). By the time Churchill's *Cloud Nine* opened at the Royal Court Theatre (again directed by Stafford-Clark), act 1 may have borne little direct resemblance to its supposed format—nor did it at the later New York staging directed by Tommy Tune in 1981 at

Lucille Lortel's Theatre de Lys (139). For while the playwright had been "inspired and nourished by the workshop" (139), she followed neither the originally suggested setting nor the placement-in-time. In her introduction to the published play, Churchill states, "When I came to write the play, I returned to an idea that had been touched on briefly in the workshop—the parallel between colonial and sexual oppression, which Genet calls 'the colonial or feminine mentality of interiorised repression' " (CHURCHILL, 245).

Churchill had first intended the play's workshop to research a typical Victorian family in the 1950s and to hypothesize its developing ideology over several decades as it approached the 1980s (245–46). In her on-stage action, she had not planned to deal specifically with feminism or sexual preference, nor had she planned to separate by a hundred years the time period of the two acts, as she did later. Yet after interacting in open, sensitivity-raising exercises with Stafford-Clark and the actors, she admits to having taken what one observer called "a bold imaginative leap" to use "a different period and society to highlight themes of sexual prejudice and role-playing" (Sher, 139). Her need to expand her play's emphasis and alter its time periods, she explains, had come with her observation of the actors during their workshop exercises (Fitzsimmons, 47). The starting point for their research was "to talk about ourselves and share our very different attitudes and experiences. We also explored stereotypes and role reversals in games and improvisations, read books and talked to other people" (CHURCHILL, 245). The actors' explorations included listening to presentations by Sheila Rowbotham and other feminists. Also, each actor did "improvisations on sexual status and confidence," which one observer describes thus: "[P]eople choose a card and if it has a high number [they] have to play high sexual confidence in a scene" (Wandor, "Free Collective Bargaining," 14). The exercises drew emotional responses from the actors, and the talk turned at once to attitudes toward women's roles in sex and marriage. Sensitive to their comments as they discussed Victorian conventionality and old-fashioned expectations about these topics, the author saw that "it was as if everyone felt they had been born almost in the Victorian Age" (Fitzsimmons, 47).

Though Churchill had initially conceived the play's first act as a "structured, conventional romantic experience . . . dominated by men . . . brightly colored and speedy" (quoted in Thurman, 56) and the second act as a series of monologues to be delivered by women and gays, the cast's open and emotional discussions of their backgrounds led her, ultimately, to focus on a feminist perspective. As a result, she set act 1 in British Imperial Africa in the 1870s and linked "the macro-political dynamic (the public) with the micro-political (the personal)"; she situated act 2 in a London park in 1979, where act 1 "sexual liaisons continue to abound, but with less repression and guilt" (Fitzsimmons, 41). One reviewer interpreted the two acts as invitations to the audience "to examine their own moral and sexual codes" (Solomon, 118).

From the workshop's revelations on sexual politics, Churchill and Stafford-Clark tried to cast roles to emphasize strongly "the artificiality and conventionality of the characters' sex roles": they mismatched the actors' genders and races with those appropriate to the various roles they were playing (Asahina, 565). Clive, a colonial administrator and the head of his family, is played by a woman; unknowingly he forces a homosexual friend to marry a governess who, the audience suspects, is lesbian. Clive's wife is played by a man, their son by a woman, their daughter by a doll, and their black servant Joshua, by a white. Some critics said the playwright and director had "spoiled the act," others that she had "produced a fine piece" with "just the right balance of rowdiness and sensitivity" to draw a "caricature of the world we grew up in" (Fitzsimmons, 44–45). What the two, collaborating, added to the act might be "all the current disparaging ideas about the colonial era," but viewers realized that "we are these people's heirs, their repressions ours"; and though some frowned at "uproariously coarse jokes" that they felt "were at the expense of Victorian pieties," others, with "uneasy giggles," tried to view the work as "a study in sexual evolution . . . another ludicrous chapter in the history of the White Man's Burden" (42).

But overall, as Churchill must have hoped, reviewers applauded, viewing the play as a demonstration of the profound changes they had been forced to make in their own lives as a result of the sexual evolution: "We get the message—we get it, in fact, within seconds of the curtain rising" (Fitzsimmons, 42). In an interview with John Simon entitled "Sex, Politics, and Other Play Things," Churchill said that the play's subject matter supported Genet's idea that "colonial oppression and sexual oppression are similar" (quoted in Simon, 130). The relationship had been apparent to Churchill and Stafford-Clark as they watched the actors' emotional reactions to Victorian ideology in the initial workshop. In 1984 Churchill wrote, "Though the play's situations and characters were not developed in the workshop, [*Cloud Nine*'s text] draws deeply on this material, and I wouldn't have written the same play without it" (CHURCHILL, 245).

MAD FOREST

A much longer and far more complex interaction brought Churchill and Wing-Davey's 1991's *Mad Forest* onto the stages of London, Bucharest, and New York. The play shows two Romanian families, one working class, one professional, before, during, and after a revolution. Churchill dramatizes their reactions to their country's suffering. In the course of the play's development in 1990, the author and director took an exploratory trip to Romania "in order to experience the effects of revolution and its aftermath" (Botto, 44).

The idea for the play originated with its principals' wish to familiarize their audiences with the plight of people in a twentieth-century nation devastated by a revolution. Since Romania was at the time experiencing the aftermath of revolution, the deprivation of the populace, and events like the assassinations of the Ceausescus, Romania seemed to the author and her director a place to begin. They sought firsthand reactions of men and women to breadlines, fear and turmoil, wanting to know how it felt to function "under a sort of incipient paranoia" (Botto, 43). These emotions they and the actors would incorporate into the play's text.

Mad Forest by Caryl Churchill, Manhattan Theatre Club, 1993. Courtesy of Martha Swope Photography, Inc.

Rather than take the Joint Stock actors to Romania immediately, Churchill and Wing-Davey opted to go alone, to approach the country sentiently to insure a compassionate dramatization of its sorrow. For a week in March 1990, the two did so, with funds contributed by the British Consul. They observed the populace and tried to master a few native phrases. After long days in the streets of the capital studying what they hoped were "typical Romanians—doctors, translators, bulldozer drivers, soldiers, house painters"—they had specific feelings and matter to offer the actors (Botto, 43).

Returning to London, they selected ten of their group to help them develop the play. Churchill's printed casts of characters often list dozens of names; but when her actors double roles, each production can use less than a dozen (Klaus et al., 1098). *Mad Forest* has sixty roles played by ten actors. Having selected ten, the playwright and director backtracked to Romania a month later. By April, all were "engaging in exercises that Wing-Davey had devised at the London Central School of Speech and Drama"; the director took his actors around Bucharest, "observing the long queues for buying meat, somehow communicating with the people who had gone through the revolution"—in the hope that when the actors returned to London, they could convincingly render the roles of ravaged survivors of a revolution (Botto, 43). Churchill's dramas are "rigorously contextualized in particular historical moments"; she has been characterized as a writer who "does dangerous history" (Randall, 146). Wing-Davey used the group's experience in the physical aftermath of revolution to help his actors feel like visitors to a foreign nation. To that end, he wanted each phrase that the actors would subsequently read on stage to seem "like a phrase from a tourist guide" (Botto, 43). When they returned to London and the play was mounted, the actors could speak brief Romanian sentences, Wing-Davey reports, "in an accent that makes the audience aware that Westerners are speaking them" (43). The workshop had made the play's characters believable; it had accomplished a Churchill goal: "to situate and set in motion historical events and their effects" (Randall, 169).

An unexpected benefit of the on-location workshop arose when the artistic head of the Romanian National Theatre, familiar with the London run, asked Churchill to return to Bucharest with the play. The playwright must have wondered whether her ability to "historicize, to present history as a complex discursive formation" would upset postrevolutionary Romanians in their own country (Randall, 169). Any playwright might fear that the actors' portrayals would estrange, put off, the actual victims of revolution being rendered on their own stage. And perhaps the Romanians would suspect the actors of patronizing them. "After all," Wing-Davey said, "this was the first play written about the revolution" (Botto, 44). But Churchill, director, and cast accepted the opportunity and took themselves and their fifty or more costumes back to Romania, where they performed the play with simultaneous translations (44). The reaction was immediate. At one point, the actors read words of poetry in Romanian: "[The] audience shed tears. . . . It was a very emotional moment. Just to hear these foreigners speak their language was some sort of identification" (44).

Ultimately, Churchill and Wing-Davey were asked to produce the play in New York. To do so, they determined to use more than the ten or so actors who had rendered the play's many roles in Romania. With more actors, Churchill could play with a technique for which she has become known: "frantic pacing and simultaneous lines," overlapping dialogue that can show "frenzy and jumble in personal transactions" (Randall, 7). Since the sponsors of the production had specified that the cast be comprised of Americans who, without the on-location experience, would know no Romanian phrases and would not identify with Romanian culture, they would lack what a workshop needs: "a communal exploration of a topic . . . a link between personal, inner experience and the larger world of public events" (Cousin, 15). Such an experience for the American actors would be vital.

Hence, in New York City, the director arranged for a workshop where his actors could mingle in churches, work places, and restaurants with people in the Romanian community in Queens. Moving even more familiarly among the area's native speakers than they could in Bucharest, they found it stimulating to master the feel of the first- and second-generation Romanians on the streets of Queens (Botto, 45). Through this exercise, the actors tried to identify with a people who had survived a revolution; they hoped to gain at least a rudimentary human bonding to their counterparts.

After workshops and rehearsals, when the new production of *Mad Forest* premiered Off-Broadway in December 1991 by critical and popular demand, it was a sell-out, leaving many theatre lovers deprived of an opportunity to enjoy and comment on it. Now, with its remounting at popular request by the Manhattan Theatre Club, the reception for this command performance will be fascinating to assess. And having triumphed in London, Bucharest, and New York's first stagings, what can come but high acclaim for its playwright, director, and performers? For, as with *Light Shining in Buckinghamshire* and *Cloud Nine*, from inception to completion, Churchill's workshop goals seem realized: to let actors experience the subject while it develops; to let the drama unfold on the stage with truth to life; and to take advantage of the creativity of all three artistic sectors of play production: author, director, and performers.

Churchill's work with directors and casts is a model for creativity in theatre for contemporary writers who find it appropriate that a play's production style should be determined "not only by a playwright's script, but also by a director's creative influence upon the script" (Klaus et al., 923). In matters of style, setting, action, and dialogue, England's Peter Brook encourages directors "to make individual choices" from many "possible understandings" of an author's intentions (Berry, 114). Indeed, theatre anthologists call Brook "the most striking example of the creative director in contemporary theater," one whose stagings of Shakespeare have inspired phrases like "Brook's *King Lear*" and "Brook's *A Midsummer Night's Dream*" rather than "Shakespeare's" (Klaus et al., 924). On the other hand, a Churchill and Mark-Davey staging might be spoken of in passing as "that Churchill/Mark-Davey *Mad Forest*."

   Other dramatists abroad have, like Churchill, leaned toward workshops to draft scripts with actors and directors. Noteworthy are productions in Paris by Ariane Mnouchkine, "whose company of actors and musicians, like that of Peter Brook, has worked with established writers to create the script for productions" (Klaus, 925). In Great Britain, "a long tradition of repertory companies has led to commissioning plays or sometimes creating elaborate adaptations [such as] Dickens's *Nicholas Nickleby*, which grew out of a collaboration between directors Trevor Nunn and John Caird, playwright David Edgar, and forty-some actors of the Royal Shakespeare Company" (925).

   Moreover, theatre's new acting styles (improvisation, confrontation, asides) and the less-realistic thrust of many works may soon demand even more communication among author, director, and cast. Whatever the moving force, theatre has never been static; and our traditional author/director hierarchy seems up for modification, maybe overripe and due for change. Perhaps the preproduction techniques by which Caryl Churchill has been developing text may soon prevail in the theatre world. Then Artaud *would* rise up and cheer!

PART FOUR

Theatre Aesthetics and the Law

Contractual Provisions of the Dramatists' Guild, Inc.

Playwrights and directors think it appropriate that their functions in production should be addressed by copyright and contract. But after a contract is negotiated, periodic crises in playwright/director collaboration may hint at inadequacy or bias in the legal document agreed to by the principals (see Figure 1). Perhaps the law cannot easily extend a playwright's control beyond initial production rights and into performance aesthetics—matters of tone, style, focus, and costuming. Yet here the protection of a playwright's intent seems sensible.

Theatre by its very nature is a collaborative medium. Directors may protest that our present documents already show a cultural bias toward playwrights as creators, ignoring those directors who want to weigh a text in their own soul and thus become a determinant in artistic creation.[1] Because of the accumulated knowledge and experience from which all talented directors work, their spontaneous productions will be applications of this knowledge and experience; though the script they produce may be an improvisation on an author's actual text, it would be "improvised from resources and disciplines that have become second nature" to the interpreter (Canaday, 134).[2]

What we must determine is how to approve this "improvisation" of a text but not its "distortion." For in the event of less dedicated or talented directors, can legal phrasing itself touch "corruption of intention . . . disrespect for text . . . directorial vulgarity . . . salacious shortchanging of production . . . lax and insensitive turns by leading performers"—any of which undermine a venture and misrepresent an author's script (Albee, viii)? Or would further attempts at regulation (by inserting

Figure 1
Comprehensive Writer's Contract

Membership Privileges:

• Use of the Approved Production Contract:

Members use the Guild's Approved Production Contract—the most comprehensive writer's contract in the world today—for productions of their plays and musicals. Under it:

—No additions, omissions, or alterations may be made in your script without your consent.

—You and your producer have approval of cast and director and confer on many other elements of the production.

—If your producer does not pay your royalties, the rights granted to him cease immediately.

—Any dispute between you and your producer is subject to arbitration. Often, when necessary, a hearing may be convened within 72 hours.

—You own the copyright and all other rights to the play.

—You have the right to formulate contracts for all other performances and uses of the play.

• *Addendum*: Legal advice; members' hotline; royalty collection.

Source: The Dramatists' Guild Brochure, 1993.

more explicit legal phrasing into contracts) unwisely limit *all* directors' creativity, relegating them to the functions of stage managers?

On such grounds, the League of New York Theaters and Producers and the Dramatists' Guild periodically renegotiate the standard contract instituted in 1926 (Kanin et al., 27–28). Figure 1 shows the current contract between playwrights and producers. Figure 2 is a typical contract between playwrights and publishers.

The Dramatists' Guild's current council members and officers are among our decade's most distinguished writers; the legal advisors to the council and the editor of its quarterly journal are leading figures in their fields:

Officers: Peter Stone, president; Terrence McNally, vice-president; Arthur Kopit, secretary; Richard Lewine, acting treasurer; Andrew Farber, executive director.

Council: Lee Adams, Edward Albee, Jon Robin Baitz, Gretchen Cryer, Christopher Durang, Jules Feiffer, Maria Irene Fornes, Herb Gardner, James Goldman, Adolph Green, John Guare, Sheldon Harnick, Tina Howe, David Henry Hwang, John Kander, Arthur Kopit, Jerome Lawrence, Ira Levin, Craig Lucas, Terrence McNally, Marsha Norman, Mary Rodgers, Joseph Stein, Peter Stone, Julie Styne, Alfred Uhry, Wendy Wasserstein, Michael Weller, Lanford Wilson, and George C. Wolfe.

Ex Officio: Robert Anderson, Frank D. Gilroy, Sidney Kingsley, and Stephen Sondheim.

Andrew Farber, executive director, Dramatists' Guild, Inc. Courtesy of
Susan Johann Photography.

Emeritus: Betty Comden, Ruth Goetz, Garson Kanin, Arthur Laurentis, and Richard
Lewine.

Advisors to the Council: Cahill Gordon & Reindel, counsel; Ben Pesner, quarterly editor;
the Professional Association of Playwrights, Composers & Lyricists; a corporate member
of the Authors League of America, Inc.

Figure 2
Standard Contract Between Playwright and Publisher

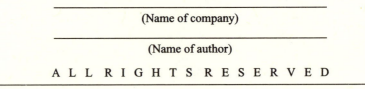

*** N O T I C E ***

The amateur and stock acting rights to this work are controlled exclusively by the
_____Publishing Company without whose permission
in writing no performance of it may be given. Royalty fees are given in our current cata-
logue and are subject to change without notice. Royalty must be paid every time a play is
performed whether it is presented for charity or for profit and whether or not admission is
charged. *A play is performed anytime it is acted before an audience.* All inquiries concerning amateur and stock rights should be addressed to:

COPYRIGHT LAW GIVES THE AUTHOR OR HIS AGENT THE EXCLUSIVE
RIGHT TO MAKE COPIES:

This law provides authors with a fair return for their creative efforts. Authors earn their
living from the royalties they receive from performance of their work and from book sales.
Conscientious observance of copyright law is not only ethical; it encourages authors to continue their creative work.

(N A M E   O F   P L A Y)

is fully protected by copyright. No alterations, deletions or substitutions may be made in the
work without the prior written consent of the publisher. No part of this work may be repro-
duced or transmitted in any form or by any means, electronic or mechanical, including pho-
tocopy, recording, videotype, film or any information storage and retrieval system, without
permission in writing from the publisher. It may not be performed either by professionals or
amateurs without payment of royalty. All rights, including but not limited to the professional, motion picture, radio, television, videotype, foreign language, tabloid, recitation,
lecturing, publication, and reading are reserved. On all programs this notice should appear:
Produced by special arrangement with:

_____
(Name of company)

_____
(Name of author)

A L L   R I G H T S   R E S E R V E D

Source: U.S. Copyright Act of 1976, Article I, Section 8.

CORRESPONDENCE WITH THE DRAMATISTS' GUILD, INC.

Dana S. Singer, former Acting Executive Director of the Dramatists' Guild,
Inc., and editor Jeane Luere discussed the provisions of the Guild's contract.
The following comments address the degree of protection afforded playwrights, composers, and lyricists against unlicensed productions (October 23,
1992).

Luere: I missed the pleasure of the annual Inge Festival and Theatre Symposium this year, and did not have the chance to ask these specific questions on legal protection for playwrights.

To begin, directors reputedly have leeway to alter a classic that lies in the public domain by shortening the text or changing its setting. Theorists like W. K. Wimsatt Jr. call these privileges "Battering the Object: The Ontological Approach" (61). Alvin Kernan objects to them as having "disintegrated and redistributed the parts of such great literary monuments as *The Iliad*, *King Lear*, *The Brothers Karamazov* that had stood at the center of humanistic literature making permanent statements about absolute truths" (76). With regard to Shakespeare, clearly authentic texts do not exist. Then where is the line in staging the work of *living* playwrights? And is the ethic of altering their plays dependent solely on the legal phrasing of the contract?

Singer:The line drawn in altering the work of a living playwright whose work is not in the public domain, using the two methods you raise of shortening the script or changing its setting, by way of example, is a clear one—one has to first obtain the playwright's permission.

The "ethic" of altering a play is not dependent solely on the legal phrasing in the contract. The playwright's ownership rights in the work are grounded in the federal copyright laws; and on top of those laws rests the customary phrase found in all production contracts between playwrights and producers: "no changes, alterations and/or omissions shall be made in the play without the prior written consent of the author." So the playwright could be said to have double protection.

I always recommend that the playwright be protected in both ways since the language in the contract with the producer only reinforces the issue and makes the limitations on the producer's rights very clear.

Luere: Your comprehensive writer's contract offers "legal advice, a members' hotline, and royalty collection." How frequently do unauthorized (noncontracted) productions of plays occur? Do most groups follow the law and get permission from dramatists?

Singer: As to actual cases, in my experience most of the producers do properly obtain permission. There are of course those situations where this does not occur, but they appear to be the exception, not the rule. In addition, the Guild is not made aware of every such situation, so it is impossible to make any absolute statements in this area.

Luere: The standard contract in your *Dramatists' Guild Brochure* reads: "Any dispute between you and your producer is subject to arbitration. Often, when necessary, a hearing may be convened within 72 hours."

Are those who do not follow the procedure to obtain legal rights from the playwright inclined to relent readily if your group approaches them?

Singer: With respect to those producers who do not obtain permission, they appear to acquiesce when confronted with their "misdeed"—whether [they are confronted] by the author, the author's representative (agent or lawyer), or the Dramatists' Guild. Please keep in mind, however, that the author might not discover the situation until after the production has been presented.

Luere: Would the more usual crisis be that the producer had no right of production at all, or that the producer's staging violated the author's aesthetic intention for his play? I am thinking of Arthur Miller's 1983–85 problems with the Wooster Group's use of his 1953 classic, *The Crucible*, and, too, of Edward Albee's suits in the 1980s over miscasting of his 1962 masterwork, *Who's Afraid of Virginia Woolf?*

Singer: It is impossible to quantify the problems distinguishing between a producer not obtaining permission at all, and the director (or whomever) interpreting a work contrary to the vision of the author. I'm afraid I have no statistics as to the frequency of either of these problems, but, again, in my experience they appear to [be] rare occurrences.

NOTES

1. From comments on "independence from a source" in Vasili Kandinsky's *Concerning the Spiritual in Art*, 47, 50, 67.

2. A paragraph on page 134 of John Canaday's *What Is Art?* upholds independence in modifying/interpreting a source by reason of the accumulated knowledge and experience from which talented renderers or modifiers work.

Collaboration and American Law

The Dramatists' Guild's efficacy in protecting playwrights from unlicensed productions is evident. But beyond rights of production lie less tangible aesthetic rights that may need to be addressed with each play: the naturalistic (representational) or confrontational (presentational) style of its delivery, the nature of its stage business, its physical mounting, and other concerns encompassed by the relatively new term "performance theory." About these concerns, many playwrights and directors communicate explicitly and settle their individual differences easily; others do not. For the aesthetic rights, the Guild's standard contract may need much more explicit stipulations. Still, many analysts feel that the eminence of the Guild, the very presence of its protection against totally unlicensed stagings, can permeate and shore up those broader aesthetic areas of performance not tightly covered by copyright or contract phrasing itself.

In one of our most prestigious theatre publications, *The Journal of Dramatic Theory and Criticism*, a recent article on performance theory and American law suggests that the theatre world may need not more laws but more awareness of the conjoint nature of theatre production. The author, Robert Hapgood, has cited many of the same sources that appear in this volume and has used them to distinctly different ends. Yet his discussions and those in our volume are mutually enhancing. His article is reprinted here to draw the first three sections of this volume into a composite picture of the playwright/director issue.

The Rights of Playwrights:
Performance Theory and American Law by Robert Hapgood

How much authority should playwrights have over the ways in which their plays are performed? In recent years Edward Albee has several times intervened to close all-male productions of *Who's Afraid of Virginia Woolf?* in which the play's heterosexual couples were portrayed as homosexual. Legally, there is no doubt about his authority to do so. "All of the copies of my plays," Albee has explained, "have a number of clauses which say they must be performed without any changes or deletions or additions and must be performed by actors of the sex as written" ("Albee," C5). But aesthetically is it justifiable for Albee to exercise his legal rights over the presentation of his play? Isn't he thereby infringing on the interpretive freedoms of his performers and violating the collaborative spirit upon which dramatic performance depends? Albee concedes that there is a place for "directorial creativity" while maintaining that "it doesn't give permission to distort." Yet what precisely is the fine line between creativity and distortion and who is to draw it? Was Tennessee Williams justified in intervening against a 1974 Berlin production of *A Streetcar Named Desire* in which, among other alterations, Stanley Kowalski was to be played as a black? (Shaland, 19). In these instances both playwrights seem clearly in the right: one of Albee's couples (who married because of a hysterical pregnancy), must at first believe the other couple to be parents; Williams' treatment of Kowalski involves issues of class rather than race. In general this essay will argue that interpretive controls granted the playwright under American contractual and copyright law—while subject to improvement—are basically desirable and that contemporary playwrights have by and large exercised their legal rights wisely in this respect. Together, I believe, the legal framework and the way playwrights have operated within it comprise a sound working aesthetic for the playwright's role in putting on a play, one that can provide a timely corrective to current tendencies in performance theory that unduly favor performers yet without reverting to the older idea that they are no more than subservient "interpreters" of the playwright's words.

The place of the playwright in the performance process has been largely neglected by such exponents of performance theory as Schechner (who coined the term), Chaikin, and Michael Goldman. It is true that for centuries the contributions of performers have been virtually disregarded by dramatic theorists, who have concentrated on dramatists and dramas. The recent concern with the importance of performance thus fills a genuine gap. Yet since performance theory has been written mostly by performers, it in turn has tended to disregard or minimize the playwright's involvement. Robert Brustein, for example, has held that close adherence to a playwright's text "not only robs collaborative artists of their respective freedoms, but threatens to turn the theater into waxworks" (Garbus, 2). Indeed, following Artaud's declaration of independence from the "tyranny" of playwrights, theorists of his persuasion have often aggressively resisted "author centered" views. The most extreme challenge to "logocentrism" in the theatre has been set forth recently in these pages by Stratos E. Constantinidis. Following Derrida he presents the case for deconstructing all "the structures of domination/subordination which regulate western theatrical production," whether the lines of authority proceed from the dramatist, the director, the designer, the actors, or God. Yet such theorizing is far removed from common practice. Since playwrights and their plays continue to be integral to most dramatic productions, a timely next step for performance theory is to take playwrights fully into account, not as they may figure in hypothetical situations but as they have participated in preparing actual productions.[1]

Unfortunately, individual contemporary playwrights have not addressed these matters in an extended and general way, although many have commented briefly to newspaper reporters and in interviews and symposiums. As it happens, these comments and the attitudes and practices they reflect are remarkably consistent: as diverse as the playwrights are, they share many common views on the subject. One of the purposes of this article is to piece together these scattered comments into a composite picture of the way playwrights today are seeing their contributions to the production of their own plays.

From the legal point of view, too, relatively little attention has been paid to these questions. This is the more surprising because the parallels between literary and legal interpretation have received unprecedented comment in the past decade, prompting the growing "literature and the law" movement in law schools. It must be admitted with Richard Posner that intriguing as such parallels may be, they can often prove facile, as when comparing the interpretation of a Shakespearian sonnet with that of the United States Constitution (Fried, 751). Such is not the case, however, where dramatic production is concerned. Since a playwright is legally entitled to a performance that he or she judges to be satisfactorily in accord with its script, interpretive disputes could potentially end up in court. There is thus special point in pursuing points of overlap between theatre aesthetics and the law. Yet to date only a few articles have done so.[2]

When a new play is being performed under "first-class" (Broadway) auspices, authorial rights are well protected by the standard Dramatists' League "Approved Production Contract for Plays." Its provisions have set the pattern for first productions in the United States whatever the venue. Explicitly recognizing that "the Play is the artistic creation of Author," it assures the right of the playwright to attend rehearsals; it provides that the producer and the playwright must agree on the director, designers, and casting; and it guarantees that no changes in the script may be made by either without the other's approval. When the playwright resists a proposed change, the producer may invoke intermediaries provided by the League to try to resolve the dispute; but the playwright can still say "no" decisively.

It might be objected that in certain respects the playwright's interpretive rights are too well protected in the standard contract, to the detriment of the director, designers, and actors (whom I will henceforth refer to collectively as "performers"). In particular the standard contract provides that "any change of any kind whatso-

ever in the manuscript, title, stage business or performance of the play made by
Producer or any third party and which is acceptable to Author shall be the property
of Author." Unless there is written agreement to the contrary, the contributions of
the performers are understood to be "for hire" and compensated by their salaries.
From a financial point of view, this arrangement may be fair enough where the immediate production is concerned (since the performers benefit from its success),
but it leaves uncompensated their contributions to subsequent productions. And
where aesthetic values are concerned, the law here certainly does less than justice
to the author's associates. Tennessee Williams is not alone among playwrights in
paying tribute to the gifts of an actor like Laurette Taylor and a director like [Elia]
Kazan, finding them decisive in the initial success of his plays (Williams, 93).

In general, though, the standard contract seems to me justified in the support it
gives the playwright. To begin with, it should be remembered that this support is
by no means unqualified: the producer has equal rights with the author. Furthermore, the author has special vulnerabilities that deserve protection. Faithful performance is of the first importance for a playwright because, apart from
closet-dramas, plays are not fully themselves except when they are performed. A
play may be published, it is true; but its publication does not provide the same direct access to the playwright's work as does the publication of a work by a poet or
novelist. However the latter may be misrepresented by a reviewer or interpreting
critic, readers can simply read the original and judge for themselves. A play is cru-
cially different. It is one thing to read a play privately, quite another to see and hear
it acted publicly. Theatrical mediation is of the essence.

In addition, the playwright's function is of particular concern because he or she
is the "silent partner" in the encounter that produces a theatre event. At a performance it is the players and playgoers for whom the encounter is face-to-face, and
the contribution of the playwright to the event may very well be slighted. A playwright's work is especially vulnerable at its first major production. Most members
of the audience, including many reviewers, cannot distinguish between the author's
contributions and those of the director, actors, and designers. And indeed such distinctions are sometimes hard to make, since the performers bring their special cre-
ativities to the realization of the playwright's conceptions to such a degree that
"interpretation" is sometimes not strong enough a word to indicate their contributions. At times, as just mentioned, these contributions may enhance the play beyond its intrinsic merits; at other times, however, they may detract. Since initial
failure may well foreclose possibilities for future productions and publication,
there seems to be general agreement that the author should have every opportunity
to insure that the first production fulfill his or her intentions.

There is also a pragmatic argument in favor of the standard contract: it has functioned remarkably well, although its institution in 1926 was hard-won and its provisions still must at times be defended.[3] A key factor in its success has been the
cooperative spirit that most recent playwrights have brought to the performance
process. Some playwrights, it is true, have wished for the kind of total control over
the performed play that a poet exercises over a poem. In the throes of trying-out

Two for the Seesaw, for example, William Gibson looked back longingly to the time when, as a young poet, he would sacrifice publication rather than allow an editor to change a word. His *Seesaw Log* remains the fullest account of the backstage tensions between the playwright, the producer, the director, and the actors as they interacted within the framework of the standard contract.[4] It rewards some special attention.

With admirable candor, Gibson details in the *Log* the painful process by which *Two for the Seesaw*, a two-character play, was shaped into a Broadway hit. The *Log's* chief antagonists are Gibson and Henry Fonda. Fonda felt that his role was "underwritten"; Gibson felt that Fonda was miscast. There was truth on both sides. Contractually, Gibson could have stood his ground, probably lost his star, and very likely had a flop. Instead he chose, reluctantly, to be his own "play doctor," adapting Fonda's part (though never to his complete satisfaction) and adjusting the whole script to the no less implacable demands of try-out audiences, as tactfully diagnosed by the director and producer. The up-shot, he was obliged to admit, was an improved play; yet one that he no longer felt to be his own. In the end, however, even Gibson was converted to a more receptive attitude. The version of the play he chose to publish with the *Log* included many of the changes from the original that he had earlier felt to be compromises forced on him by others.

Other playwrights have entered more readily into the teamwork of theatre. Seeing theatre as "an art which reposes upon the work of many collaborators," Thorton Wilder observes: "The dramatist through working in the theatre gradually learns not merely to take account of the presence of the collaborators, but to derive advantage from them" (117). Tennessee Williams has traced this learning process in his own career. Like many inexperienced playwrights, he was at first excessively deferential toward famous performers; after his early successes he then went through a period of arrogant self-assertion; eventually he achieved a more mature attitude: while never forgetting that "Nobody knows a play better than the man who wrote it" (97), he learned to participate in a working partnership with the performers. This last is an attitude that John Guare shares. He welcomes the rehearsal of one of his plays: "everything should go through the director, but I don't want to hand my play over to a director and say, 'Do what you want, this is a libretto for your intentions.' I work with the director and the lighting designer, the set designer, the costume designer, to focus in so that everybody's telling the same story. That to me is what the theatrical experience is—the audience watching a group of people all trying to produce the same effect. It's truly democratic" (Savran, *In Their Own Words*, 88). All the same, the "story" to be told is clearly Guare's.

Gibson makes a useful distinction between the creativity of playwrights and that of performers. That of a playwright is "primary": "where nothing was, he ordains a world" (113); that of performers is "secondary." The two are mutually dependent, but it is the solitary act of the playwright that is originating, that necessarily comes first. At the end of his career Tennessee Williams felt keenly the difficulty of keeping these priorities in order. While welcoming advice, he maintained: "I have the longest acquaintance with the play and I must not place anyone else's counsel regarding the script above my own." When at rehearsals he felt himself "an outsider to my own play" because "everyone else seems to be working but me," he reminded himself:

> For two or three years I was the solitary worker: all those working mornings—the bad ones when I wondered if a good working day would ever come again. With all these pressures upon me, I must try to remember that bittersweet time when my life was the play and the play was my life. (Smith, 116)

Within the provisions of the standard contract, playwrights have found various ways of exercising the special authority that comes with primary creativity. As confirmed by Savran's interviews in *In Their Own Words*, American playwrights today have felt free to adapt their involvement in a production to their own predilections and those of their producers. At one extreme, Maria Irene Fornes insists on directing her own plays; at the other, Marsha Norman thinks "it would be ideal to have the first production done by people you really trusted but who were far away. You'd simply get on a plane and go see it" (187). In the real world, however, she reluctantly goes to rehearsals "out of self protection." Wallace Shawn agrees that an author should attend rehearsals to avoid being "totally shocked at what has been made of his play" since otherwise the audience members "will go to their grave believing that that was the way the author intended it" (213). But for the most part he advises authors to intervene only when "the director is doing something that violates your most profound beliefs about the play." David Mamet's involvement has varied from play to play. He worked closely with the production of *American Buffalo* whereas with *Edmond* he only "went to the first rehearsal and said hello to the cast and showed up at the opening" (138). Exercising their contractual prerogative, many of the playwrights have repeatedly chosen favorite directors, as Michael Weller did with Alan Schneider and Lanford Wilson has done with Marshall Mason, August Wilson with Lloyd Richards, Tina Howe with Carole Rathman, David Mamet with Gregory Mosher. Most rewrite readily during rehearsals; Shawn is not so inclined, however, explaining that his lines typically have not just one purpose but five and are so interwoven that any attempt to provide single-purpose lines on demand seems "so crude and bad and superficial it stands out." The contract has thus provided a firm yet flexible structure within which all concerned have usually been able to find a comfortable fit and get on with their work.

Problems, of course, do arise. David Rabe is frank to admit that his "intentions" in *Hurlyburly* were not at first clear to himself; it was only in the process of rehearsal that he realized that he and the director, Mike Nichols, were working at cross purposes: "the end result was something that was neither his nor mine and thus, I think, it didn't make a lot of sense at certain points" (200). With the first New York production of Sam Shepard's *True West*, produced by Joe Papp at the Public Theater, the difficulties occurred because true agreement was not reached between the producer and the playwright concerning the director and casting. Reservations were harbored on both sides that led to disagreements so acute that the resulting production was publicly disavowed both by its director and Shepard (Ferretti). In neither of these instances, however, was the problem with the prevailing system but with individual failures to clarify and resolve differences.

In general, thus, the Dramatists' Guild contract supplies a sound framework for striking a working balance among priorities. By requiring agreement on essentials between Producer and Author, it recognizes the collaborative nature of the dramatic enterprise while insuring that the playwright may play a major and integral role in the performance process, decisive yet not all-dominating.

After the first, major production of a play, what should be the playwright's role? For revivals, the playwright is usually not physically present during rehearsals and try-outs or previews. As years pass, the play's relevance may need updating. What degree of control should the playwright exercise in these circumstances? Legally, the matter is largely one of copyright (Nimmer). Article I, Section 8 of the United States Constitution vests Congress with the power: "to promote the progress of science and useful arts by securing for limited times, to authors and inventors, the exclusive right to their respective writings and discoveries." The right of "public performance in dramatic compositions" has specifically been so regulated since 1856. Current law, under the Copyright Act of 1976, guarantees playwrights absolute control over whether, where, or when their works are performed. Under this Act, the period of protection is the author's lifetime plus fifty years.

In the United States, these rights are financial. Many other countries, especially France and other Continental nations, also give distinct protection to various categories of "moral rights" to personal expression. Of these, the most pertinent is the "right of integrity," by which authors are protected from distortions of their works that would harm their "fame and reputation" (Stewart, 59–61). Although the United States does not have an equivalent as such, playwrights have been able to resist such distortions through stipulations in granting permission for performance like those Edward Albee has made for *Who's Afraid of Virginia Woolf?* When objectionable plans are known in advance, a playwright (or heir or agent) may simply deny permission to perform, as when Samuel Beckett refused to allow an all-woman production of *Waiting for Godot*, on the grounds that such casting "made it something other than what he had written" (Bair, 632). Once permission is granted, if the terms for permission have been violated, the playwright may take legal action against this infringement of copyright. This right has also been bolstered by the Lanham Act, which is designed to protect consumers from deception as to the source or origin of goods or services.[5]

In practice, the general rule for revivals has been for the play's dialogue to be carefully respected but for much more latitude to be allowed with staging and sets. In the words of Mel Gussow, A *New York Times* theatre-critic, the script's stage directions "are usually treated as suggestions rather than as commands from the author."[6] Although many take this common practice to be definitive, there is reason to question whether this should necessarily be so.

This issue was at the heart of the dispute concerning the 1984 production of Beckett's *Endgame* at Harvard by the American Repertory Theatre (ART), directed by JoAnne Akalaitis. Much discussed in newspapers at the time, the dispute very nearly came to trial. As reported by Martin Garbus, Beckett's lawyer, ART had duly obtained permission to perform the play, on the express condition that "no changes shall be made in the manuscript or the book of the play for the purpose of your production"; the license agreement further stated that "failure to meet any of the conditions will result in the immediate and automatic withdrawal of this release" (Garbus, 2). Incited by reports from his American agent and publisher Barney Rosset that these conditions had not been met, Beckett (who never saw the production) decided to take legal action against it. The ART, in turn, was prepared to go to court. An out of court settlement was reached only after around-the-clock negotiations.[7]

The main point of contention was the ART stage-design by Douglas Stein. Beckett's opening stage-directions are stark:

Bare interior. Grey light. Left and right back, high up, two small windows, curtains drawn. Front right, a door. Hanging near door, its face to wall, a picture. Front left, touching each other, covered with an old sheet, two ashbins. Center, in an armchair on castors, covered with an old sheet, Hamm. Motionless by the door, his eyes fixed on Hamm, Clov. Very red face. Brief tableau.

Stein's striking set was elaborate. Kalb describes it as:

a burned-out subway tunnel with implied windows high, but no picture. . . . Broken steel girders outline the top of the back wall, which is about twenty feet high and made of metal plates. Thus, each time Clov needs to look out of a window, he must climb all the way up this wall on two tall structural ladders. To the left and right are partial life-size subway cars, situated diagonally, no track in sight, as if strewn there by a tremendous explosion. Their windows have no glass and are charred at the top edges, indicating a fire. The electric lights on the cars are unaccountably illuminated, as are a line of theater striplights offhandedly lying in a rubbish pile in front of Nagg and Nell's ashbins. Centered in the floor of black mud is a large puddle that reflects the various stage lights, and beside the puddle is a charred human body. (88–89)

Part of the compromise, out-of-court settlement allowed Beckett to include the following statement in the playbill:

Any production of *Endgame* which ignores my stage directions is completely unacceptable to me. My play requires an empty room and two small windows. The American Repertory Theater production which dismisses my directions is a complete parody of the play as conceived by me. Anybody who cares for the work couldn't fail to be disgusted by this.

In the playbill also was a statement by Robert Brustein, ART's artistic director, in which he maintained that "like all works of theatre, productions of *Endgame* depend upon the collective contributions of directors, actors, designers to realize them effectively, and normal rights of interpretation are essential in order to free the full energy and meaning of the play." And so the issue was explicitly joined: the subway set, which the ART lawyer James Sharaf later insisted "fell within a designer's legitimate right to interpret from the script" (Freedman, "Playwrights Debate") was found by the script's author to be "completely unacceptable." Whose rights should prevail? Legally, no resolution was reached, although both sides claimed some satisfaction; Brustein felt that "the solution is perfectly in keeping with our feeling that people have the right to express themselves freely and creatively"; Garbus felt that the "settlement would dissuade other theaters from veering from Mr. Beckett's text and stage directions for *Endgame*" (Freedman, "*Endgame*").

Aesthetically, the dispute calls in question the extent to which liberties should be taken with authorial stage directions, some of which may be as integral to the author's intention as the spoken words. As Gussow observes, while some plays have wildly fantastic directions that are very much open to interpretation, "a realistic play sets more stringent guidelines"; with Beckett, as with Pinter and Ionesco, the plays "are rooted in particular environments" organic to their meaning. Furthermore, stage directions often help the playwright to create a distinctive kind of theatre experience for the audience. Garbus well describes the kind of experience indicated by Beckett:

Everything is set in place for total concentration. There are no extraneous props, costumes or sounds. The drama has a crystal purity, providing its own insights, posing its own questions. It allows the audience to create their own personal vision of what is happening to the actors and to themselves. (2)

Convincingly, he argues that these values were diminished when ART "based its production on a contemporary milieu and experience." Even so sympathetic an observer as Kalb, whose account of the production is the most detailed and appreciative available, acknowledges that: "Akalaitis makes it too easy for spectators to take intellectual possession of what they see as familiar and direct it toward ordinary or banal meanings. . . . The specificity of the new metaphor, the subway, does undercut some of the play's deeper resonances. Productions that occur in the bare room apart from any identifiable history or time convey a certain proud recalcitrance, a durability of symbol, that this production lacks" (90–91).

In statements to the press apart from those in the playbill, Brustein went further than claiming "normal rights of interpretation, October 7, 1993" to assert that the production brought "new values to an extraordinary play" (Freedman, "Associates") and later to look back on the dispute as part of "a growing conflict between playwrights who insist on a very pure rendering of their work, years after it was written, and theater companies that are inspired by visionary artists to bring something new to the play" (Freedman, "Who's to Say"). In Garbus' view, a playwright has the legal right under the Lanham Act to repudiate a distorted production as "a false representation and a deception upon the public." Simple truth in advertising would seem to point to labelling the ART *Endgame* an "adaptation," which would have satisfied Beckett, but which ART refused to do. Instead an elaborate—and from the public's point of view unsatisfactory—compromise was reached whereby Beckett's name was not used in advertising unless the playbill statements were also published. Unsuspecting playgoers who knew only that *Endgame* was to be performed may have felt that it was late in the day to be told, as they opened their playbills, that they had paid their money to see what the author regarded as a "parody" of his play.

Although the result was compromised, the support that the law provided the playwright seems again to have been aesthetically justified. It is of course conceivable that a performer might hit upon a production idea that would constitute a genuine improvement on the original yet that the playwright would not recognize as such. Where this was plausible, one would hope that playwrights would follow Beckett's example and be willing to modify their right to prohibit production, as long as the production was clearly labelled an "adaptation."

In New York, another back-stage drama was under way at about the same time as the one in Cambridge, in which another famous playwright felt that his work was being parodied. At issue was the experimental Wooster Group's use of Arthur Miller's *The Crucible* in *L.S.D. (. . . Just the High Points . . .)*, directed by Elizabeth LeCompte. At stake were the rights of a playwright when his or her work is in the hands of performers whose intentions are not interpretive but frankly adaptive, to the point of being deconstructive.

The Wooster Group never received permission to perform *The Crucible*. Initially, in 1983, they presented work-in-progress rehearsals open to the public, in which they performed a 45 minute version of Miller's play, using the final sections of its four acts, preceded by the playing of 20 minutes of excerpts from Timothy Leary's record album *L. S. D.* In the face of resistance by Miller, they then reduced the Miller excerpts to 25 minutes (hence "Just the High Points" in the title) as part of an enlargement and reworking of the whole piece completed in 1984; it included a later segment designed to "disintegrate" Miller's play by exactly reenacting a drugged rehearsal they had videotaped in which, amid scenes of partying, portions of Act III of *The Crucible* sporadically appeared (Savran, *The Wooster Group*, 200). When Miller threatened legal action against this revised version, LeCompte, having offered to perform the 20 minute portion in pantomime, then reduced the dialogue of the portion to gibberish. Finally, she substituted parts of the play written for this purpose by Michael Kirby, *The Hearing*, which updated the witch-hunt to the 1950s. Parallel passages in *The Crucible* were announced by act and scene so that spectators might follow the Miller text in the copies of the play that were placed behind chairs in the audience; "accidental" slips by the actors into Miller's language were silenced by a buzzer (Aronson, 70). In January 1985, when Miller's lawyers still demanded that the Group cease and desist performance, threatening a suit "based upon all past, present and future performances," *L.S.D. (. . . Just the High Points . . .)* was closed.

Such reworking of classics is a feature of the Wooster Group. Parts of *The Cocktail Party* and *Long Day's Journey into Night* were similarly incorporated into other works; *Our Town* was controversially juxtaposed with black-face routines and pornography. Like other features of the Wooster Group's work, there is a deliberately transgressive aspect to these appropriations. Savran aptly subtitles his book on the Group: "Breaking the Rules."[8] LeCompte's attitude toward the classic plays she has appropriated appears not to be simply challenging; she has expressed affection and admiration for them as well. But her ambivalence results in treatments that are at the least disturbingly interrogatory of the plays as cultural icons, and the contexts the Wooster Group invent characteristically undercut the affirmations of the originals.[9]

What legal defense does a playwright have against unwelcome appropriation? Miller is the only living playwright whose work the Group has thus far used. His stated objections were at first economic. According to members of the Group, Miller seemed "bemused" after seeing the 45 minute version. Through his agent, he a few days later refused performance rights on the grounds that "extensive use of language, characters and scenes amounts to an unacknowledged 'complete' rendering of the play" which "might tend to inhibit first-class productions" of it. To a reporter he referred to it as a "blatant parody" (Massa). Later, he is reported to have said that his real reasons were artistic: "I'm not interested in the money. The esthetics are involved. I don't want the play mangled that way. Period" (Shewey).

Regarded simply as an "abbreviation" (Miller's word) of *The Crucible*, the Wooster Group's 45 and 25 minute abstracts obviously infringe upon Miller's copyright since they were performed without his permission. Savran does not challenge the legality of Miller's prohibition, but he does attack its aesthetic justice, arguing that Miller's "reading" has no more authority than anyone else's except that it is supported by the law. In Savran's view, Miller's insistence on his own interpretation aligns him with the very authority figures *The Crucible* deplores, "who exercise their power arrogantly and arbitrarily to ensure their own continued political and cultural dominion" (Savran, *Wooster Group,* 219). Harsh words! . . . But a production is not equivalent to a "reading." The sorts of interpretive freedom enjoyed by a reader or spectator cannot be simply extended to performers because in a performance there is an element of *presenting* a playwright's work as well as interpreting it, and the two are not readily distinguishable. Furthermore, Miller has not indicated that there is only one "correct" way of presenting his play; he has denied that view: "I am not saying that every production has to be the same. That would be boring. But if the playwright or his representatives say the spirit of the play is violated, that's got to be honored. When the playwright's alive he's got to know best" (Freedman, "Who's to Say"). And since a work is identified with its author, doesn't he—like John Proctor in the play—have a right to protect his "name"? Miller's summary seems to be sound: "Maybe at some point in the future the play will become a kind of public classic. But I'm still around and I should have a say about how the play is done as long as I am" (Freedman, "Play Closed").

There is more of a legal question, however, concerning the final versions, which were undertaken in consultation with a copyright lawyer, especially the version employing Kirby's "The Trial," since the law protects "derivative" works such as parodies as long as the derived work is not too close to the original and displays a considerable degree of independent creativity.[10] If the Wooster Group had begun with its final version, it might well have been legally defensible and thus allowed LeCompte to fulfill her aim of using "irony and distancing techniques to cut through to the intellectual and political heart of *The Crucible*" (Savran, "The Wooster Group," 102). However offensive this dissection may have been to Miller, it seems to me aesthetically justifiable as well since no work should be exempt from appraisal, even if the appraisal is to a degree in its own identifiable terms, whether by way of criticism or homage.

In both the Beckett and Miller disputes, the problems arose from the performers taking the same sorts of liberties that, without legal challenge, they may take with classic plays in the public domain. Why should contemporary "classics" be treated any differently? What finally justifies a living playwright's acting as arbiter of stage interpretations of his work? In the *Endgame* dispute, the celebrated constitutional lawyer, Lawrence H. Tribe, charged that Beckett, in violation of the first amendment rights to free expression of the ART performers, was trying to act as a "censor." But is it "censorship" for Beckett to oppose what he regards as the misrepresentation of his own work? And what of Beckett's own rights? Do not performers who alter his explicit directions deny or vitiate his freedom of expression? I would argue that in cases of conflict it is to the benefit of society to give precedence to the playwright. For as the history of the theatre shows, it is the great playwrights who have led the way in redefining what is "dramatic" for their times and in enlarging the range of dramatic possibility for times to come. The innovations of great performers have been less freshly original and enduring, tending to "date" rapidly. Even great dramatists, however, eventually lose their currency. Miller seems to be right in repeatedly referring to his lifetime as the limit of his artistic control. Legally extending copyright fifty years beyond the owner's lifetime properly protects the financial interest of heirs. But where aesthetic control is concerned, I would propose that a play in effect enter the public domain when its playwright dies, whether by law or common understanding.[11] It seems unwise to try to retain interpretive control after that, as did Tennessee Williams in his will:

No play which I shall have written shall for the purpose of presenting it as a first-class attraction on the English-speaking stage, be changed in any manner whether such change shall be by way of completing it, or adding to it, or deleting from it, or in any other way revising it, except for the customary type of stage directions. (Garbus, 2)

Should an heir or agent exercise such total control? Who but the playwright can truly say whether changes are or are not true to the spirit of the work? As times and styles change, there is more and more need for renovative mediation between the play and its audience. In turn, performers might refrain from attempting to update plays whose authors are still alive, without explicit approval in advance, devoting more of their efforts instead to plays already in the public domain and labelling their freer versions with phrases like "adapted from" and "based upon."

There is a final way in which American law and the views of playwrights can enlighten theory about the performance process. The law's large-minded concern for both the general good and individual incentives to create raises a question not often asked in current theory: why should an author labor to make from nothing works that are no more than raw materials for others to do with as they will?[12]

Here the testimony of film scriptwriters is a help. It should give pause to those inclined to erode the rights of playwrights. Traditionally, reversing the theatre's pattern, it is the screenwriters' work that has been done "for hire." As F. Scott Fitzgerald's hack screenwriter Pat Hobby put it, with unconscious irony, in films "They don't want an author. They want writers—like me" (Fitzgerald, 149). Playwrights who have worked as screenwriters often celebrate the job-satisfactions of artistic control that the Dramatists' Guild contracts insure while lamenting the (highly paid) frustrations of Hollywood, when that control is lost. Peter Stone points out that since someone else owns the copyright, "You have sold away your right of approval. They can do anything, and will, without consultation" (Kanin et al., 31). The novelist William Goldman, who wrote the film *Butch Cassidy and the Sundance Kid*, has expressed the sense of "mourning" he feels at parting with a screenplay, over which he will have no say whatsoever at any future stage of its career (Goldman, *Adventures*, 399–403).

Certain screenwriters have countered these frustrations by becoming directors as well (Robert J. Thompson has recently shown that the same is true of certain writers for television). Lately, the auctioning of screenplays written on speculation has come into practice (Harmetz, "Thrills?" H14). The author runs the risk of writing for nothing; but when successfully carried out, this method can yield not only millions of dollars but the satisfaction of artistic creation through informal rights of approval. Joe Eszterhas, who wrote *Jagged Edge*, and John Patrick Shanley, who wrote *Moonstruck*, are two screenwriters who have in this way succeeded in defending their scripts against changes proposed by stars and directors. To be sure, they do not have the independent authority stipulated in the Dramatists' Guild contract; they are dependent on the moral support of their producers. But they are by no means in so abjectly subservient a position as William Goldman has depicted: "I'm always nice to Dustin Hoffman—he can fire me" (Goldman, *Hype*, 101). The disincentive to productive work of such subservience has been expressed by Shanley:

It means from the day you start to write, somebody else owns what you write. They can take it away from you anytime they want, they can tell you how it should be changed. But, even more basic—in the soul of a human being—if you know that every word you write belongs to somebody else, it doesn't make you feel very good and I don't think it makes you do your best work. (Dent, 16)

Eszterhas emphasizes the positive side of the same coin. With the elation of fresh discovery, he finds that the independent screenwriter has an impetus: "Your belief in what you are saying. Not what the studio is saying. Not what the producer is saying. Not what the director is saying. Not what the actors are saying. You.

Alone" (H12). The co-writer of *Rainman*, Ron Bass, enters more readily into collaborative partnerships, taking it as a challenge when dealing with someone else's
alternative notion "to go beyond what I thought was good and make something
that's brand new, that's better for him and better for me." Even Bass, though, cher-
ishes writing his first draft: "Just for me, I write it just my way, it's heaven. That's
the thing I would really do for nothing" (Dorff, 31). Deploring the usual assembly-
line system, Goldman discerns that what is at stake is nothing less than the writer's
creative urge: "if you are the kind of weird person who has a *need* to bring something into being, and all you do with your life is turn out screenplays, I may covet
your bank account, but I wouldn't give two bits for your soul" (Goldman, *Adventures*, 78).

A decisive role for playwrights in the production process thus not only derives
from their primary creativity but fosters it. This may be the deepest guidance that
the law's wisdom and the views of playwrights can give performance criticism.

NOTES

Reprinted with permission from *Journal of Dramatic Theory and Criticism* 6, no. 2
(1992): 41–59.

1. In *Shakespeare the Theatre-Poet* I make this suggestion, surveying a range of performance theorists (Hapgood, 7–12) and categorizing the various roles that Shakespeare
and other playwrights through the centuries have played in the performance process
(49–60).

2. Rabkin helpfully ventilates many of the issues discussed here, especially emphasiz-
ing analogies with literary theory. Himself a lawyer, Garon emphasizes legal aspects, particularly the rights of performers; he has not found a single case litigated in which a
playwright alleged improper interpretation of his script (286).

3. Middleton gives a firsthand account of the institution of the contract (299–373); its
terms are periodically renegotiated with the League of American Theaters and Producers,
with royalties a particular issue (Kanin et al., 27–28).

4. See also Gray's accounts of the first productions of *The Common Pursuit*, Odet's
diary of his failure, *Night Music*, and the interviews with contemporary women playwrights
by Betsko and Koenig.

5. Eysner reports the 1976 suit in which the Monte Python scriptwriters won an injunction from the United States Court of Appeals, based on Section 43(a) of the Lanham
Act, against broadcast of their work from which unauthorized cuts had been made.

6. Notice, however, that the standard contract in the clause quoted above gives the playwright control over "stage directions" among other features that may have been altered during rehearsals.

7. There were a number of points of difference, including introductory and incidental
music by Philip Glass (the use of which was made clear in the request for permission) and
ART's usual "color blind" casting of white and African-American actors. For a fuller discussion of this production by Jonathan Kalb, see his *Beckett in Performance* (78-87); it includes his interview with Akalaitis (165–72). The latter prompted a denunciation of Rosset
by Actors Equity to which Rosset responded that "taking all the factors together—that the
father and son are black and the mother was white—added a dimension to the play Beckett

had not put there" (Freedman, "Actors Equity," C17). Complicating factors in the background were a series of freewheeling productions of Beckett done by Akalaitis and her associates in the Mabou Mines company, plus other recent productions of *Endgame* that were much more freely interpretive than ART's. Hitherto, Beckett had taken no legal action against such productions but contented himself with wry criticisms and indirect (but effective) resistance to performances in France of Andre Gregory's 1973 environmental production in which spectators were caged by chicken wire. Beckett's general position was summed up by Bair in her 1978 biography: "whenever possible, he tries to maintain absolute control over all productions; when not possible, he ignores them" (634). He had accordingly instructed his zealous agent Rossett that "he would not interfere with productions of his plays on aesthetic grounds even if he had the right to do so, because, once started, there would be no end." For instance, Beckett is said to have known and done nothing about Marcel Delval's 1984 *Endgame* in Brussels, which was staged in waist-deep water (Kalb, "The Underground Endgame," 92). Productions of *Endgame* with which Beckett himself had been associated had not been strictly in accord with the printed directions. According to Ruby Cohn the set for the production Beckett directed was "spare rather than bare" (239); he accepted the ornate design of the George Devine production in London as being in keeping with his English translation as contrasted with the harsher French original (Bair, 499–500). It's not clear why Beckett took particular exception to the ART version.

8. For example, in *Rumstick Road* LeCompte and the actor Spalding Gray deliberately violated confidences. After telling the audience that his grandmother asked him not to play a tape of her reading Mary Baker Eddy, Gray proceeded to do so. Later he played a tape he had made of a telephone conversation with his mother's psychiatrist about her electric shock therapy; the tape was made without the doctor's knowledge, and its public presentation, needless to say, did not have his approval.

9. Savran, *The Wooster Group, Part III*. See also Auslander and Erickson.

10. The relative rights due the original and the derivative works is a favorite current issue among lawyers; volume after volume of the annual *Copyright Law Symposium* include articles on the subject. Bernstein's is of particular interest because it includes not only parodies but "serious and substantial" secondary uses, such as Woody Allen's tribute to Fellini's *8½* in *Stardust Memories*.

11. French law, for example, keeps moral rights distinct from financial ones; in France, *droit moral* is perpetual.

12. Compare the 1986 opinion of the Seventh Circuit Court of Appeals in the case of *Baltimore Orioles v. Major League Baseball Players*, *Federal Reporter, Second Series*, vol. 805. St. Paul, Minn.: West, 1987. 678 (cited in Garon, 283):

> The purpose of federal copyright protection is to benefit the public by encouraging works in which it is interested. To induce individuals to undertake the personal sacrifices necessary to create such works, federal copyright law extends to the authors of such works a limited monopoly to reap the rewards of their endeavors.

Afterword

Part One of this volume linked current performance theory in the theatre world to earlier discourse in the field of literature, where old views on authorial potency had been challenged. Directors, apparently released from once-imposed restraints, now frequently challenge the language of a dramatic text; they discover a play's meaning beyond its playwright's conscious intention. By supplementing, displacing, and replacing text, some sought to enlarge the potential for their own interpretive authority, often with recognized success.

Still, the commentary by playwrights and directors in Part Two gave divergent views of these trends and of the primary function of performance. Some saw performance as a service to a composed text, an interpretation of that text. Others viewed a text as but one of many components brought together to produce a piece of theatre—equal to (but not more important than) scenery, sound, and costuming. Those questioned, whether author or director, often agreed that facets of what they variously term a composed text, a full text, or a through-composed text must be respected, while a text that "asks for improvisation" might be experimented with (Albee, "Beckett on Stage," Alley Theatre Panel Discussion). Part Three's case studies—five tiers of theatre interchange or collaboration—suggested that in the complex area of production, we are still searching for theatrical solutions that encourage the creativity of directors but also follow the artistic intent of playwrights. From midcentury on, production prototypes were evolving rather than remaining static, in time returning full circle to their earlier configuration. First, strong, talented "directors' directors" succeeded in altering the work of cooperative and appreciative authors. Soon more assertive types—the "tyrant directors"—could commercialize the work of insecure and compliant playwrights. Later, determined and aggressive directors sometimes distorted the staging of modern classics so far that heretofore cooperative playwrights rebelled. After a time, other playwrights, to guard their own work, mastered the art of directing; they modified and enhanced their own authorial vision. Several authors-turned-directors later took a turn at staging the works of other authors whether living or deceased, altering and enhancing their texts. A return to the tonic has now sounded as some of these playwright-directors opt to free up their own plays to other directors rather than stage their premieres themselves. One author-director's readily stated motivation was to discover how an objective interpreter might envision and stage his play.[1] And increasingly, a few author-and-director teams have developed dramatic text both before and during its staging to make full use of each partner's artistic potential.

In Part Four, the legal and aesthetic issues of production and the Dramatists' Guild's standard contract were assessed. Its legal language provides "a timely corrective to current tendencies in performance theory" (Hapgood, 47) which may have raised directors over authors. The contract's phrasing grants authors legal rights to a satisfactory performance that follows the script but does not make the director an inconsequential figure. Since the producer as well as the playwright signs the contract, what theatre groups want—normal freedom of interpretation (Garbus, 2)—should be possible.

A greater awareness of the complexities of play and performance might bring fruitful cooperation between authors and directors; voluntarily, producers could bill performances as "adaptations" if they are not close interpretations of playwrights' works. Yet without explicit oral and written guidelines in our contracts, it may be unrealistic to expect to see at once this reflex cooperation between production groups and authors; for the backdrops of persons involved in matters of play or performance differ uniquely. How can playwrights reared in an author-centered culture welcome a rationale that moves directors to center front—even gifted and serious ones? And will directors nurtured in a performance-aligned climate discern that granting them a fuller role in artistic creation might blur the line that playwrights see between interpretation and distortion of their texts? Who can change human nature!

Hereafter, whether an author's work has or has not entered the public domain, we may need to approach (and risk) the task of expanding and rephrasing our standard legal contracts to delineate aesthetic as well as legal facets of licensing and to mandate suitable use on playbills of terms like "production" versus "adaptation." In this ticklish and risky semantic process, the onus for production failures might then fall equally on overly rigid disciples of authorial potency and capricious, less than serious distorters of works of art. The gamble might win us a treasure: years of theatre from teams of glowing authors and gleaming directors.

NOTE

1. Edward Albee's remark to me before the American Premiere of his *Three Tall Women*, which he did not direct at the River Arts Theatre, Woodstock Arts Festival, Woodstock, New York, July 30–August 15, 1992.

Works Cited

**PREFACE AND PART ONE, THEORIES OF AUTHORSHIP
AND INTERPRETATION**

Albee, Edward. "Introduction." In *Selected Plays of Edward Albee*. New York: Doubleday, 1987.

———. *Marriage Play*. Unpublished. (World premiere at Vienna's English Theatre, June 1987. American premiere at the Alley Theatre, Houston, Tex., January 8–February 2, 1992.)

Artaud, Antonin. *The Theatre and Its Double*. Trans. Mary C. Richards. New York: Grove Press, 1958.

Barthes, Roland. "From Work to Text," In *Image/Music/Text*. Trans. Stephen Heath. New York: Hill and Wang, 1977.

———. "Literature and Signification." In *Barthes: Critical Essays*. Trans. Richard Howard. Kingsport, Tenn.: Kingsport Press, 1963.

Benston, Kimberly W. "Being There: Performance as Mise-en-Scène, Abscene, Obscene, and Other Scene," *Publications of the Modern Language Association* 107, no. 3 (May 1992): 434–49.

Blau, Herbert. "Follow the Bright Angels." *Tulane Drama Review* 5, no. 1 (September 1960): 89-101.

Ciment, Michel. *Kazan on Kazan*. New York: Viking Press, 1974.

Davis, Robert Con. *Contemporary Literary Criticism*. New York: Longman, 1986.

Derrida, Jacques. *De La Gramatologie*. Baltimore: Johns Hopkins University Press, 1976.

Eco, Umberto. *A Theory of Semantics*. Bloomington: Indiana University Press, 1984.

Foucault, Michel. "The Discourse on Language." In *The Archaeology of Knowledge*. Ed. R. D. Laing. Trans. A. M. Sheridan Smith. New York: Random House, 1972.

————. "What Is an Author?" Reprinted in Harari.

Freedman, Samuel J. "Play Closed after *Crucible* Dispute." *New York Times*, Nov. 28, 1984, E21.

————. "Who's to Say Whether a Playwright Is Wronged?" *New York Times*, December 23, 1984, E6.

Harari, Josue V., ed. *Textual Strategies: Perspectives in Post-Structuralist Criticism*. Ithaca, N.Y.: Cornell University Press, 1979.

Hirsch, E. D., Jr. *Validity in Interpretation*. New Haven, Conn.: Yale University Press, 1967.

Hobson, Harold. "Miss Vivien Leigh." *Sunday Times* (London), Nov. 13, 1949, 2.

Hodge, Francis. *Play Directing*. 3d ed. Englewood Cliffs, N.J.: Prentice-Hall, 1988.

Issacaroff, Michael, and Robin F. Jones. *Performing Texts*. Philadelphia: University of Pennsylvania Press, 1988.

Jones, David Richard. *Great Directors at Work: Stanislavsky, Brecht, Kazan, Brook*. Berkeley: University of California Press, 1986.

Kernan, Alvin. "The Battle for the Word: Dictionaries, Deconstructors, and Language Engineers." In *The Death of Literature*. New Haven, Conn.: Yale University Press, 1990.

Massa, Robert. "Arthur Miller Clings to *The Crucible*." *The Village Voice*, December 27, 1983, 52.

Pirandello, Luigi. *Six Characters in Search of an Author*. New York: Dutton, 1952.

Rabkin, Gerald. "Is There a Text on This Stage? Theatre/Authorship/Interpretation." *Performing Arts Journal* 9, no. 2 (1985):142–59.

Roof, Judith. "Testicles, Toasters and the 'Real Thing.' " *Studies in the Humanities* 17, no. 2 (December 1990): 106–19.

Schechner, Richard. "Performance/Script/Theatre/Drama." *The Drama Review* 17, no. 3 (September 1973): 6–36.

Schneider, Alan. *Entrances: An American Director's Journey*. New York: Viking Press, 1986.

Smith, Barbara Herrnstein. "The Ethics of Interpretation" and "Authorial Intentions and Literary Ethics." In *On the Margins of Discourse*. Chicago: University of Chicago Press, 1978.

Suchy, Patricia A. "When Words Collide: The Stage Direction as Utterance." *Journal of Dramatic Theory and Criticism* 6, no. 1 (Fall 1991): 69–82.

Vincent, Michael. "Author, Authority, and the Pedagogical Scene: *Elvire Jouvet 40*." *Journal of Dramatic Theory and Criticism* 6, no. 1 (Fall 1991): 5–13.

Young, Robert. *Untying the Text: A Post-Structuralist Reader*. Boston: Routledge and Kegan Paul, 1981.

PART TWO, REMARKS OF PLAYWRIGHTS AND DIRECTORS

Berry, Ralph. "Peter Brook." In *On Directing Shakespeare*. New York: Barnes and Noble, 1977.

Brockett, Oscar G. *History of the Theatre*. 4th ed. Boston: Allyn and Bacon, 1982.

Edmonson, Andrew. *The Alley Theatre Press Release*, 17 March 1992: 1–7.

Freedman, Samuel J. "Who's to Say Whether a Playwright Is Wronged?" *New York Times*, December 23, 1984, E6.

Hodge, Francis. *Play Directing*. 3d ed. Englewood Cliffs, N.J.: Prentice-Hall, 1988.

Quintero, Jose. *If You Don't Dance They Beat You*. Boston: Little, Brown, 1974.

Rabkin, Gerald. "Is There a Text on This Stage? Theatre/Authorship/Interpretation." *Performing Arts Journal* 9, no. 2 (1985):142–59.

Review of *Prospero's Books*, with John Gielgud; dir. Peter Greenway. *Morning Edition*, National Public Radio, KCFR, Denver, Colo., November 3, 1991. [Repeated on November 29, 1991.]

PART THREE, TIERS OF DIRECTOR/ PLAYWRIGHT INTERCHANGE

Albee, Edward. "Playwright/Director Relationship." Forum at Tenth Annual William Inge Festival, Independence, Kans., April 25–28, 1991.

Artaud, Antonin. *The Theatre and Its Double*. Trans. Mary C. Richards. New York: Grove Press, 1958.

A "Director's Director"

Atkinson, Brooks. "*Streetcar* Tragedy—Mr. Williams Report on Life in New Orleans." *New York Times*, December 14, 1947, Sec. 2:1.

Bigsby, C.W.E. *A Critical Introduction to Twentieth-Century American Drama*. Vol. 2. Cambridge: Cambridge University Press, 1984.

Ciment, Michel. *Kazan on Kazan*. New York: Viking Press, 1974.

Donahue, Francis. *The Dramatic World of Tennessee Williams*. New York: Frederick Ungar, 1964.

Falk, Signi L. *Tennessee Williams*. New York: Twayne Publishers, 1961.

Freedman, Samuel J. "Who's to Say Whether a Playwright Is Wronged?" *New York Times*, December 23, 1984, E6.

Hayes, Walter. "*Streetcar*: A Triumph for the Oliviers." *Daily Graphic*, October 13, 1949, 2.

Hobson, Harold. "Miss Vivien Leigh." *Sunday Times* (London), November 13, 1949, 2.

Jones, David Richard. *Great Directors at Work: Stanislavsky, Brecht, Kazan, Brook*. Berkeley: University of California Press, 1986.

Kazan, Elia. *A Life*. New York: Alfred A. Knopf, 1988.

———. "Notebook for *A Streetcar Named Desire*." Excerpted in *Twentieth Century Interpretations of* A Streetcar Named Desire. Indianapolis: Bobbs-Merrill, 1963.

Kolin, Philip C. "The First Critical Assessments of *A Streetcar Named Desire*: The *Streetcar* Tryouts and the Reviewers." *Journal of Dramatic Theory and Criticism* (Spring 1991): 45–65.

———. "Olivier to Williams: An Introduction: 'Affectionate and mighty regards from Vivien and from me': Sir Laurence Olivier's Letter to Tennessee Williams on the London Premiere of *A Streetcar Named Desire*." *Missouri Review* 13, no. 3 (1991): 143–57.

———. "*A Streetcar Named Desire*: A Playwright's Forum." *Michigan Quarterly Review* 39, no. 2 (Spring 1990): 173-203.

Maxwell, Gilbert. *Tennessee Williams and Friends*. Cleveland: World, 1965.

Miller, Jordan Y. *Twentieth Century Interpretations of* A Streetcar Named Desire. Englewood Cliffs, N.J.: Prentice-Hall, 1971.

Oakes, Philip. "Return Ticket." *Sunday Times* (London), March 17, 1974, 35.

Pauly, Thomas H. *An American Odyssey: Elia Kazan and American Culture*. Philadelphia: Temple University Press, 1983.

Smith, Barbara Herrnstein. "The Ethics of Interpretation" and "Authorial Intentions and Literary Ethics." In *On the Margins of Discourse*. Chicago: University of Chicago Press, 1978.

Vlasopolos, Anca. "Authorizing History: Victimization in *A Streetcar Named Desire.*" *Theatre Journal* (October 1986): 322–338.

Williams, Tennessee. *Memoirs*. New York: Bantam Books, 1976.

Windham, Donald. *Tennessee Williams' Letters to Donald Windham*. New York: Holt, Rinehart and Winston, 1976.

A Tyrant Director?

Albee, Edward. "Playwright/Director Relationship." Forum at Tenth Annual William Inge Festival, Independence, Kans., April 25–28, 1991.

Arendt, Hannah. *The Life of the Mind: Willing*. New York: Harcourt Brace Jovanovich, 1978.

Berry, Ralph. *On Directing Shakespeare*. New York: Barnes and Noble, 1977.

Bigsby, C.W.E. *A Critical Introduction to Twentieth-Century American Drama*. Vol. 2. Cambridge: Cambridge University Press, 1984.

Brockett, Oscar G. *History of the Theatre*. 4th ed. Boston: Allyn and Bacon, 1982.

Brustein, Robert. "The Men-taming Women of William Inge." *Harper's Magazine* (November 1958): 52–57.

Clurman, Harold. Review of *Picnic* [Theatre Section]. *Nation* (March 7, 1953): 212–13.

Hodge, Francis. *Play Directing*. 3d ed. Englewood Cliffs, N.J.: Prentice-Hall, 1988.

Inge, William. "From *Front Porch* to Broadway." *Theatre Arts* 38, no. 4 (April 4, 1954): 32–33.

———. "More on the Playwright's Mission." *Theatre Arts* 42, no. 8 (August 1958): 19.

———. *Picnic*. New York: Random House, 1953.

———. "*Picnic*: Of Women." *New York Times*, (14 February 1953): Sec. X: 3.

———. Summer Brave: *The Rewritten and Final Version of The Romantic Comedy* Picnic. New York: Dramatists' Play Service, 1962.

Jones, Therese. "Critics and Characters." Chap. 3, unpublished doctoral dissertation, University of Colorado, Boulder, Colo., 1992.

Logan, Joshua. *JOSH: My Up and Down, In and Out Life*. New York: Delacorte Press, 1976.

Nathan, George Jean. "Director's *Picnic.*" *Theatre Arts* 37 (May 1953): 14–15.

———. "William Inge." In *The Theatre of the Fifties*. New York: Alfred A. Knopf, 1953.

Reilingh, Maarten. "William Inge." In *American Playwrights since 1945: A Guide to Scholarship, Criticism, and Performance*. Ed. Philip Kolin. Westport, Conn.: Greenwood Press, 1989.

Voss, Ralph. "William Inge." In *Dictionary of Literary Biography: Twentieth Century American Dramatists* 7 (1981): 325–37.

Williams, Tennessee. *Memoirs*. New York: Bantam Books, 1976.

Wood, Audrey, with Max Wilk. "Come Back, Sweet William." In *Represented by Audrey Wood: A Memoir*. Garden City, N.Y.: Doubleday, 1981.

A Director's Distortion of a Modern Classic

Aronson, Arnold. "The Wooster Group's *L.S.D. (. . . Just the High Points . . .).*" *The Drama Review* 29 (1985): 65-77.

Ciment, Michel. *Kazan on Kazan.* New York: Viking Press, 1974.

Ferres, John H., ed. *Twentieth Century Interpretations of* The Crucible. Englewood Cliffs, N.J.: Prentice-Hall, 1972.

Foucault, Michel. "What Is an Author?" Reprinted in Harari.

Freedman, Samuel J. "Play Closed after *Crucible* Dispute." *New York Times,* November 28, 1984: E21.

———. "Who's to Say Whether a Playwright Is Wronged?" *New York Times,* December 23, 1984: E6.

Harari, Josue V., ed. *Textual Strategies: Perspectives in Post-Structuralist Criticism.* Ithaca, N.Y.: Cornell University Press, 1979.

Jones, David Richard. *Great Directors at Work: Stanislavsky, Brecht, Kazan, Brook.* Berkeley: University of California Press, 1986.

Kazan, Elia. *A Life.* New York: Alfred A. Knopf, 1988.

Levin, David. "Salem Witchcraft in Recent Fiction and Drama." *New England Quarterly* 28 (December 1955): 537-46.

Massa, Robert. "Arthur Miller Clings to *Crucible.*" *The Village Voice,* December 27, 1983, 52.

Miller, Arthur. *Arthur Miller: Eight Plays.* New York: Doubleday, 1981.

———. *The Crucible* (Acting Edition). New York: Dramatists' Play Service, 1954.

———. "Journey to *The Crucible.*" *New York Times,* February 8, 1953, II–3.

———. *Timebends: A Life.* New York: Grove Press, 1987.

Rabkin, Gerald. "Is There a Text on This Stage? Theatre/Authorship/Interpretation" *Performing Arts Journal* 9, no. 2 (1985):142–59.

Rovere, Richard. "Arthur Miller's Conscience." *New Republic* 136 (June 17, 1957): 13–15.

Savran, David. "The Wooster Group, Arthur Miller and *The Crucible.*" *The Drama Review* 29 (1985): 99–109.

———. *The Wooster Group, 1975–1985: Breaking the Rules.* Ann Arbor: UMI Research Press, 1986.

Trewin, J. C. "Plays in Performance." *DRAMA: British Theatre Performance* 3, no. 15 (Winter 1949): 7–8.

Walker, Phillip. "Arthur Miller's *The Crucible*: Tragedy or Allegory?" *Western Speech* 20 (Fall 1956): 222–24.

Windham, Donald. *Tennessee Williams' Letters to Donald Windham.* New York: Holt, Rinehart and Winston, 1976.

A Playwright-Director Opens Up a Classic

Abrams, M. H. *A Glossary of Literary Terms.* 5th ed. New York: Holt, Rinehart and Winston, 1988.

Albee, Edward. "Author's Note." In *Tiny Alice.* New York: Dramatists' Play Service, 1965.

———. *Box and Quotations from Chairman Mao Tse-Tung.* New York: Dramatists' Play Service, 1969.

———. Class session of Professor Albee's "Advanced Playwriting" course at the University of Houston, prior to opening of "Albee Directs Beckett" bill, Alley Theatre, Houston, Tex., February 11, 1991. [Transcribed by editor.]

———. "Director Albee Says Plays by Beckett Not That Difficult." Interview by Everett Evans. *Houston Chronicle*, February 17, 1991, 20, 32, 33.

———. "Game of Truth: Talk with the Author." Interview in *Newsweek*, October 29, 1962, 52–53.

———. "Some Thoughts on Viewing Beckett." *Houston Performances: The Arts and Theatre Magazine*, February 1991, 9.

Albee, Edward, et al. "Beckett on Stage." Panel discussion on Albee's direction of two Beckett plays. Alley Theatre, Houston, Tex., March 11, 1991.

———. "Playwright/Director Relationship." Forum at Tenth Annual William Inge Festival, Independence, Kans., April 25-28, 1991.

Albright, William. "Albee Ensures Beckett Plays Are Accessible." *Houston Post*, February 22, 1991, E5.

Bair, Dierdre. *A Biography: Samuel Beckett*. New York: Harcourt Brace Jovanovich, 1978.

Barthes, Roland. "Literature and Signification." In *Barthes: Critical Essays*. Trans. Richard Howard. Kingsport, Tenn.: Kingsport Press, 1963.

Beckett, Samuel. "Beckett Continues to Refine His Vision." Interview by Mel Gussow. *New York Times*, December 26, 1976, D1, D27.

———. *Krapp's Last Tape and Other Dramatic Pieces*. New York: Grove Press, 1981.

———. *Ohio Impromptu*. In *Rockaby and Other Short Pieces*. New York: Grove Press, 1981.

Bigsby, C.W.E. *A Critical Introduction to Twentieth-Century American Drama*. Vol. 2 (Cambridge: Cambridge University Press, 1984).

Blau, Herbert. "Follow the Bright Angels." *Tulane Drama Review* 5, no. 1 (September 1960): 89–101.

Brockett, Oscar G. *History of the Theatre*. 4th ed. Boston: Allyn and Bacon, 1982.

Cohn, Ruby. "Explosive Cocktails." *Journal of American Drama and Theatre* 1, no. 2 (Fall 1989): 5–17.

———. *Samuel Beckett: The Comic Gamut*. New Brunswick, N.J.: Rutgers University Press, 1962.

Cronyn, Hume. *A Terrible Liar: A Memoir*. New York: William Morrow, 1991.

Davis, Robert Con. *Contemporary Literary Criticism*. New York: Longman, 1986.

Evans, Everett. "Alley Program Shows Why Beckett's Plays Still Divide Audiences." *Houston Chronicle*, February 22, 1991, E1, E4.

Frye, Northrop, Sheridan Baker, and George Perkins. *The Harper Handbook to Literature*. New York: Harper, 1985.

Gussow, Mel. "Odd Man in on Broadway." Interview with Edward Albee. *Newsweek*, February 4, 1963, 48–54.

Holman, C. Hugh, and William Harmon. *A Handbook to Literature*. 5th ed. New York: Macmillan, 1986.

King, Michael. "True to the Words." *Houston Press*, February 28, 1991, 12.

Kolin, Philip C. *American Playwrights since 1945: A Guide to Scholarship, Criticism, and Performance*. Westport, Conn.: Greenwood Press, 1989.

———. "Olivier to Williams: An Introduction: 'Affectionate and mighty regards from Vivien and from me': Sir Laurence Olivier's Letter to Tennessee Williams on the London Premiere of *A Streetcar Named Desire*." *Missouri Review* 13, no. 3 (1991): 143–57.

Kolin, Philip C., and J. Madison Davis, eds. *Critical Essays on Edward Albee*. Boston: G. K. Hall, 1986.

Krejci, Anna. "Albee's Ego Overpowers Beckett." *Public News* (February 27, 1991): 10, 15.

Lahr, John. *Notes on a Cowardly Lion*. New York: Ballantine Press, 1969.

Luere, Jeane. "A Turn at the Top: Albee's Direction of Beckett." *South Atlantic Review* (South Atlantic Modern Language Association) (November 1993).

McCarthy, Gerry. *Edward Albee*. New York: St. Martin's Press, 1987.

Paolucci, Anne. "Albee and the Restructuring of the Modern Stage." *Studies in American Drama* 1 (Summer 1986): 4–16.

———. *From Tension to Tonic: The Plays of Edward Albee*. Carbondale: Southern Illinois University Press, 1972.

Review of *Prospero's Books*, with John Gielgud; dir. Peter Greenaway. *Morning Edition*, National Public Radio, KCFR, Denver, Colo., November 3, 1991. [Repeated on November 29, 1991.]

Roof, Judith. "Testicles, Toasters and the 'Real Thing.' " *Studies in the Humanities* 17, no. 2 (December 1990): 106–19.

Roudané, Matthew. *Who's Afraid of Virginia Woolf? Necessary Fictions, Terrifying Realities*. Boston: G. K. Hall, 1990.

Schneider, Alan. *Entrances: An American Director's Journey*. New York: Viking Press, 1986.

Schumach, Murray. "Why They Wait for Godot." *New York Times Magazine* no. 6 (September 21, 1958): 36, 38, 41.

Seitz, William C. *Abstract Expressionism in America*. Cambridge: Harvard University Press, 1983.

Spence, David. " 'Albee Directs Beckett' on the Neuhaus Arena Stage." *The Jewish Herald-Voice* (February 28, 1991): 26.

Staib, Philippe. "Apropos Samuel Beckett." In *Beckett at Sixty: A Festschrift*. London: Calder and Boyars, 1967.

Director, Playwright, and Cast

Artaud, Antonin. *The Theatre and Its Double*. Trans. Mary C. Richards. New York: Grove Press, 1958.

Asahina, Robert. Review of *Cloud Nine*. *The Hudson Review* 34 (1981): 565.

Berry, Ralph. *On Directing Shakespeare*. New York: Barnes and Noble, 1977.

Botto, Louis. "Revolutionary Theatre." *Playbill* 22, no. 1 (October 31, 1992): 42–45.

Campbell, Donald. "Traditional Movement." *Plays and Players* (November 1976): 20–21.

CHURCHILL: PLAYS: ONE. New York: Routledge, Chapman and Hall, 1985.

Cousin, Geraldine. *Churchill: The Playwright*. London: Methuen Drama, 1989.

Fitzsimmons, Linda. *File on CHURCHILL*. London: Methuen Drama, 1989.

Hayman, Ronald. "Double Acts." *Sunday Times Magazine*, March 2, 1980, 27.

Klaus, Carl H., Miriam Gilbert, and Bradford S. Field, Jr. *Stages of Drama: Classical to Contemporary Masterpieces of the Theater*. 2d ed. New York: St. Martin's Press, 1991.

Mairowitz, David Zane. "God and the Devil." *Plays and Players* (February 1977): 24.

Randall, Phyllis R. *Caryl Churchill: A Casebook*. New York: Garland, 1988.

Sher, Antony. *The Joint Stock Book: The Making of a Theatre Collective*. Ed. Rob Ritchie, London: Methuen, 1987.

Simon, John. "Sex, Politics, and Other Play Things." *Vogue* (August 1983): 126–39.

Solomon, Alisa. Review of *Cloud Nine*. *Theatre Journal* 34, no. 1 (March 1982): 117–18.
Thurman, Judith. "Caryl Churchill: The Playwright Who Makes You Laugh about Orgasm, Racism, Class Struggle . . ." *Ms* (May 1982): 56.
Wandor, Michelene. "The Fifth Column: Feminism and Theatre." *Drama*, no. 152 (1984): 7.
———. "Free Collective Bargaining." *Time Out* (March 3–April 4, 1979): 14.

PART FOUR, THEATRE AESTHETICS AND THE LAW

Contractual Provisions of the Dramatists' Guild, Inc.

Albee, Edward. "Introduction." In *Selected Plays of Edward Albee*. New York: Doubleday, 1987.
Canaday, John. *What Is Art?* New York: Alfred A. Knopf, 1988.
Kandinsky, Wassily. *Concerning the Spiritual in Art*. New York: George Wittenborn, 1947.
Kanin, Garson, Schary Dore, and Peter Stone. "The Minimum Basic Agreement and Artistic Integrity." *Dramatists' Guild Quarterly* 16 (1979): 27–32.
Kernan, Alvin. *The Death of Literature*. New Haven, Conn.: Yale University Press, 1990.
Wimsatt, W. K., Jr. "Battering the Object: The Ontological Approach." In *Contemporary Criticism*. Stratford-Upon-Avon Studies, 12. London, 1970.

Collaboration and American Law

"Albee Seeking to Close an All-Male *Woolf*." *New York Times*, August 3, 1984, C5.
Aronson, Arnold. "The Wooster Group's *L.S.D. (. . . Just the High Points . . .)*." *The Drama Review* 29 (1985): 65–77.
Artaud, Antonin. *The Theatre and Its Double*. Trans. Mary C. Richards. New York: Grove Press, 1958.
Auslander, Philip. "Toward a Concept of the Political in Postmodern Theatre." *Theatre Journal* 39 (1987): 20–34.
Bair, Dierdre. *Samuel Beckett: A Biography*. New York: Harcourt Brace Jovanovich, 1978.
Beckett, Samuel. *Endgame*. New York: Grove Press, 1958.
Bernstein, Richard A. "Parody and Fair Use in Copyright Law." Copyright Law Symposium 31. New York: Columbia University Press, 1984.
Betsko, Kathleen, and Rachel Koening. *Interviews with Contemporary Women Playwrights*. New York: William Morrow, 1987.
Cohn, Ruby. *Just Play: Beckett's Theater*. Princeton, N.J.: Princeton University Press, 1980.
Constantinidis, Stratos E. "Is Theatre under Deconstruction? A Retroactive Manifesto in a Language I Do Not Own." *Journal of Dramatic Theory and Criticism* 4 (1989): 31-52.
Dent, Skye. "John Patrick Shanley." *Writers Guild of America West Newsletter*, May 1988.
Derrida, Jacques. "The Theatre of Cruelty and the Closure of Representation." In *Writing and Difference*. Trans. Alan Bass. Chicago: University of Chicago Press, 1978.
Dorff, Matt. "Pencils Notebooks." *Writers Guild of America West Newsletter*, July 1989.
Erickson, Jon. "Appropriation and Transgression in Contemporary American Performance: The Wooster Group, Holly Hughes, and Karen Finley." *Theatre Journal* 42 (1990): 225–36.
Eszterhas, Joe. "From a Writer's Standpoint, Rewards Are Worth the Risks." *New York Times*, July 6, 1990, H11–13.

Eysner, Jason. "Mutilation of Script Actionable under Lanham Act." *Art and the Law* 3 (1977): 7–8.

Ferretti, Fred. "Joseph Papp: A 'Divisive Force' or a 'Healing' One?" *New York Times*, December 20, 1980, 16.

Fitzgerald, F. Scott. *The Pat Hobby Stories*. New York: Charles Scribner, 1970.

Freedman, Samuel J. "Actors Equity Protests Beckett Cast Criticism." *New York Times*, January 9, 1985, C17.

———. "Associates of Beckett Seek to Halt Production." *New York Times*, December 8, 1984, A14.

———. "*Endgame* Opens in Wake of Pact." *New York Times*, December 13, 1984, C14.

———. "Miller Fighting Group's Use of Segment from *Crucible*." *New York Times*, November 17, 1984, A14.

———. "Play Closed after *Crucible* Dispute." *New York Times*, November 28, 1984: E21.

———. "Playwrights Debate Staging." *New York Times*, March 14, 1985, C21.

———. "Who's to Say Whether a Playwright Is Wronged?" *New York Times*, December 23, 1984, E6.

Fried, Charles. "Sonnet LXV and the 'Black Ink' of the Framers' Intention." *Harvard Law Review* 100 (1987): 751–60.

Garbus, Martin, and Gerald E. Singleton. "Playwright-Director Conflict: Whose Play Is It Anyway?" *New York Law Review* (December 28, 1984): 1–2.

Garon, Jon. "Director's Choice: The Fine Line Between Interpretation and Infringement of an Author's Work." *Columbia-VLA Journal of Law and the Arts* 12 (1988): 277–306.

Gibson, William. *The Seesaw Log*. New York: Alfred A. Knopf, 1959.

Goldman, Michael. *The Actor's Freedom*. New York: Viking, 1972.

Goldman, William. *Adventures in the Screen Trade*. New York: Warner, 1983.

———. *Hype and Glory*. New York: Willard Books, 1990.

Gray, Simon. *How's That for Telling Them, Fat Lady?: A Short Life in the American Theatre*. London: Faber, 1988.

———. *An Unnatural Pursuit and Other Pieces: A Playwright's Journal*. London: Faber, 1985.

Gussow, Mel. "Enter Fearless Director, Pursued by Playwright." *New York Times*, January 3, 1985, C14.

Hapgood, Robert. *Shakespeare the Theatre-Poet*. Oxford: Clarendon Press, 1988.

Harmetz, Aljean. "Glory and Humiliation in the Screen Trade." *Esquire* 1, no. 16 (1991): 79-84.

———. "Thrills? Millions? 'Spec' Scripts Bring Big Bids." *New York Times*, July 6, 1990, H11, H14.

Kalb, Jonathan. *Beckett in Performance*. Cambridge: Cambridge University Press, 1989.

———. "The Underground Endgame." *Theater* 16 (1985): 88–96.

Kanin, Garson, Schary Dore, and Peter Stone. "The Minimum Basic Agreement and Artistic Integrity." *Dramatists' Guild Quarterly* 16 (1979): 27–32.

Massa, Robert. "Arthur Miller Clings to *The Crucible*." *The Village Voice*, December 27, 1983, 52.

Middleton, George. *These Things Are Mine: The Autobiography of a Journeyman Playwright*. New York: Macmillan, 1947.

Nimmer, Melville B., and David Nimmer. *Nimmer on Copyright—A Treatise on the Law of Literacy, Musical and Artistic Property and the Protection of Ideas*. 4 vols. New York: Matthew Bender, 1990.

Odets, Clifford. *The Time Is Ripe: The 1940 Journals of Clifford Odets*. New York: Grove Press, 1988.

Posner, Richard A. *Law and Literature: A Misunderstood Relation*. Cambridge: Harvard University Press, 1988.

Rabkin, Gerald. "Is There a Text on This Stage? Theatre/Authorship/Interpretation." *Performing Arts Journal* 9, no. 2 (1985): 142–59.

Savran, David. *In Their Own Words: Contemporary American Playwrights*. New York: Theatre Communications Group, 1988.

———. "The Wooster Group, Arthur Miller and *The Crucible*." *The Drama Review* 29 (1985): 99–109.

———. *The Wooster Group, 1975–1985: Breaking the Rules*. Ann Arbor: UMI Research Press, 1986.

Schechner, Richard. *Essays on Performance Theory 1970–6*. New York: Drama Book Specialists, 1977.

Shaland, Irene. *Tennessee Williams on the Soviet Stage*. Lanham, Md.: University Press of America, 1987.

Shewey, Don. "Miller's Tale." *The Village Voice*, November 27, 1984, 123.

Smith, Bruce. *Costly Performances—Tennessee Williams: The Last Stage*. New York: Paragon House, 1990.

Stewart, Stephen M. *International Copyright and Neighboring Rights*. London: Butterworths, 1983.

Thompson, Robert J. *Adventures on Prime Time: The Television Programs of Stephen J. Cannell*. New York: Praeger, 1990.

Tribe, Lawrence H. "First Amendment Endgame." *Boston Globe*, December 15, 1984, 19.

Wilder, Thornton. "Some Thoughts on Playwrighting." In *American Characteristics*. New York: Harper and Row, 1979.

Williams, Tennessee. "Author and Director: A Delicate Situation." In *Where I Live: Selected Essays*. Ed. Christine R. Day and Bob Woods. New York: New Directions, 1978.

AFTERWORD

Albee, Edward. "Beckett on Stage." Panel discussion on Albee's direction of two Beckett plays, Alley Theatre, Houston, Tex., March 11, 1991.

"Comprehensive Writer's Contract." *Dramatists' Guild*, Exec. Dir. David Levine. 1992:4.

Garbus, Martin, and Gerald E. Singleton. "Playwright-Director Conflict: Whose Play Is It Anyway?" *New York Law Review* (December 28, 1984): 1–2.

Hapgood, Robert. "The Rights of Playwrights: Performance Theory and American Law." *Journal of Dramatic Theory and Criticism* 6, no. 2 (1992): 41–59.

General Bibliography

Abrams, M. H. *A Glossary of Literary Terms*. 5th ed. New York: Holt, Rinehart and Winston, 1988.

Albee, Edward. "Author's Note." In *Tiny Alice*. New York: Dramatists' Play Service, 1965.

———. *Box and Quotations from Chairman Mao Tse-Tung*. New York: Dramatists' Play Service, 1969.

———. Class session of Professor Albee's "Advanced Playwriting" course at the University of Houston, prior to opening of "Albee Directs Beckett" bill, Alley Theatre, Houston, Tex., February 11, 1991. [Transcribed by editor.]

———. "Director Albee Says Plays by Beckett Not That Difficult." Interview by Everett Evans. *Houston Chronicle*, February 17, 1991, 20, 32, 33.

———. "Game of Truth: Talk with the Author." Interview in *Newsweek*, October 29, 1962, 52–53.

———. "Introduction." In *Selected Plays of Edward Albee*. New York: Doubleday, 1987.

———. *Marriage Play*. Unpublished. (World premiere at Vienna's English Theatre, June 1987. American premiere at the Alley Theatre, Houston, Tex., January 8–February 2, 1992.)

———. "Some Thoughts on Viewing Beckett." *Houston Performances: The Arts and Theatre Magazine*, February 1991, 9.

Albee, Edward, et al. "Beckett on Stage." Panel discussion on Albee's direction of two Beckett plays, Alley Theatre, Houston, Tex., March 11, 1991.

———. "Playwright/Director Relationship." Forum at Tenth Annual William Inge Festival, Independence, Kans., April 25–28, 1991.

Albright, William. "Albee Ensures Beckett Plays Are Accessible." *Houston Post*, February 22, 1991, E5.

"Alley Press Release." The Alley Theatre, Houston, Tex., February 1991.

Arendt, Hannah. *The Life of the Mind: Willing*. New York: Harcourt Brace Jovanovich, 1978.

Aronson, Arnold. "The Wooster Group's *L.S.D. (. . . Just the High Points . . .)*." *The Drama Review* 29 (1985): 65–77.

Artaud, Antonin. *The Theatre and Its Double*. Trans. Mary C. Richards. New York: Grove Press, 1958.

Atkinson, Brooks. "*Streetcar* Tragedy—Mr. Williams Report on Life in New Orleans." *New York Times*, December 14, 1947, Sec. 2:1.

Auslander, Philip. "Toward a Concept of the Political in Postmodern Theatre." *Theatre Journal* 39 (1987): 20–34.

Bair, Dierdre. *A Biography: Samuel Beckett*. New York: Harcourt Brace Jovanovich, 1978.

Barthes, Roland. "From Work to Text," In *Image/Music/Text*. Trans. Stephen Heath. New York: Hill and Wang, 1977.

———. "Literature and Signification." In *Barthes: Critical Essays*. Trans. Richard Howard. Kingsport, Tenn.: Kingsport Press, 1963.

Beckett, Samuel. *Cascando and Other Short Dramatic Pieces*. New York: Grove Press, 1967.

———. *Endgame*. New York: Grove Press, 1958.

———. Ohio Impromptu. In *Rockaby and Other Short Pieces*. New York: Grove Press, 1981.

Benston, Kimberly W. "Being There: Performance as Mise-en-Scène, Abscene, Obscene, and Other Scene." *Publications of the Modern Language Association* 107, no. 3 (May 1992): 434–49.

Bernstein, Richard A. "Parody and Fair Use in Copyright Law." Copyright Law Symposium 31. New York: Columbia University Press, 1984.

Berry, Ralph. *On Directing Shakespeare*. New York: Barnes and Noble, 1977.

———. "Peter Brook." In *On Directing Shakespeare*. New York: Barnes and Noble, 1977.

Betsko, Kathleen, and Rachel Koening. *Interviews with Contemporary Women Playwrights*. New York: William Morrow, 1987.

Bigsby, C.W.E. *A Critical Introduction to Twentieth-Century American Drama*. Vol. 2. Cambridge: Cambridge University Press, 1984.

Blau, Herbert. "Follow the Bright Angels." *Tulane Drama Review* 5, no. 1 (September 1960): 89–101.

Botto, Louis. "Revolutionary Theatre." *Playbill* 22, no. 1 (October 31, 1992): 42–45.

Brockett, Oscar G. *History of the Theatre*. 4th ed. Boston: Allyn and Bacon, 1982.

Brustein, Robert. "The Men-taming Women of William Inge." *Harper's Magazine* (November 1958): 52–57.

Campbell, Donald. "Traditional Movement." *Plays and Players* (November 1976): 20–21.

Canaday, John. *What Is Art?* New York: Alfred A. Knopf, 1988.

Ciment, Michel. *Kazan on Kazan*. New York: Viking Press, 1974.

Clurman, Harold. Review of *Picnic* [Theatre Section]. *Nation* (March 7, 1953): 212–13.

Cohn, Ruby. "Explosive Cocktails." *Journal of American Drama and Theatre* 1, no. 2 (Fall 1989): 5–17.

———. *Just Play: Beckett's Theater*. Princeton, N.J.: Princeton University Press, 1980.

———. *Samuel Beckett: The Comic Gamut*. New Brunswick, N.J.: Rutgers University Press, 1962.

"Comprehensive Writer's Contract." *Dramatists' Guild*, Exec. Dir. David Levine. 1992:4.

Constantinidis, Stratos E. "Is Theatre under Deconstruction? A Retroactive Manifesto in a Language I Do Not Own." *Journal of Dramatic Theory and Criticism* 4 (1989): 31–52.

Cousin, Geraldine. *Churchill: The Playwright*. London: Methuen Drama, 1989.

Cronyn, Hume. *A Terrible Liar: A Memoir*. New York: William Morrow, 1991.

Davis, Robert Con. *Contemporary Literary Criticism*. New York: Longman, 1986.

Dent, Skye. "John Patrick Shanley." *Writers Guild of America West Newsletter*, May 1988.

Derrida, Jacques. *De La Gramatologie*. Baltimore: Johns Hopkins University Press, 1976.

———. "The Theatre of Cruelty and the Closure of Representation." In *Writing and Difference*. Trans. Alan Bass. Chicago: University of Chicago Press, 1978.

Donahue, Francis. *The Dramatic World of Tennessee Williams*. New York: Frederick Ungar, 1964.

Dorff, Matt. "Pencils Notebooks." *Writers Guild of America West Newsletter*, July 1989.

Duckworth, Colin. *Angels of Darkness*. London: George Allen and Unwin, 1972.

Eco, Umberto. *A Theory of Semantics*. Bloomington: Indiana University Press, 1984.

Edmonson, Andrew. *The Alley Theatre Press Release*, March 17, 1992, 1–7.

Erickson, Jon. "Appropriation and Transgression in Contemporary American Performance: The Wooster Group, Holly Hughes, and Karen Finley." *Theatre Journal* 42 (1990): 225–36.

Eszterhas, Joe. "From a Writer's Standpoint, Rewards Are Worth the Risks." *New York Times*, July 6, 1990, H11–13.

Evans, Everett. "Alley Program Shows Why Beckett's Plays Still Divide Audiences." *Houston Chronicle*, February 22, 1991, E1, E4.

Eysner, Jason. "Mutilation of Script Actionable under Lanham Act." *Art and the Law* 3 (1977): 7–8.

Ferres, John H., ed. *Twentieth Century Interpretations of* The Crucible. Englewood Cliffs, N.J.: Prentice-Hall, 1972.

Ferretti, Fred. "Joseph Papp: A 'Divisive Force' or a 'Healing' One?" *New York Times*, December 20, 1980, 16.

Fitzgerald, F. Scott. *The Pat Hobby Stories*. New York: Charles Scribner, 1970.

Fitzsimmons, Linda. *File on CHURCHILL*. London: Methuen Drama, 1989.

Foucault, Michel. "The Discourse on Language." In *The Archaeology of Knowledge*. Ed. R. D. Laing. Trans. A. M. Sheridan Smith. New York: Random House, 1972.

———. "What Is An Author?" Reprinted in Harari.

Freedman, Samuel J. "Actors Equity Protests Beckett Cast Criticism." *New York Times*, January 9, 1985, C17.

———. "Associates of Beckett Seek to Halt Production." *New York Times*, December 8, 1984, A14.

———. "*Endgame* Opens in Wake of Pact." *New York Times*, December 13, 1984, C14.

———. "Miller Fighting Group's Use of Segment from *Crucible*." *New York Times*, November 17, 1984, A14.

———. "Play Closed after *Crucible* Dispute." *New York Times*, November 28, 1984, E21.

———. "Playwrights Debate Staging." *New York Times*, March 14, 1985, C21.

———. "Who's to Say Whether a Playwright Is Wronged?" *New York Times*, December 23, 1984, E6.

Fried, Charles. "Sonnet LXV and the 'Black Ink' of the Framers' Intention." *Harvard Law Review* 100 (1987): 751–60.

Frye, Northrop, Sheridan Baker, and George Perkins. *The Harper Handbook to Literature*. New York: Harper, 1985.

Garbus, Martin, and Gerald E. Singleton. "Playwright-Director Conflict: Whose Play Is It Anyway?" *New York Law Review* (December 28, 1984): 1–2.

Garon, Jon. "Director's Choice: The Fine Line Between Interpretation and Infringement of an Author's Work." *Columbia-VLA Journal of Law and the Arts* 12 (1988): 277–306.

Gibson, William. *The Seesaw Log.* New York: Alfred A. Knopf, 1959.

Goldman, Michael. *The Actor's Freedom.* New York: Viking Press, 1972.

Goldman, William. *Adventures in the Screen Trade.* New York: Warner, 1983.

———. *Hype and Glory.* New York: Willard Books, 1990.

Gray, Simon. *How's That for Telling Them, Fat Lady?: A Short Life in the American Theatre.* London: Faber, 1988.

———. *An Unnatural Pursuit and Other Pieces: A Playwright's Journal.* London: Faber, 1985.

Gussow, Mel. "Beckett Continues to Refine His Vision." *New York Times*, December 26, 1976, D1, D27.

———. "Enter Fearless Director, Pursued by Playwright." *New York Times*, January 3, 1985, C14.

———. "Odd Man in on Broadway." Interview with Edward Albee. *Newsweek*, February 4, 1963, 48–54.

Hapgood, Robert. "The Rights of Playwrights: Performance Theory and American Law." *Journal of Dramatic Theory and Criticism* 6, no. 2 (1992): 41–59.

———. *Shakespeare the Theatre-Poet.* Oxford: Clarendon Press, 1988.

Harari, Josue V., ed. *Textual Strategies: Perspectives in Post-Structuralist Criticism.* Ithaca, N.Y.: Cornell University Press, 1979.

Harmetz, Aljean. "Glory and Humiliation in the Screen Trade." *Esquire* 1, no. 16 (1991). 79–84.

———. "Thrills? Millions? 'Spec' Scripts Bring Big Bids." *New York Times*, July 6, 1990, H11, H14.

Hayes, Walter. "*Streetcar*: A Triumph for the Oliviers." *Daily Graphic*, October 13, 1949, 2.

Hayman, Ronald. "Double Acts" [Churchill interview]. *Sunday Times Magazine*, March 2, 1980, 27.

Hirsch, E. D., Jr. *Validity in Interpretation.* New Haven, Conn.: Yale University Press, 1967.

Hobson, Harold. "Miss Vivien Leigh." *Sunday Times* (London), November 13, 1949, 2.

Hodge, Francis. "Starting Point: Basic Assumptions; Improvisation as a Tool." In *Play Directing.* 3d ed. Englewood Cliffs, N.J.: Prentice-Hall, 1988.

Holman, C. Hugh, and William Harmon. *A Handbook to Literature.* 5th ed. New York: Macmillan, 1986.

Inge, William. "From *Front Porch* to Broadway." *Theatre Arts* 38, no. 4 (April 4, 1954): 32–33.

———. "More on The Playwright's Mission." *Theatre Arts* 42, no. 8 (August 1958): 19.

———. *Picnic.* New York: Random House, 1953.

———. "*Picnic*: Of Women." *New York Times,* February 15, 1953, Sec. 2: 3.

———. Summer Brave: *The Rewritten and Final Version of The Romantic Comedy* Picnic. New York: Dramatists' Play Service, 1962.

Issacaroff, Michael, and Robin F. Jones. *Performing Texts.* Philadelphia: University of Pennsylvania Press, 1988.

Jones, David Richard. *Great Directors at Work: Stanislavsky, Brecht, Kazan, Brook.* Berkeley: University of California Press, 1986.

Jones, Therese. "Critics and Characters." Chap. 3, unpublished doctoral dissertation. University of Colorado, Boulder, Colo., 1992.

Kalb, Jonathan. *Beckett in Performance*, Cambridge: Cambridge University Press, 1989.
———. "The Underground Endgame." *Theater* 16 (1985): 88–96.
Kandinsky, Wassily. *Concerning the Spiritual in Art*. New York: George Wittenborn, 1947.
Kanin, Garson, Schary Dore, and Peter Stone. "The Minimum Basic Agreement and Artis-
tic Integrity." *Dramatists' Guild Quarterly* 16 (1979): 27–32.
Kazan, Elia. *A Life*. New York: Alfred A. Knopf, 1988.
———. "Notebook for *A Streetcar Named Desire*." Excerpted in *Twentieth Century Inter-
pretations of* A Streetcar Named Desire. Indianapolis: Bobbs-Merrill, 1963.
Kernan, Alvin. "The Battle for the Word: Dictionaries, Deconstructors, and Language Engi-
neers." In *The Death of Literature*. New Haven, Conn.: Yale University Press, 1990.
King, Michael. "True to the Words." *Houston Press*, February 28, 1991, 12.
Klaus, Carl H., Miriam Gilbert, and Bradford S. Field, Jr. *Stages of Drama: Classical to
Contemporary Masterpieces of the Theater*. 2d ed. New York: St. Martin's Press,
1991.
Kolin, Philip C. *American Playwrights since 1945: A Guide to Scholarship, Criticism, and
Performance*. Westport, Conn.: Greenwood Press, 1989.
———. "The First Critical Assessments of *A Streetcar Named Desire*: The *Streetcar* Tryouts
and the Reviewers." *Journal of Dramatic Theory and Criticism* (Spring 1991): 45–65.
———. "Olivier to Williams: An Introduction: 'Affectionate and mighty regards from Vivien
and from me': Sir Laurence Olivier's Letter to Tennessee Williams on the London Pre-
miere of *A Streetcar Named Desire*." *Missouri Review* 13, no. 3 (1991): 143–57.
———. "*A Streetcar Named Desire*: A Playwright's Forum." *Michigan Quarterly Review*
39, no. 2 (Spring 1990): 173–203.
Kolin, Philip C., and J. Madison Davis, eds. *Critical Essays on Edward Albee*. Boston:
G. K. Hall, 1986.
Krejci, Anna. "Albee's Ego Overpowers Beckett." *Public News* 27 (February 1991): 10, 15.
Lahr, John. *Notes on a Cowardly Lion*. New York: Ballantine Press, 1969.
Lampe, Eelka. "From the Battle to the Gift: The Directing of Anne Bogart." *Drama Review*
36, no. 1 (Spring 1992): 14–47.
Levin, David. "Salem Witchcraft in Recent Fiction and Drama." *New England Quarterly* 28
(December 1955): 537–46.
Logan, Joshua. *JOSH: My Up and Down, In and Out Life*. New York: Delacorte Press, 1976.
Mairowitz, David Zane. "God and the Devil." *Plays and Players* (February 1977): 24.
Massa, Robert. "Arthur Miller Clings to *The Crucible*." *The Village Voice*, December 27,
1983, 52.
Maxwell, Gilbert. *Tennessee Williams and Friends*. Cleveland: World, 1965.
McCarthy, Gerry. *Edward Albee*. New York: St. Martin's Press, 1987.
Middleton, George. *These Things Are Mine: The Autobiography of a Journeyman Play-
wright*. New York: Macmillan, 1947.
Miller, Arthur. *Arthur Miller: Eight Plays*. New York: Doubleday, 1981.
———. *The Crucible* (Acting Edition). New York: Dramatists' Play Service, 1954.
———. "Journey to *The Crucible*." *New York Times*, February 8, 1953, B3.
———. *Timebends: A Life*. New York: Grove Press, 1987.
Miller, Jordan Y. *Twentieth Century Interpretations of* A Streetcar Named Desire. Engle-
wood Cliffs, N.J.: Prentice-Hall, 1971.
Nathan, George Jean. "Director's *Picnic*." *Theatre Arts* 37 (May 1953): 14–15.
———. "William Inge." In *The Theatre of the Fifties*. New York: Alfred A. Knopf,
1953.

Nimmer, Melville B., and David Nimmer. *Nimmer on Copyright—A Treatise on the Law of Literacy, Musical and Artistic Property and the Protection of Ideas*. 4 vols. New York: Matthew Bender, 1990.

Oakes, Philip. "Return Ticket." *Sunday Times*. (London), March 17, 1974, 35.

Odets, Clifford. *The Time Is Ripe: The 1940 Journals of Clifford Odets*. New York: Grove Press, 1988.

Paolucci, Anne. "Albee and the Restructuring of the Modern Stage." *Studies in American Drama* 1 (Summer 1986): 4–16.

———. "Edward Albee." In *American Dramatists*, ed. Matthew C. Roudané. Detroit: Gale Research, 1989.

———. *From Tension to Tonic: The Plays of Edward Albee*. Carbondale: Southern Illinois University Press, 1972.

Pauly, Thomas H. *An American Odyssey: Elia Kazan and American Culture*. Philadelphia: Temple University Press, 1983.

Pirandello, Luigi. *Six Characters in Search of an Author*. New York: Dutton, 1952.

Posner, Richard A. *Law and Literature: A Misunderstood Relation*. Cambridge: Harvard University Press, 1988.

Quintero, Jose. *If You Don't Dance They Beat You*. Boston: Little, Brown, 1974.

Rabkin, Gerald. "Is There a Text on This Stage? Theatre/Authorship/Interpretation." *Performing Arts Journal* 9, no. 2 (1985): 142-59.

Randall, Phyllis R. *Caryl Churchill: A Casebook*. New York: Garland, 1988.

Reilingh, Maarten. "William Inge." In *American Playwrights since 1945: A Guide to Scholarship, Criticism, and Performance*. Ed. Philip Kolin. Westport, Conn.: Greenwood Press, 1989.

Review of "Prospero's Books," with John Gielgud; dir. Peter Greenaway. *Morning Edition*, National Public Radio, KCFR, Denver, Colo., November 3, 1991. [Repeated on November 29, 1991.]

Ritchie, Rob. *The Joint Stock Book: The Making of a Theatre Collective*. London: Methuen Theatrefile, 1987.

Roof, Judith. "Testicles, Toasters and the 'Real Thing.' " *Studies in the Humanities* 17, no. 2 (December 1990): 106–19.

Roudané, Matthew. *Understanding Edward Albee*. Columbia: University of South Carolina Press, 1987.

———. *Who's Afraid of Virginia Woolf? Necessary Fictions, Terrifying Realities*. Boston: G. K. Hall, 1990.

Rovere, Richard. "Arthur Miller's Conscience." *New Republic* 136 (June 17, 1957): 13–15.

Savran, David. *In Their Own Words: Contemporary American Playwrights*. New York: Theatre Communications Group, 1988.

———. "The Wooster Group, Arthur Miller and *The Crucible*." *The Drama Review* 29 (1985): 99–109.

———. *The Wooster Group, 1975–1985: Breaking the Rules*. Ann Arbor: UMI Research Press, 1986.

Schechner, Richard. *Between Theatre and Anthropology*. Philadelphia: University of Pennsylvania Press, 1985.

———. *Essays on Performance Theory 1970–6*. New York: Drama Book Specialists, 1977.

———. "Performance/Script/Theatre/Drama." *The Drama Review* 17, no. 3 (September 1973): 6–36.

Schneider, Alan. *Entrances: An American Director's Journey*. New York: Viking Press, 1986.

Schumach, Murray. "Why They Wait for Godot." *New York Times Magazine* no. 6 (September 21,1958): 36, 38, 41.

Seitz, William C. *Abstract Expressionist Painting in America*. Cambridge: Harvard University Press, 1983.

Shaland, Irene. *Tennessee Williams on the Soviet Stage*. Lanham, Md.: University Press of America, 1987.

Shewey, Don. "Miller's Tale." *The Village Voice*, November 27, 1984, 123.

Smith, Barbara Herrnstein. "The Ethics of Interpretation" and "Authorial Intentions and Literary Ethics." In *On the Margins of Discourse*. Chicago: University of Chicago Press, 1978.

Smith, Bruce. *Costly Performances—Tennessee Williams: The Last Stage*. New York: Paragon House, 1990.

Spence, David. " 'Albee Directs Beckett' on the Neuhaus Arena Stage." *The Jewish Herald-Voice* (February 28, 1991): 26.

Staib, Philippe. "Apropos Samuel Beckett." In *Beckett at Sixty: A Festschrift*. London: Calder and Boyars, 1967.

Stewart, Stephen M. *International Copyright and Neighboring Rights*. London: Butterworths, 1983.

Suchy, Patricia A. "When Words Collide: The Stage Direction as Utterance." *Journal of Dramatic Theory and Criticism* 6, no. 1 (Fall 1991): 69–82.

Thompson, Robert J. *Adventures on Prime Time: The Television Programs of Stephen J. Cannell*. New York: Praeger, 1990.

Trewin, J. C. "Plays in Performance." *DRAMA: British Theatre Performance* 3, no. 15 (Winter 1949): 7–8.

Tribe, Lawrence H. "First Amendment Endgame." *Boston Globe*, December 15, 1984, 19.

Vincent, Michael. "Author, Authority, and the Pedagogical Scene: *Elvire Jouvet 40*." *Journal of Dramatic Theory and Criticism* 6, no. 1 (Fall 1991): 5–13.

Vlasopolos, Anca. "Authorizing History: Victimization in *A Streetcar Named Desire*." *Theatre Journal* (October 1986): 322–38.

Voss, Ralph. "William Inge." In *Dictionary of Literary Biography: Twentieth Century American Dramatists* 7 (1981): 325–37.

Walker, Phillip. "Arthur Miller's *The Crucible*: Tragedy or Allegory?" *Western Speech* 20 (Fall 1956): 222–24.

Wilder, Thornton. "Some Thoughts on Playwrighting." In *American Characteristics*. New York: Harper and Row, 1979.

Williams, Tennessee. "Author and Director: A Delicate Situation." In *Where I Live: Selected Essays*. Ed. Christine R. Day and Bob Woods. New York: New Directions, 1978.

———. *Memoirs*. New York: Bantam Books, 1976.

Wimsatt, W. K., Jr. "Battering the Object: The Ontological Approach." In *Contemporary Criticism*. Stratford-Upon-Avon Studies, 12. London, 1970.

Windham, Donald. *Tennessee Williams' Letters to Donald Windham*. New York: Holt, Rinehart and Winston, 1976.

Wood, Audrey, with Max Wilk. "Come Back, Sweet William." In *Represented by Audrey Wood: A Memoir*. Garden City, N.Y.: Doubleday, 1981.

Young, Robert. *Untying the Text: A Post-Structuralist Reader*. Boston: Routledge and Kegan Paul, 1981.

Index

About the Editors

JEANE LUERE, Professor Emeritus at the University of Northern Colorado, has published extensively in the fields of English literature and the humanities. Luere has received grants from the Ford Foundation and the National Endowment for the Humanities, and has conducted research on theatre for thirteen months at the library of the University of Firenze, Italy, and for fourteen months at the University of Teheran, Iran, while teaching humanities at these universities. She has published articles and research in many journals such as *Theatre Journal, Studies in American Drama: 1945–Present*, and *South Atlantic Review*.

SIDNEY BERGER is Director, School of Theatre, University of Houston, and Producing Director, Houston Shakespeare Festival. He has directed over 100 productions and is the author of many articles.

ISBN 0-313-28679-5

90000>

EAN

9 780313 286797

HARDCOVER BAR CODE